MUMS to MUMS

Volume I:
Pregnancy – preparing for a revolution in your life

by 1200 mums

Project initiated and compiled
by Barbara Falenta

2021

Mums to Mums
Vol. I: Pregnancy – preparing for a revolution in your life

Online shop: MumsToMums.com

Athors: 1 200 Mums

Project Coordinator: Barbara Falenta, barbara.falenta@MumsToMums.com

Cover Design: Kayah Grochowalska

Internal Illustrations: Xenia Potepa

Internal Design: Bukebuk.pl

Copyright © 2020-2021 for English edition by Barbara Falenta. All rights reserved.

ISBN/EAN: 978-83-959481-0-7

Mums to Mums Publishing, www.MumsToMums.com

The coordinator and the authors have made every effort to ensure that the information contained in this book is complete and reliable. However, it cannot be regarded as a substitute for advice from experts, including medical, pharmaceutical, psychological or legal experts. The coordinator and the authors are not liable for any damages resulting from the use of information contained in the book.
The responsibility of the Coordinator and Authors is appropriate for this form of publication. The Authors and the Project Coordinator are not responsible for the use of this information and related possible patent or copyright infringement.
Mention of specific companies, organizations, or authorities in the book does not imply endorsement by the publisher, nor does mention of specific companies, organizations, or authorities imply that they endorse this book.
Making copies by photocopier, photographic methods or copying the book on film, magnetic or other medium will infringe the copyright of this publication. This publication, or any part of it, may not be copied, reprinted or in any other way reproduced. It also cannot be read aloud on public media without the written consent of the coordinator (Barbara Falenta).
All rights reserved.

Table of contents

Dear Mum... and Dad, Grandma and Grandpa!	7
We couldn't have written this book without the following people	9
How to use this book	11

STARTING OUT RIGHT

1. "I've got good news!" When to announce your pregnancy?	15
2. Classic or modern? Choosing a name can be tricky	16

YOUR BABY

Health and development

3. I'm growing and growing! The main stages of your baby's development during pregnancy	21
4. Playing with the little one in my belly – supporting your growing baby	25
5. Hello, it's Mum! How to build a relationship with your baby during pregnancy?	28
6. Stress and its effects on your pregnancy and your baby	31
7. Cancer prevention during pregnancy – how to reduce the risk of cancer for your child?	33
8. Preterm babies – happiness that comes early	36
♦ My story... Susanna	41

Baby essentials

9. The nesting instinct – fact or excuse?	45
10. An oasis of peace and development. Arranging your baby's room	47
11. Making your home safe for your baby	54
12. Baby essentials – do we have it easier than our mums?	57
13. Baby essentials – putting it all together sensibly	59
14. Baby essentials – clothes	61
15. Baby essentials – cosmetics. The basics of baby care	64
16. Baby essentials – vegan cosmetics	66
17. Baby essentials – first aid kid	67
18. Baby essentials – equipment. Things you didn't even know existed!	72
19. Baby essentials – prams. Your child's first 4 wheels	78

20. Baby essentials – the car seat.. 84
21. Reusable nappies. Back to the past or a modern solution? 87
22. Help! Twins!.. 92
♦ My story... Annette 96

MUM

A healthy and well-cared future mum

23. Under good care – how do I choose the right doctor to lead me
    through pregnancy? 101
24. Caution advised! What medical test should you avoid in pregnancy? 103
25. Nausea, drowsiness and hypersensitivity to smells... How to deal
    with pregnancy ailments?.. 105
26. Don't ignore them! Things you should be concerned about
    during pregnancy 109
27. Sugar and spice... A few words about gestational diabetes 112
28. A pregnant woman walks into a pharmacy... Basic principles of medicine
    use during pregnancy.. 116
29. You mean folic acid isn't enough?! What supplements to take
    in pregnancy.. 124
30. Pregnancy is not like illness? Lifestyle choices during pregnancy................... 134
31. Nourishing both of you, without eating for two. A healthy diet
    during pregnancy 137
32. Pregnancy diet for vegetarians and vegans.. 140
33. Munching cucumber with chocolate. The science behind
    pregnancy cravings 140
34. How much coffee can a mum-to-be drink? Stimulants during pregnancy 144
35. Staying active – physical exercise and movement during pregnancy 148
36. Pregnant yoga – exercise for health! 152
37. 50 shades... of a future mother – sex during pregnancy 153
38. A pampered mum-to-be. What cosmetic treatments can you have
    during pregnancy?... 155
39. Read the label! What kind of cosmetics can you use during pregnancy? 163
40. Pregnancy cosmetics for vegans and vegetarians 165
41. It's not always rosy... Getting through a difficult pregnancy 166
♦ My story... Martina... 170

Emotions and the mental health of the future mum

42. Give me some space! Hormones and their effect on a pregnant woman's emotions 173
43. It's not just physical – taking care of your mental health during pregnancy. 176
44. Meditation and the well-being of the future mother 180
- My story... Caroline 181
45. Lions and tigers and bears, oh my! The fear of giving birth and other pregnancy worries 183

What else should you know?

46. Shopping with your bump... and not necessarily replacing your entire wardrobe 189
47. Mum's essentials – must-haves in the home medicine cabinet 192
48. There are two of you now. Staying safe during pregnancy 197
49. On the plane with a baby bump?! Travel during pregnancy 200
50. The baby shower – your child's first party 205
51. Crazy for animals. Preparing pets for a baby's appearance 207

THE BIRTH

52. Attitude matters – preparing mentally for childbirth 215
53. Yes, yes, you can (and should) prepare your body for delivery! 217
54. Natural childbirth, caesarean section, vbac – different forms of childbirth 220
55. Back to school – choosing an antenatal class 230
56. Choosing where to give birth 233
57. Preparing for childbirth at home 240
- My story... Agatha 243
58. Who to give birth with? A companion in the delivery room 245
- My story... Daria 247
59. Occupation: Midwife 249
60. Occupation: Doula 252
61. Birth plan – oxymoron or useful practice? 254
62. Pack up! What to take to the birth? 257
63. Is this it? How you know when the birth has begun? 261
- My story... Olga 264
64. Ouch! Methods for relieving labour pain 265
65. Cord blood – what we know to date 270

66. The kid scored! About the Apgar score.. 273
67. Kangaroo care – wonderfully close to baby, straight after birth 274
68. Breastfeeding – preparation during pregnancy 276

THE POSTPARTUM PERIOD

69. The postpartum period – an important time after the birth.
 The physiological aspect... 283
70. The postpartum period – an important time after the birth.
 The psychological aspect 291

TIPS & TRICKS

71. Organisational tips & tricks to make starting motherhood easier 295
72. 20 things to do while you're pregnant... 297
 ◆ My story... Magdalene 298

MISCARRIAGE. WE RECOMMEND THAT YOU ONLY READ THESE CHAPTERS IF THEY SADLY APPLY TO YOU

73. Losing your baby – the medical side... 305
74. Losing your baby – the psychological impact 308
 ◆ My story... Monica 311
 ◆ My story... Eve 313

Us Mums, we are strong!... 317
It's (almost) over.. 319
What's next?.. 321
Bibliography... 323
The Authors of the book "Mums to Mums" 337

Dear Mum...
and Dad, Grandma and Grandpa!

There is an extraordinary book awaiting you, the result of a unique international project undertaken by more than **1200 women. Each is an expert in her field, and also a mother. Among us there are doctors, psychologists, pharmacists, midwives, doulas, lactation counsellors, dieticians, educators, physiotherapists and pedagogues**. All of them decided to share their expertise and practical knowledge about children, motherhood and the family. For more than a year we have had long, exciting and emotional discussions, with the aim of together creating a valuable book for you.

From the beginning, it was meant to be different. Informative, because it is written by female experts, but at the same time taken from real life. Practical, because it is written by mothers, not 'upbringing theorists'. Close, honest and from the heart – as if you are talking to your sister or friend.

In this book you will find the topics that we, women who are already on the path of motherhood, consider the most important for every mother who is at the beginning of that path. **We found a lack of such knowledge when we were beginning our own adventures into motherhood.** We weren't afraid to address difficult, often controversial, subjects. We focused not only on the needs of the child, but we also remembered your needs, and the needs of the whole family – motherhood is a big change in life and you need support.

Treat this book as an inspiration, not as a universal recipe for motherhood – because nothing like that exists. Every child, every mother and every family is unique.

Feel free to make notes in the book, stick in cards and draw on them – we do it ourselves! This is your guide, to which you can return at any time.

We believe that if you read one book about pregnancy and motherhood, it should be this one. It has expert knowledge and practical guidance, guidance in a nutshell – from mums for mums (and all the family!). Or maybe you have a loved one who would love to receive this valuable gift?

As authors who have put a lot of work, energy and heart into this project, we are curious to know if you liked it, if it was useful to you or if you would change anything? Please share your opinions with us in the way you prefer:
- contact@MumsToMums.com
- facebook.com/MumsToMumsBook
- instagram.com/MumsToMums
- www.MumsToMums.com

Happy reading and good luck! You can do it! :)

With love,
Barbara Falenta and 1200 mums & experts

We couldn't have written this book without the following people

The initiator and coordinator of the "Mums to Mums" project, the cause of all the fuss:
Barbara Falenta – mother of two little men, Peter's wife, a fan of far off travels

The Authors of chapters of the book "Mums to Mums" – mums and experts in their fields, including doctors, pharmacists, midwives, doulas, dieticians, psychologists and pedagogues. They often worked on the book at night, spending every spare moment between job and childcare on the computer. A complete list of Authors can be found at the end of the book.

Co-authors of the book – participants in the "Mums to Mums" project, who took part in exciting and emotional discussions, shared their knowledge and experiences. A complete list of them can be found at the end of the book.

Project team – women who turned visions and ideas into reality:
Camilla – mother of three children, Tobias's wife
Lena – Arletta's mother, Michael's partner, Persian cat lover ;)
Violet – Tosia's mum, Thomas's wife; the right hand of the coordinator, woman for special ops

Editorial staff – professionals who spent many long hours eradicating commas in the wrong places:
Agnes – Editor-in-Chief; Casilda's mother and Michael's wife; writer, editor, baby wraps lover, bibliophile
Annette – Frank's mum, editor
Annette – Olive and Lena's mum
Eve "Thori" – writer, blogger, editor
Kate – Hubert's mum, editor

Internal illustrations:
Xenia – mother of two children, illustrator, author of web comics on motherhood

Cover illustration and cover design:
Kayah — blogger, mum of two children

Good spirits of the project — women who believed in it from the very beginning, who shared their knowledge, supported it and came in at critical moments: Agnes B., Agnes W., Annette, Anna, Camilla, Kaya, Magdalene, Magda, Martina, Violet

Thank You all ♡! — Barbara

P.S. Peter, thank you. You made it through!
P.P.S. My dear sons, I would like to thank you too. If it weren't for you, this book would have been written six months earlier ;). But without you, it would never have been written at all ♡.

How to use this book

In a moment, you will start to read 74 chapters on how you can prepare for having a baby. Each chapter has its own author, but they are the result of discussions with over 1000 mothers.

Were the discussions exciting and emotional? Of course they were.
Did we always agree? Of course not. Because there is no single answer to the question "How do you bring a child into the world?"

Don't treat this book as a universal recipe for maternity because one doesn't exist. Let it be a compendium of valuable, practical knowledge and a source of inspiration for you and your loved ones. Choose what you feel will be helpful for you and your family.

If you've reached for this book, it means that you've chosen the path of conscious motherhood and we congratulate you on that. Because knowledge and maternal intuition are not mutually exclusive – they complement each other.

Some practical information:
1. This symbol ▸ placed in brackets refers to a chapter on a given topic in this volume or the second one (indicated by the number I or II respectively), e.g. (▸ II – 36) refers to volume II, chapter 36.
2. Numbers in square brackets, e.g. [8], refer to the corresponding footnote number in the bibliography at the end of the book, chapter by chapter.
3. The table of contents is at the beginning of the book.
4. All quotations contained in this book come from discussions in the "Mums to Mums" group.

Once again, we invite you to share your impressions after reading the book:
- on our Facebook: facebook.com/MumsToMums
- at goodreads.com (each volume of the book is evaluated separately)
- write to us at contact@MumsToMums.com

Find us at:
- www.MumsToMums.com
- www.instagram.com/MumsToMums
- www.facebook.com/MumsToMumsBook

We're planning more projects for mums! Why don't you join us in writing the next part? :)

STARTING OUT RIGHT

1. "I've got good news!"
When to announce your pregnancy?

One day you see two magic lines on the pregnancy test... What are your initial feelings: Fear? Euphoria? Excitement? You'll almost certainly have some doubts and uncertainties. Once you and the father get used to the idea, you'll want to tell your loved ones about the pregnancy. Who should you tell first, and how? There isn't really a perfect answer to this.

Before you tell others, think about whether you want to share this information at all before the first 3 months. The 1st trimester is the most risky, the period when miscarriages or other complications are more common. If you've had difficulties getting pregnant or have had miscarriages before, you may not necessarily feel like sharing the news right away. Catherine writes: "I know too many stories where people started telling the world about the news in the 4th or 5th week and then had a miscarriage. And then they had to deal with all the questions: 'When's the due date?'. 'Do you know the gender?' etc."

Another thing to consider is who you want to tell first: Your parents? Your friends? Margaret just told her mother and sisters straight away and "the rest after the 12th week." Likewise Annette: "Your closest family (parents, siblings) can be told earlier, everyone else can wait."

Think carefully about when and how you share in the workplace. Dorothy provides a cautionary tale: "I told my employer a week after taking the pregnancy test. Honesty in my case didn't work. I had been in line to get a raise, but when I was asked where I saw myself in the company next year, I replied: 'On maternity leave'... They soon forgot about the raise and the promotion." However, remember that you must inform your employer about your pregnancy if you want to take advantage of your working rights, such as a ban on overtime, night work or heavy lifting. Rights do vary from country to country, so you might want to check what your working rights are where you live.

However, the most important thing is whether you feel the need to tell others your news. What does your gut tell you? As Anna stressed, the best moment is simply when you feel it is time to share. Betty added that it's worth waiting until you're ready, and that's probably the most sensible answer – because each mum is ready when she's ready.

There are as many voices and opinions as there are women. Sometimes you're able to think it over and plan it carefully, and sometimes life will write the script for you because you may start throwing up at the least convenient moment! Or maybe you want the announcement of your pregnancy to be a special and unforgettable moment? One thing is certain – always listen to your intuition and to your heart. These are good and proven counsellors. ◆

Joanna – wife and mother. A special needs educator by profession, currently a full-time mum to Lena and John.

2. Classic or modern? Choosing a name can be tricky

What do we take into account when choosing a name for a child? It is a personal matter, and we often make our choice long before the birth or even conception. Various factors influence the decision – here are some of them:

- **Our taste and experience.** We immediately reject certain names because they have negative associations for us or because there are already several people with that name in our family, while others we like immediately – for example the name of a beloved grandparent or childhood hero. There's also the issue of matching the name and the surname.
- **Form.** Some of us prefer names which can't be shortened, like Jane or Simon, others want names with diminutives but with a more formal full form (Kate – Katie – Katherine, or Bob – Bobby – Robert). In intercultural families – apart from a fondness for a name – the spelling and ease of pronunciation by members of both families should also be taken into account.
- **Origin.** Every parent becomes a specialist in onomatics! This is a specialised field of linguistics – the study of the history and origin of proper names, especially personal names. Some people take the origin of the word as their point of reference e.g. the Greek word Agatha means "good, wonderful" while Sofia means "wisdom".
- **(Almost) mathematical formulas.** You can make a list of your favourite names, rating them with a points system to choose the perfect name. There may be arguments with parents and in-laws, and even annoyance towards friends

who 'stole' a chosen name for their own child. A ready-made formula is provided by Anna: "I must admit that for us the choice of a name was a bit of an ordeal. Somehow it brought us us more frustration than pleasure. That's why we approached the matter methodically for our second child. First we chose 10 names from the annual list released by the national statistical office which we liked. Then each of us independently evaluated the names on a scale of 1-10. We compared the results and chose the 3 highest scores. Then we checked how they sounded with the second name and surname and their popularity in recent years – then chose the least popular one."

- **Alphabetically.** You can use an alphabetical system and name your children starting with the same letter, like Rebecca, Robert and Richard.
- **Religious reasons.** Sometimes you can check if there is a saint with your chosen name. Agatha writes: "We wanted the name to have had a long cultural tradition, and the children to have a patron saint."
- **The influence of a name on character.** Thoughts about the future of your children may also be important to you. Maggie writes: "The meaning of a name is important to me because I put a lot of emphasis on the child being a good husband/wife and parent one day. This is an absolute priority for me. I think that a name has a strong influence on character."

Name rankings. Every year independent rankings of the most popular names are produced. The most reliable seem to be those prepared by the government which then appear on various websites. There are also several books with names, in which there is always a lot of detailed information on the origin, meaning and character traits of each name [2]. As parents, however, you should remember first and foremost – a name must not be damaging or harmful to the child in any way. It can also be troubling for a child to have a foreign, unfamiliar name, pronounced or written in different ways. And you need to keep in mind that the official form of the first name is used in official situations and documents (on ID cards, school certificates, etc.), and should be unambiguous. Family and friends can of course use any diminitive form they choose.

One or two names? While it is worth taking more care over the first name, the second name carries a smaller, but often no less important, emotional charge. Parents usually give them in memory of relatives who may have passed away, or other people important to them. Another reason might be to keep a name in the family. In other words, the first name is the one we like and the second is after the grandfather or grandmother. Some say there's no need for a second name at all, as it only makes signing documents take longer or causes confusion. In practice, it sometimes happens that parents or grandparents start talking to their children using their second name, meaning the first name – chosen with reverence – appears only in documents.

How to avoid mistakes and misunderstandings when naming your baby?
Parents often have the irresistible temptation to give their children such unusual names that even officials have trouble deciding whether to accept or reject them. We encourage you to familiarize yourself with the position of your national language authority [3]. You will find there are hints about which rules should be followed, e.g. whether the correct name is Clare or Klare, Kymena or Xymena, Jon or John. ♦

Margaret – mum of Anna, Matthew and Kuba, owner of a creative cafe.
Dominica – ICF coach, supervisor.

YOUR BABY

Health and development

3. I'm growing and growing!
The main stages of your baby's development during pregnancy

A positive pregnancy test usually results in a lot of mixed emotions, often extreme. Thoughts crowd your head: "What now?", "Will I manage?", "When do I go to the doctor or gynaecologist?". After all, once the first wave of feelings has passed, you need to come back to earth and approach it with common sense. Two lines. Okay, I'm pregnant. How many weeks pregnant am I? What size is my baby now?

In the beginning... Fertilization is no more than the combination of an egg cell and a sperm, resulting in a zygote. The first division of the zygote results in two cells. On the 3rd day of development, the zygote reaches the morula stage (8-16 cells), transforming into a multicelled blastocyst after the next 2 or 3 days. By about the 12th day of its intrauterine life, it has completely nested or implanted itself into the uterine wall. In the prenatal development of the human embryo there are 3 stages: Pre-germ (1st week of intrauterine life), embryonic, also called the organogenesis stage (from 2nd to 8th week) and fetal (from 9th week after fertilization until the end of the pregnancy) [1].

Two dashes and then what? After you've taken the pharmacy's pregnancy test, look at your calendar and remember the first day of your last period. Why? The first day of your last period is considered the beginning of your pregnancy. So, the fertilization actually occurs in the second week of pregnancy. Yes, it sounds strange, but for the purpose of calculating the date of birth, this is the assumption. Then you can go to the doctor and do a blood test for a hormone produced in pregnancy called Human chorionic gonadotropin (hCG). On the first day of your expected period , assuming regular cycles, the result should already indicate about 200 U/L of hCG. hCG doubles its value every 48 hours, so on the basis of this, we can conclude that the pregnancy is still developing. hCG positive? It is time to make an appointment with your doctor or gynaecologist! The baby bump is only visible at the end of the 5th week of pregnancy. This is important because if at this stage your hCG levels are more than 1,000 U/L and you do not see a gestational sac baby bump, it's possible this could, sadly, be an ectopic pregnancy, so it's definitely worth checking.

First ultrasound. In early pregnancy (up to week 11), you should have at least one ultrasound examination to confirm the pregnancy and determine the baby's position and stage of development. Ultrasounds up to this period are usually performed vaginally, although it varies from country to country. Only later, when the fetus is large enough, is the ultrasound performed through the abdominal wall.

The first ultrasound examination is usually performed about 3 weeks after fertilization, which is about the 5th week of a healthy pregnancy. At this stage, you should already have a gestational sac baby bump, but you don't yet see the yolk sac, which appears a few days later (and from which the placenta will develop in the future). The fetus's heartbeat cannot yet be picked up. About 1-2 days after the appearance of the yolk sac, an embryo about 3 mm long (CRL – *crown-rump length*) is visible. At this point the doctor should also be able to detect the heartbeat. This long-expected throbbing dot appears at the end of the 6th week of pregnancy and is visible in the ultrasound image. It may happen that at this visit the gynaecologist won't be able to detect the heartbeat and will ask you to come back in a few days. This happens and you shouldn't worry, because the pregnancy may be earlier on than initially calculated. On the other hand, if there is a clear gestational sac in the 6th week of pregnancy and you do not see a yolk sac, it may be what they call an empty fetal egg. If the doctor does not see the heartbeat until the baby reaches 6 mm (CRL), it means that the pregnancy is sadly not developing properly.

Once you see the beating heartbeat you can check the baby's heart rate, which initially conforms to the mother's heart rate and gradually increases to a target rate of 160 beats a minute. Now – from the 8th week of pregnancy – is usually the time to assess the baby's heart rate.

We can only talk about a fully-developed human placenta at the end of the 1st trimester of the pregnancy. This performs the essential functions of: gas exchange between the mother and fetus, the supply of nutrients necessary for the baby's development, the removal of metabolic products and the production of the many hormones necessary during pregnancy [1].

How does the little one develop? Each week of pregnancy brings huge changes in the body of the developing fetus:
- 5 – a visible gestational follicle with a yolk follicle,
- 6 – the heartbeat starts,
- 7 – arms and legs begin to appear, the heart beats harder, the lungs start to form,
- 8 – you can clearly see the head and... a small tail, which will disappear in the following week,
- 9 – the embryo already has eyelids, there is a membrane between the fingers and toes,
- 10 – **the embryo becomes a fetus**, nose holes and tear ducts are visible, the membrane between the fingers and toes disappears and your little one can fold its arms and legs,
- 11 – ears are developing,
- 12 – in the jaw, milk teeth appear, the baby's muscles develop,
- 13 – the baby starts its first breathing, swallowing and sucking reflexes,
- 14 – the skeleton of the baby begins to form,
- 15 – nails appear, the baby starts to grow very fast,
- 16 – the little one is covered with a waxy like substance called *vernix caseosa* (vernix), which is intended to maintain temperature and protect its skin; the wax may be visible for days or even weeks after birth,
- 17 – the reproductive organs are fully formed,
- 18 – you can feel the first movements of your baby; it starts to make faces and the bone marrow starts to produce blood cells,
- 20 – muscle mass increases quickly, fetal mass appears on the skin and, in girls, egg cells appear in the ovaries (about 6 million of them),
- 22 – eyebrows and hair are already growing, lungs start to produce surfactant (a substance supporting their proper functioning, preventing their collapse and the sticking of alveoli),
- 23 – **from this week on, the baby has a chance to survive outside the womb** thanks to the progress of modern medicine and the help of specialized equipment,
- 24 – the baby already has its own daily routine, usually waking up when you're asleep, and falling asleep to the sway of your walking motion,

- 28 – the eyes open, the baby can already see light, smell the smells in the fetal water and hear,
- 29-36 – the baby develops rapidly, increasing in weight and generally preparing for life outside its mother's belly,
- 37 – from this week on, the baby is completely ready for independent survival outside the mother's body, with fully developed lungs.

Prenatal ultrasounds, also known as fetal genetic testing or (non invasive) Prenatal Testing (NIPT), is still considered controversial. It differs from ordinary ultrasounds in that it assesses the anatomy of the fetus very precisely, whereas the ordinary ultrasound only assesses the heart rate and estimated mass of the baby.

The question is: do you do it or not? You make the decision yourself. No one will force you, but it is recommended that you do it because some birth defects that are not visible during a regular examination can be treated before the child is born. Generally a prenatal ultrasound is performed three times during a pregnancy, although of course it varies from country to country, and often within a country:
- 11-14 weeks – the so-called 12 week or nuchal translucency scan with an assessment of the risk of genetic defects,
- 18-22 weeks – the so-called half-way ultrasound or anatomy scan; this is when you can best see the baby and all its organs, so that the doctor can evaluate whether the child is developing properly,
- 28-32 weeks – the development of pregnancy in the third trimester is evaluated.

Prenatal ultrasounds, as opposed to ordinary ultrasounds, are performed for a fee, unless you belong to a higher risk group (e.g. are 35 years or older, have a child with a genetic irregularity from a previous pregnancy, have a chromosome aberration in one of the parents or if you have had an abnormal screening result), then in many countries this is covered by the country's national health service.

Miscarriage or birth? If the birth occurs before the 22nd week of pregnancy, then it's technically considered a miscarriage. From the 23rd week, then it's a birth. Full term pregnancy is from the 37th week. Before the 36th week, it's considered a premature birth.

Pregnancy can be a very beautiful period in a woman's life, but it can also be stressful. It is important to have regular checkups to confirm the well-being of your little one. Keep in mind that it is only in the first trimester of pregnancy that the baby develops at a universal pace. After this it is a completely individual matter and you shouldn't compare your pregnancy with that of your friend or sister. ◆

Agnes – Pola's mum and midwife.

4. Playing with the little one in my belly — supporting your growing baby

Your baby learns a lot of things in your belly. Firstly, it exercises the reflexes that will be needed to adapt to life outside the womb, for example the sucking reflex. These abilities are biologically programmed and appear in all children. The lack of such abilities or their excessive persistence after birth can be signs of problems in development. But is there anything you can teach your baby inside the womb?

During the prenatal period the child is aware of its inner world and remembers these impressions. Your baby is getting used to the rhythm of the day and is beginning to create musical or taste preferences [3]. The baby is able to learn and remember certain stimuli as early as 3 months before birth, and the ability to gradually get used to sounds appears as early as the 23rd week [8]. If you want to provide your baby with the best possible conditions for development, take care of yourself first. This means: eat healthily, take care of your movement, and rest.

Eat healthily. For the development of the brain and the entire nervous system of your child, omega-3 acids, including DHA and folic acid, are extremely important. They influence both physical and intellectual development. Try to eat good quality foods containing these nutrients, including fish, green vegetables, whole grains and eggs [5] (▶ I – 29).

Exercise and touch. Your baby loves your touch, like stroking your belly – it helps it develop well. This is something that all women – from all corners of the earth, regardless of their level of education and social status – may do. It's the oldest and most common form of establishing a bond with your child [2]. Scientists have also developed special programmes to stimulate its development, such as haptonomy or "Prenatal University". The first, by F. Veldman, uses a special way of touching the abdomen, allowing not only you to have contact with the baby, but also your partner or another person.

Another, devised by R. Van de Carr, is based on a special routine of patting and stroking your belly, combined with speaking and singing. You don't have to use these methods of course – it's fine just to sit back, relax and try to feel your baby's position with gentle movements. Massage your belly, embrace it, and encourage your partner and older children to do the same. Dancing is wonderful, and will be a pleasure for both you and the little one [3]. In Montreal, a study was carried out on a group of women who exercised for 20 minutes three times a week. Their children after birth had better cognitive development than children of mothers who were physically inactive [4]. Do talk to your doctor or midwife, though, about any activity you want to do.

Relax. Stress has a negative impact on the baby in your belly and can affect brain function throughout its life. Studies on extreme stress have been carried out, however, according to some scientists, even moderate doses of stress may influence the intelligence of a child, especially its linguistic abilities [1]. So do make sure you get enough rest, and find time for hobbies and relaxation.

You can influence your little one not only with good health and well-being, but also by playing with him or her! Below are some ideas.

Talk, read and sing to your child. Singing stimulates the development of synapses in the brain, improves its well-being and has a calming influence [3]. The child prefers to "listen to the voice of the mother rather than the voice of another woman; a female voice rather than a male voice; and any human voice rather than silence" [8]. Don't worry if you think you can't sing – your baby will love it regardless! It recognizes not only your voice, but also those around you. When someone is often in your company, especially when he or she turns directly to your belly, the child will recognize this person's voice after birth [6]. The fetus also remembers fairy tales and poems read to it during pregnancy. It learns the language the mother speaks more quickly and can recognize the emotions of her speech [8]. Research shows that children whose mothers talked to them directly in the womb, developed language and communication skills faster. However, exposure to ambient sounds such as TV, radio or voices of strangers, had no effect [2, 7].

Play music and lullabies. The baby's environment in the womb is not one of silence: it not only hears external sounds, but also all the sounds coming from the mother's body, such as the heartbeat and organs at work. Tunes are imitated through tempo and rhythm. Music can be part of your daily activities, but you can also treat listening to music as a special time. Classical music is best (it calms the heart and brain waves), like Bach, Mozart, Schumann, Debussy, Tchaikovsky or Vivaldi. Either way, the child will show you with his or her movements, what kind of music makes it happy and relaxed, and which kind makes it excited or emotional. [3]. Children who were stimulated by music during pregnancy are statistically calmer, more joyful, better at sucking, and then at babbling, chattering and learning to speak. This is the case not only for intellectual but also physical abilities [3]. In the USA, research was conducted using a "fetal walkman", through which music was played directly to the abdomen. This is quite a controversial practice, with unknown long-term effects, so it is probably better to limit yourself to listening to music in the traditional way [3]. Be careful of the noise level, though; pregnant women shouldn't be in an environment louder than 85 decibels. From as early as five months excessive noise can frighten a baby and damage its hearing [8].

Stimulation and playing with the baby in your belly can affect its development, but there's no guarantee that you will raise a future Nobel Prize winner! All ideas should be tailored to you and your baby's needs. Do what you enjoy. Playing classical music to your baby to the point where it annoys you will certainly not be beneficial. If touching your belly is not for you, think about other forms of play. The most important thing is always you and your baby's health. All ideas contained in this chapter are inspiration for spending time together, not absolute recommendations. If you don't feel like doing them, don't have time, or simply don't believe in their effectiveness, that's ok. The most important thing is that you love your baby and you care for it to the best of your ability. ♦

Beatrice – Angel's mother, special needs educator, therapist.

5. Hello, it's Mum! How to build a relationship with your baby during pregnancy?

Pregnancy is not always planned, and even if it is, sometimes it inspires fear and worry instead of tears of joy. Not every woman gives her whole heart to a child as soon as she sees two lines on a test. This is confirmed by the mothers who contributed to our discussions and backed up by scientific research. Usually it takes time to get used to the new situation and your bond with your baby is formed gradually [4].

You perceive yourself and your baby in different ways at different stages of pregnancy. This is due to changes in your body and psyche, and is influenced by your mental and physical state and those of the people around you. "When a mother experiences a feeling of joy and contentment, various chemicals such as endorphins are released into her blood. When a mother feels good, the child is bathed in 'happy hormones' and produces them on its own', and this happens as early as 6 weeks after conception [5].

Establishing a connection. Babies subconsciously pick up attitudes towards them. Even if the baby is an 'unexpected surprise', it doesn't mean that there will be any problems. Give yourself and others time to adapt to the situation, talk frankly with those close to you [4]. Below you will learn about ways in which you can build a relationship with your little one.

Visualization. Probably every woman expecting a child wonders what it will look like, whose eyes will it inherit and whose hair colour will it get? This will help you see the child as a real person, not a strange creature in your belly. Try to take a moment every day to relax and imagine your child's future. You can get family members – particularly your older children, if you have any – to draw the baby, both what it looks like in the belly now and what it will look like in the future. It will be fun and a beautiful souvenir to look back on.

A boy or a girl? Knowing your child's sex can help not only in choosing a name, but also choosing baby clothes or arranging a room for him or her. If there are children in the family, it will be easier for them to find their new role as older siblings if they know what kind of playmate they are waiting for. Of course, the decision to find out the gender of a child is an individual matter. Interestingly, more and more parents are opting for a surprise at birth.

What's in a name? The easiest way to make your child's presence real is to give them a name, or even a nickname. Personally, for a long time I didn't want to know the sex of my child, which meant that, until its very birth, we didn't have a name ready. So we called it "Pea". Giving a baby a name helps us treat it as a family member.

Talking to the baby. What do you say to your baby? Everything! You can tell it what you're doing, what you're afraid of, how you feel, how you imagine him or her, what you'll do in the future. Do they have to be just positive topics? No, any subject is good. If you have a difficult pregnancy, you will have different fears and you can share them with your baby. It subconsciously feels the signals you give off, and saying things out loud can give both you and the baby respite and relief. When you have a free moment, sit or lie down comfortably, breathe deeply and enjoy the moment with your baby. This applies to both you and those around you, especially older siblings who are waiting – often impatiently – to meet their brother or sister [4].

Singing. Singing used to be one of the few forms of entertainment available to everyone. Singing can make us feel shy or embarrassed, but our voice is lovely for the baby. What kind of songs to sing? It's up to us. By singing we show our baby that we accept it, that we love and care for it, and it involves him or her in our community. We can sing the lullabies we used to listen to – our family's favourite songs. Additionally, singing is a great opportunity to practice our breathing and diaphragm movement, which is extremely important during childbirth and influences the development of your baby's brain [4].

Observing movement. Studies have shown that after birth babies continue to behave like they do in the womb, so you can try to predict its temperament by the way it behaves in the belly.

Learn to listen to the signals coming from your little one. If it hasn't been active for a while, it's not a bad idea to check in with your doctor to see that your pregnancy is going well.

Touching your belly. Studies have shown that unborn babies react to touch far more than to their mother's voices [2]. You can use a technique called haptonomia, created by F. Veldman, which involves particular ways of touching your belly, and allows both you and your partner or another person to communicate with your baby. Lie down in a comfortable position and breathe calmly. Stroke your belly gently and tenderly, and try to feel what position your baby is in. You can rock your baby using breathe and gentle movements. It is important that your partner or another person joins in with you.

Here are some ideas for activities you can do to deepen your relationship with your baby [3]:
- baby-focused activities: positive thinking about your baby; visualising your baby, your interactions, your games; talking to your baby aloud or in thought; telling him or her what is happening; writing fairy tales, diaries, letters to your baby; painting on your belly; having constant awareness of your baby's presence; involving him or her in your family's life; meditation, prayer,
- listening activities: telling stories, reading, listening to music, singing, playing instruments, tapping rhythms,
- movement activities: swaying your belly, dancing, stroking, massaging, hugging, playing with your baby, observing its movements,
- other forms of activity: artistic, making things for your baby, preparing or buying clothes, arranging its room.

Parents who try to establish a relationship with their baby during the prenatal period feel better prepared for their role and become more sensitive to the signals their baby sends, which definitely helps in the early days of parenthood. ◆

Beatrice – Angel's mother, special needs educator, therapist.

6. Stress and its effects on your pregnancy and your baby

The word "stress" usually has a negative meaning. Yet a state of stress can also produce a positive response which aids development. In particularly difficult situations stress responses can save lives.

Here we look at ways in which the mother's mind can influence the development of the baby in the womb. We will also cover the impact of the emotional and postnatal aspects of the mother's mind on the development of her baby and on her relationship with her unborn child. Professor David Barker's epidemiological research has helped us better understand fetal programming, a theory which suggests that the environment in the womb can affect the development of the baby and therefore have a lasting effect on its later health and wellbeing – even into adulthood – and especially concerning illnesses such as obesity, diabetes and cardiovascular diseases. [4]. It's known that fetal programming may result from subtle changes in the environment of the womb, such as an alteration in the mother's diet or stress level.

The impact of stress in fetal programming. The period of embryonic development occurs when the basic structures of the body are formed. In the 9th week of pregnancy, the embryo becomes a fetus. From the 24th week the fetus is considered viable to live outside the mother's belly. During fetal development there are critical periods that may affect the child's progress. For example, during the first few weeks of pregnancy, the baby's arms and legs grow, whereas other organs – such as the brain – develop at every stage of pregnancy. The consumption of alcohol or certain medicines may affect the development of the baby's nervous system and brain throughout the whole pregnancy. Your emotional state can also affect the development of your baby in the womb and have a long-term effect on your child. Studies have shown that unborn babies may be affected by parental quarrels, anxiety felt by the mother, and even stress caused by natural disasters [2]. Effects can be long-term. The child may have greater emotional or behavioural problems, as well as a slower learning capacity. But keep in mind that children are affected by stress in different ways.

Of course, we can't eliminate all stress in our lives. You can be happy and at peace one moment, and feel anxious and depressed the next. Anxiety during pregnancy is common, and to some degree it can be an inherent part of it. However, by taking due care of your emotional state, the risk of problems in later life can be reduced.

The impact of severe stress during pregnancy. Considering how sensitive a pregnancy is to the psychological state of the mother, it's important to emphasize the influence of traumatic stress on the developing baby. Mental health problems in women during pregnancy are common. As many as 20% of pregnant women show symptoms of anxiety. Both anxiety and depression during pregnancy may later be linked to postpartum depression. Many women also experience other issues during this time. Studies carried out over the last decade have focused on the neurobehavioural and psychological functioning of the newborn [2]. There is clear evidence, for example, that high levels of stress experienced by the mother impact on the neurodevelopmental functioning of the newborn, including an increase in anxiety, a difficult temperament and sleep problems. In older children between the ages of 3 and 16, studies indicate an increased risk of emotional problems, especially anxiety, depression, the symptoms of attention deficit hyperactivity disorder (ADHD) and behavioural problems.

So, the more anxious a mother is, the greater the risk of problems for the child. However, you should keep in mind that not only toxic or extreme stress has an impact. Some studies have shown increased risk for the child if the mother is exposed to more everyday problems, or experiences strong anxiety related to her pregnancy [2]. Therefore both long-term, chronic stress and short-term every day stress, particularly if intense, can be harmful to the developing baby.

Stress and support during pregnancy. Partners, families and employers have a very important role to play. It's crucial that you receive comprehensive care. The role of the partner or close support network is probably the most important of all. Their support may be a kind of buffer for the experiences of the mother. In contrast, an unsupportive partner can make the situation significantly worse. Awareness is essential here, mainly an awareness of the needs and experiences of both the pregnant woman and her partner by society at large, including employers. There are women who love to work and will want to work until the end of their pregnancy, but there are also women for whom professional activities will be too demanding. Ideally a pregnant woman has a choice here. As far as professional help is concerned, there are usually many forms of support available, like antenatal classes. The knowledge that is passed on in these classes or in women's groups can help to alleviate many of the fears of the expectant mother, but is not enough in the case of more serious problems such as severe anxiety, high risk pregnancy or depression. In such cases a psychiatrist, psychologist or psychotherapist should be consulted.

Feeling stressed, regardless of the external situation, is a part of this special time of pregnancy. However, experiencing a great deal of permanent stress does not serve the woman or her baby's best interests. It is therefore important to surround the mother and child, and even the whole family, with proper care. ◆

Alexandra – mother of Sofia and George, psychologist and psychotherapist.

7. Cancer prevention during pregnancy — how to reduce the risk of cancer for your child?

More and more people are talking about the prevention of cancer and it is worth bringing it up early on. A malignant cancer is the result of genetic errors in DNA that lead to the uncontrolled division and multiplication of defective (cancerous) cells. We have no influence over some of the genetic conditions that can cause cancer in a child. As parents, however, you can reduce the risk of cancer to a certain extent by taking care of your own health – even before you start trying for a baby.[1]

How to minimise the risk of babies falling ill during pregnancy? Lifestyle changes, a healthy diet and physical activity support the body in the process of correct cell division. The elimination of factors that may cause DNA damage or hinder protection against genetic changes (including chemicals, cigarette smoke, alcohol or pollution) are concrete steps you can take to reduce the risk of cancer for your baby and for yourself.[2]

It's worth considering a few things during pregnancy, such as:
- quitting smoking – preferably before you start trying to have a baby (the sooner, the better); avoiding exposure to tobacco smoke (passive smoking can be harmful to the unborn baby),
- giving up alcohol,
- a healthy diet – with large portions of fruit and vegetables (wash them thoroughly before eating them), avoiding products that are highly processed, fast food, artificial additives and preservatives; take great care with food quality,
- avoiding harmful compounds or ingredients, for example in cosmetics, toys, and – not least – the air; it's worth checking lists of dangerous ingredients and read labels when shopping,
- taking care of the appropriate concentration of vitamin D3 (doses should be determined with your doctor on the basis of the results of vitamin D3 concentration in blood),
- avoiding drugs that may have teratogenic effects (toxic to the embryo or fetus); all drugs taken by a pregnant woman must be consulted with a doctor,
- avoiding viral infections, mainly measles, smallpox, rubella and flu – it is worth considering vaccination for these diseases during pregnancy planning.

---

[1] Cancer Prevention, "Recommendations and public health and policy implications 2018", World Cancer Research Fund/American Institute for Cancer Research.
[2] "Diet, Nutrition, Physical Activity and Cancer: a Global Perspective", Continuous Update Project Expert Report 2018, World Cancer Research Fund/American Institute for Cancer Research.

Extra measures to keep a future mother healthy include:
- reducing unhealthy fats and sugar, banning sweetened drinks (excessive sugar consumption interferes with pancreatic function and insulin production, which increases the risk of diabetes and obesity in the mother and her offspring),[2]
- taking care of your weight before and during pregnancy – you don't have to eat "for two" when you're pregnant, it's enough on average to add about 300 more calories,[3]
- outdoor exercise,
- getting enough good sleep.

The role of the father. Future fathers can also influence the health of their offspring. More and more research shows that a man's preconception lifestyle is linked to the quality of semen and the risk of serious diseases in the child[4]. Avoiding chemicals, ensuring a healthy diet, reducing alcohol and not smoking (also in the company of a pregnant woman) are measures that should all be taken to help reduce the risk of your child developing cancer.

These actions, which should already be taken when you are planning to grow your family, will certainly have a positive impact on both your health and the health of your child. ◆

Eve – mother of three sons, the youngest of whom beat leukemia. Editor-in-chief of a website which provides information about cancer in children.

Consultation: Prof. Thomas Szczepanski – Head of Department of Pediatric Hematology and Oncology in Zabrze, Medical University of Silesia in Katowice, Poland.

---

[3] "Nutrition Recommendations in Pregnancy and Lactation", collective work, 2016, https:// www.ncbi.nlm.nih.gov/pubmed/29842836.
[4] Schmidt CW, "Chips off the Old Block: How a Father's Preconception Exposures Might Affect the Health of His Children", Environ Health Perspect, 2018, https:// www.ncbi.nlm.nih.gov/pmc/articles/PMC6066336/

8. Preterm babies — happiness that comes early

A premature baby is a baby born before week 37 of the pregnancy. Before week 28 is termed 'extremely premature', while after week 34 is 'late premature'. At this stage the organs are basically formed, although there remain the issues of independent eating and breathing, as well as catching up on weight. Extremely premature babies are in the most difficult situation and they are the ones fighting the toughest battle for life.

Premature birth. The causes of preterm birth are extremely varied. They can be caused by problems in your physiology, incorrect development during pregnancy or by external factors such as infections. Sometimes, however, despite a healthy lifestyle and frequent medical check-ups, a preterm birth happens. It can happen without any previous symptoms – the birth simply begins and nothing can stop it. In this case the most important thing is to get to the hospital quickly, preferably – if possible – one with a neonatal unit for premature babies. Any bleeding or pain similar to that which accompanies a stomach or menstrual disorder, is a signal that something isn't right and you need to go for check-up. Also, a lack of physical activity or movement from the baby throughout the day should be a concern, and it's advisable to go to a medical expert. When a premature birth begins, after you have been admitted to the hospital and examined, you may receive steroids designed to accelerate the development of the child's lungs and probably an IV with a drug to delay delivery (usually by a few days, sometimes a few hours – but there are times when it will not delay it at all). If you can be transported to a hospital with a neonatal ward, your baby will be admitted to it immediately after birth. If not, he or she will be transported to a hospital where the personnel are able to provide the right level of care. At this point, unfortunately, you can remain in a different hospital from your child until you are discharged.

The birth of a premature baby looks slightly different to that of a classic hospital birth. Nobody pays attention to the birth plan. The priority is the welfare of the baby. The standard procedure for preterm birth is an episiotomy to protect the baby's head. The whole birth takes place with the assistance of a doctor. If a midwife is present, it is the doctor – not the midwife – who is in charge of the birth. The father of the child or partner may also be present.

First moments after the birth. An extremely premature baby isn't handed to you after birth. It is immediately examined and, if necessary, intubated, and immediately afterwards it goes into an incubator. You will be transferred to the postpartum ward alone, while the baby will be transferred – depending on its condition – to either an intensive care unit (ICU) or the Neonatal Intensive Care Unit (NICU). Extremely premature babies and babies with birth defects are transferred to the ICU. Physiologically safe, fully developed and late preterm babies weighing more than 2,500 g can stay with their mother if the doctor decides so. The rest go to the NICU.

The mother of a premature baby. Your most important task after a premature birth is to induce and maintain lactation. Doctors in the NICU ward believe that there is nothing better for a baby than breast milk, which allows the baby to develop better and make up for weight loss and development. The mother's milk is not only considered food, but also medicine. In order to stimulate and sustain lactation, you have to pump frequently, at least 6-8 times a day, at equal intervals. In the neonatology ward there are usually breast pumps available, which can be used while on the hospital premises (both until you discharged, as well as during your visits to your baby). If you have problems with inducing lactation, it's best to consult a Lactation Consultant (hospital or private) who will recommend steps to take. Also check whether there is a milk bank in the hospital or one nearby. This allows your baby to have access to natural breast milk before you start lactating.

After a premature birth, you only stay in the hospital ward for a few days, like a regular birth, and then you are discharged. If you would like to stay in or near the hospital, you should ask if there is a bed in another ward available, or sometimes there are beds available in other hospital buildings, such as mothers' dormitories. Whatever you decide, you have the right to stay with your child as long as you want. Your partner can visit at certain stated times. During this time, depending on the hospital, you can stay with your child together or you can alternate with your partner. It is sometimes the case that only the child's parents can enter the NICU and wards marked for continuous care (that is, the ones that a child will stay in after leaving the ICU).

Feeding a premature baby. If you opt for breastfeeding, you'll need to deliver your milk to the hospital. It should be stored and transported according to the instructions given by the hospital. If for some reason you do not deliver the milk, your baby will receive a milk substitute formula for premature babies or milk from the milk bank (if available in your hospital and you agree to this).

If for various reasons you cannot produce or feed your own milk, you can use the milk bank.

For preterm babies with low birth weight, the hospital sometimes adds a formula to the milk that speeds up the baby's weight gain – ask about it when you are discharged from the hospital. After consultation with your doctor you can order it from the pharmacy and add it when you return home.

The baby's time in hospital. The hospital often offers parents a free course for preterm care and first aid. During your child's stay in hospital you can (together with the baby's father) take part in care activities such as changing nappies, breastfeeding or bottle feeding, while bathing and dressing your baby is the responsibility of the medical staff.

Contact with a parent is very important for a preterm baby. You can touch him or her in the incubator and talk or sing to him or her. Your smell is very important to your baby. Ask if you can 'kangaroo' your baby (also known as 'skin to skin'). If there is no good reason not to, even babies weighing only a kilo from the incubator can be kangarooed. The staff have a duty to make this possible. It has been scientifically proven that children who receive skin to skin develop better and catch up with their peers faster than those who don't. The recommended minimum time for skin to skin is one hour. There is no upper time limit.

The medical staff have a duty to keep you informed of everything that concerns your child. Ask the doctors or nurses about any issues related to your care and the baby's general condition, progress, possible treatments or surgeries, medicines administered, examinations carried out and their results. The doctor may order an eye examination. If an abnormality is detected in the initial examination, or if it's unclear, further examinations will be ordered.

In the NICU, the doctor is fully in charge. If you disagree with any form of treatment, and the doctors consider that there is a threat to your child's life and the treatment is necessary, they can contact a court and the court can deprive you of your parental rights if it believes it is necessary to do so (legal conditions vary from country to country, so you need to check your rights here). In the neonatal ward, if there is no life-threatening situation, you can decide whether you approve of a given form of treatment (for example, blood transfusions if the child is weak and anaemic). You also have the right to decide whether or not to vaccinate your child. If you have given your consent for vaccinations but do not want your baby to have those that the hospital provides, in some countries you have the option of buying other vaccines at the pharmacy and delivering them to the ward under appropriate transport conditions.

The baby placed in the incubator is transferred to a regular cot after he or she has mastered breathing and reached a minimum weight of 1700 g. In order for the baby to be discharged from the hospital, it needs to achieve a minimum weight of 2 kg and learn how to breathe and eat independently.

Returning home. It is not possible to return to the neonatal ward once you have been discharged. If there is a problem, the discharged baby will be transferred to another ward in the children's hospital, not the maternity ward. Make sure you read the discharge notes before leaving the hospital and if you have any doubts, ask a doctor. You should also receive a number of referrals. Some of these referrals will indicate a specific date of the visit to a given institution, while others will require you to make an appointment. Try to do this as soon as possible, as waiting times can be long and time is crucial for premature babies. When you call the clinic, be clear that you are making an appointment for a premature baby as some clinics and hospitals keep spaces available. Check-ups that can be done for preterm babies include:
- eye examination (ophthalmologist; examination of the fundus every two weeks until the retinopathy ceases to be a threat),
- heart test (cardiologist),
- hearing screening,
- regular checks to a neonatologist and psychologist. It is also worth making an appointment with an orthopaedist (referral can be issued by a pediatrician).

Immunisation record. Before introducing a vaccination calendar, you can consider visiting a neurologist who will determine the neurological status of your baby. The referral must be issued by a doctor. You should also ask your doctor to refer you to the vaccination clinic, especially if there are any post-vaccination complications or reactions. Remember to indicate that your baby is a premature baby, as this may help to get an earlier appointment. The clinic will help you choose the safest possible package and will adapt the timing of the vaccinations to your baby's situation. A good time to make such a visit is after a neurological check-up, when you have the results of the tests. In many countries a premature baby is entitled to free combined vaccinations, because he or she cannot be vaccinated with a whole cell pertussis (against the whooping cough), but only with an acellular one. You need to make sure your clinic doesn't forget about this.

"Must haves" at home. Before you leave the hospital, you need to get some baby clothes specifically for a premature baby. Sometimes they're not easy to find, so try to get hold of them beforehand. A breast pump is a *must have* item for a premature baby. You will also need a thermal pack with cooling pads to transport the milk to the hospital. After discharge, a respiratory monitor is highly recommended. This device is placed under the mattress of the cot and monitors your baby's breathing. It will immediately sound an alarm if breathing stops for over 20 seconds. It's best to choose a model with a medical certificate, because a quick reaction can save a premature baby's life.

When will a premature baby catch up with its peers? The age of a preterm baby is calculated according to two dates: the date of birth and the due date (corrected age). Both dates should always be given to healthcare professionals, as they are both needed to check the progress of your baby. All developmental expectations placed on the child are compared against their age and rehabilitation activities are arranged according to their due date. The diet is extended between the actual age and the due date, and is adjusted on the basis of observation. A premature baby ceases to be treated as such when he or she is two years old (according to the due date). By this time, all developmental differences should have evened out and the toddler shouldn't stand out from its peers.

Regardless of medical progress, a premature baby, especially extreme cases, may have to deal with some effects of prematurity all their life. However, it is comforting to know that even extremely premature babies are increasingly likely to survive than in the past. Regardless of the problems you face as a premature baby's mother, remember that for your little warrior, you are always the greatest support. If you are close, loving and committed at every step, many problems can be overcome. ◆

Anna – mother of a premature child who was born in week 28.

My story

Don't raise the child you wanted, raise the one you have.

Yoda, like most newborn babies, was no beauty; the complete lack of hair on the top of his head, combined with his monk-like crown, gave the impression of a little old man. I was so happy to hold him in my arms. I was only worried about two things: a very low weight (2160 g) and his foggy eyes. But then a nightmarish procession of doctors began, which lasted for over a year.

After just a few hours, a well-known ophthalmologist was called from another hospital. The small examination room quickly became cramped. There was me, a midwife, a neonatologist, the head of neonatology and a neonatal eye specialist wearing cosmic goggles. Tiny Yoda was lying on the table, receiving anaesthetic eye drops. I watched the doctor put a metal device between his eyelids. A nightmare. No one but the midwife was talking to me directly. It was a conversation between doctors. Only when I started asking simple questions, the slightly impatient doctor said that his eyes were not reacting to light. I didn't understand, I asked for an explanation. "That means he can't see." End of test.

Yoda was wrapped up in a blanket and given back to me without a word. I didn't have time to think about it because there was a new problem. Yoda's sugar level started to drop, and since he was tiny and pretty weak, he couldn't suck well by himself yet. It was quickly decided to take him to the intensive care unit. He was given a heated cot and an IV drip. I caught up with him there, but I couldn't stay the whole night. I went down to the room where we were supposed to spend our first night, hugging him and getting to know each other. Suddenly I was caught up in all the repressed feelings and negative thoughts. I realised that my son was blind. All my plans were ruined. I felt very lost and didn't know if I was up to being the mother of a disabled child. I fell asleep, broken, with tears in my eyes and a feeling of complete helplessness.

In the morning I got up, washed, dressed and went to see my son. Holding, feeding and nurturing him gave me new strength. He was so tiny and helpless, and I knew I had to be strong. He was relying on me. Almost immediately I realised that the ophthalmologic diagnosis was wrong because his eyes squinted under the strong light of the incubator lamp. I tried to keep my emotions in check, but I was hoping that maybe he could see something. As it turned out, I was right.

After more than a week we ended up in the neonatal pathology ward in another hospital, where we were stuck for several weeks. It was the most difficult period. Yoda was subjected to various examinations almost every day, most of which prevented me from being with him. Ever more doctors found new problems in my son's body. When we finally returned home after almost a month, it was the happiest day of my life. First we got some sleep, lying down together (we slept separately in the hospital), then we started going out for walks. After weeks of being closed in a stuffy ward, where you couldn't open the windows, I felt that I could breathe again.

Now, almost two and a half years since Yoda's birth, I have managed to put that time behind me. I hope that my son remembers even less than I do. Only photos, blog and Facebook entries and a pale scar on his chest remind us of our story (that time in hospital). And there was a lot of that: laparoscopic surgery, heart coils and – immediately afterwards – open-heart surgery. Weeks of hospitals, dozens of medical visits, examinations and hours of sessions with various therapists.

Yoda is not much different from his peers. He is tiny and sometimes he moves very cautiously. We know he can see things, but we don't know to what extent. Just like other children his age, he has his favourite toys and food. He goes down slides and loves swings. He wants us to read to him endlessly the same books – books we already know by heart. He climbs on the furniture and falls off just like healthy children.

When I think about the horror I felt after the diagnosis of my son's eyes, I am a little angry with myself. In the hospitals I met parents and children with problems much worse than ours, and they didn't give up, they just went ahead. In one *book about the development of children with visual problems, I read a shocking sentence: in order to be a good parent to a disabled child, you have to first mourn the healthy child who was expected, but was never born. This is true. If I focused on everything I can't do with my son, I would miss out on what we can do. And there's more and more to do. I just found out that skiing is not completely lost and I'm already thinking about where Yoda and his dad will be able to experience the joys of the 'white madness' in two years time.*

I have the impression that today's ease of access to information is sometimes a curse. All too often we try to put our children into certain frames of reference, constantly analysing and comparing. You need to give your child space and opportunities for self-development, instead of matching them to your ideas. The process of getting to the point where I was no longer raising the child that I had wanted and had created in my head, but the one that was born, was enlightening and gave me a sense of relief, joy and fulfilment. ◆

Susanna Angelosanto – Philip and Felix's mum.

Baby essentials

9. The nesting instinct — fact or excuse?

"Nesting instinct" is a well-known term, yet no dictionary or encyclopedia defines it. How do we know whether such a thing exists at all? Perhaps it is just a made up idea by expecting mothers?

What does science say? The nesting instinct, or nesting, is a natural part of pregnancy resulting from fluctuations in hormones and changes in the woman's body. It most often occurs in the third trimester of pregnancy when there is a decrease in progesterone and an increase in oxytocin – the hormone responsible for starting the birth contractions of the uterus. Scientists say that it is probably because of oxytocin that most women feel a sudden surge of energy to 'nest'.

Will it be the same with you? It's not for certain. Some women say that the nesting instinct doesn't affect them at all, while others state that it appears early on in their pregnancy. "When I found out about the first pregnancy, it was as if I was struck by lightning," says Madelaine. "I planned, renovated, shopped, cleaned – it was madness! With the second child, I promised myself that it would be different, that I wouldn't go crazy... but it was even worse. I renovated and cleaned what I had already renovated and cleaned." There are mums who feel the nesting instinct very strongly in their first pregnancy only, spending the whole 9 months renovating or shopping for the baby. Each of us is different and will experience this condition differently – or not at all. Remember that there is nothing worse than comparing yourself to other mums. Try to experience your pregnancy as beautifully as you can, and in your own way!

The nesting instinct can also affect men. This is great news for us women. Together with the father of the child you can use the time to prepare your home for your baby's appearance. This can be a fantastic opportunity to get closer and take co-responsibility for your baby's arrival. During my coaching sessions with parents, I have met many couples who had never had such a close and warm relationship with each other as they had during pregnancy.

Take note. If you're actually experiencing the nesting instinct and you're caught up in the irresistible temptation to renovate your home or buy baby clothes and toys – give yourself the right to do so. Don't deny your emotions and don't deny yourself the right to happiness. This is a special time. Make the most of it – these moments may not come again. But you also need to put yourself first. If you want to paint the baby's room or move the furniture, don't do it all yourself! Remember that you are pregnant and there is nothing more important than the wellbeing of you and your baby. Your energy and excitement can make you move mountains, but you will feel just as happy and fulfilled supervising the renovation work, as opposed to doing it all yourself.

Use your energy. Since you know the nesting instinct is not an illness or invention by pregnant women, do your best to use your energy wisely. Try to involve the father of the child or your partner as well. This is the right time to discuss things together, plan the nursery and organise the first weeks of your new life together. It can also help you avoid conflict.

Also consider whether it is better to invest your time and energy in things that are important to you rather than in renovations and shopping. Think about what you enjoy and what you may not have time to do once the baby arrives. It's a great time to realise your dreams and develop your passions. You could, for example, take the time to make some handicrafts for your baby, or maybe learn a new language?

You have a lot to plan and prepare for, so you can welcome your baby into the world calmly. Use the power of your hormones, but don't forget that you are special and you have the best intuition about what is best for you. ◆

Dominica – a mother, ICF coach and supervisor.

10. An oasis of peace and development. Arranging your baby's room

When you're expecting a baby, you'll be planning to set up a baby room or a baby corner in one of your rooms. The media, retailers and online stores encourage you to buy lots of things, take into account current trends in interior design, and basically convince you that you need to buy all the furniture and accessories necessary to care for your child and make sure it's as comfortable as possible. Stop. Before you furnish your baby's room, think about who and what it's for? The answer to this key question will help you to arrange the space based on actual needs, rather than marketing forces.

Who is the baby room for? A baby's room – or corner, as the name suggests – is a space primarily for your BABY, not for the adult looking after the baby. When you realise this, a lot of furniture and accessories are suddenly rendered unnecessary.

In your child's room you can create a space that grows with your child, according to his or her abilities and needs. It will help him or her feel safe and enjoy playing and exploring its surroundings.

How to arrange a room for an infant up to one year old? Of course you need to consider the baby's current needs (which grow month by month), but don't forget that your baby will use its room for the next few years. You might like to take into account, for example, Maria Montessori's methodology (▶ II – 100), which has a lot in common with minimalism. Or the Japanese art of organising according to Marie Kondo (the so-called KonMarie method), and not least the limitations of your space at home. Follow the gist from them: the room should be comfortable for the baby, fit for the baby's fine motor skills, encourage activity and be well thought out.

What's useful in a child's room or corner?
- A place to sleep – if your baby sleeps with you in bed or in his or her cot in your bedroom, he or she doesn't need to have a separate sleeping area initially. However, if you choose to have your baby sleep in a separate room, remember that its sleeping place should be, above all, safe (▶ II – 32), without too many distractions or decorations. The cot needs to provide a peaceful sleep, not encourage play. Also keep in mind that there is no need for patterned bedding, which can be a sensory overload for the baby. Let the child's sleeping area be calm, subdued, quiet and secluded.
- The playmat – it is designed to be safe and can be easily fitted to any space. The baby does not have to stay in his or her cot or rocker (which is not recommended by physiotherapists by the way) all the time, he or she can freely start using a playmat or 'activity mat' and its surroundings on his or her own for tummy time and play (under supervision) whenever he or she is able to.
- A mirror on the wall – placed next to the playmat supports fine motor skills and physical development while encouraging better coordination of the body. It can also help a baby get to know its own body, and encourages movement.
- Basket with toys – initially just a few, because a baby doesn't need many. They should preferably be made from natural material like wicker, wood or cotton.
- Bookshelves – it's worth placing the baby's books low enough for them to reach themselves in time.

- Toy rack – for older babies who already have more toys. They can be divided thematically, with one shelf for instruments and another for animal figures, for example.
- Carpet – as a sensory variation on the floor.
- Wardrobe – open, with some clothes on shelves or in baskets. Even if a child does not dress itself until the age of 1 or 2, it's worth allowing him or her to experience his or her clothes in familiar surroundings. Initially, this will mean your baby throwing its clothes everywhere :) but be patient. Your baby is watching you, and when he or she sees that clothes have their place and are properly arranged, at some point he or she will also want to sort their clothes themselves.

What kind of furniture is not needed in your baby's room?
- Change table – you can put it in the bathroom or bedroom, or you can simply give it up completely by changing your child on the bed or on the sofa, with the use of a mat.
- Wardrobe – for the first few years it will probably be too tall for a child – too heavy and inaccessible (because it hides the contents, which discourages children). Besides, babies do not need many clothes, so you can keep them in your own wardrobe for the first months of its life.
- A feeding chair – it may come in handy if you've decided to have your baby sleep in its own room from birth, and you need to feed them at night, sitting down. If you are breastfeeding, it could be more comfortable for you to breastfeed lying on a sofa or taking your baby to bed for feeding.

The most important thing to remember is that a baby's room (or corner) is not a room where his or her belongings are stored, but a space where the furniture is suitable for their fine motor skills and challenges them, but does not interfere with their development or inhibit their independence.

Arranging a room for a child under 3 years old. A toddler aged 1-3 years freely explores the space in his or her own house or apartment. A sense of ownership and willingness to make decisions on everyday matters grows each day, such as the choice of what to wear. It's worth arranging his or her room or corner so that it can be used independently and safely for various activities. Remember that many activities which adults do every day in different rooms,

children do within one room. Each activity can require different things, as well as circumstances which encourage either quiet play or movement.
- **The sleep zone (sometimes combined with a relaxation zone).** Here your child sleeps, relaxes or is read to. This zone should not contain excessive stimuli, such as colours or patterns. A safe and comfortable bed, one which he or she can get into and out of by him or herself, is obviously a must. A corner is usually the best place to put the bed, away from radiators, doors or windows.
- **The fun zone.** This is where your child plays with his or her toys, which are stored and organised. The furniture shouldn't be too high for the child – he or she should be able to reach the top shelf. Little children enjoy the things they see. That is why I recommend using small wicker baskets, wooden trays and knitted bowls that show their contents, and I advise against deep baskets or crates.
- **The reading zone.** This area should not be distracted by decorations and colours, but should encourage free access to books and provide a comfortable place to read them (on a seat, pillow or carpet). The books should be placed at the front of the room, with their attractive covers on display, encouraging the child to reach for them. It should be lit appropriately, with a switch that a child can easily reach.
- **The dressing area.** Here the child's clothes are arranged and he or she can look in a mirror, building self-awareness of his or her body. Hand-eye coordination is exercised, as well as the opportunity for fine motor exercises such as hanging clothes on a hanger, fastening buttons or putting on clothes. The mirror can also help the child immediately check his or her outfit choices as the clothes are put on.
- **The music zone.** Here the child plays instruments, listens to music, sings, dances, learns about the body and expresses emotions. It can be combined with the clothing zone (with its mirror). Consider the space needed for movement such as dancing and free access to instruments.
- **The sports zone.** It could just be a swing, a rocker, a ladder or a climbing wall. Safety is key here.
- **The work zone.** Here the child can engage in creative, artistic or handiwork. This area should ideally be by a window, and remember to create space for

art materials that the child can freely use. This area should not be distracted by intense colours, patterns and excessive decorations.

When we create areas that support activities and allow our child to use all the furniture on his or her own, the child will feel 'at home' and will be happy to spend time in his or her room, encouraging us to accompany him or her.

Furniture for the baby's room. Remember to choose furniture that is functional and useful for your child. Unfortunately, most children's furniture on the market is not suited for little ones – even from well-known brands or designer boutiques. Keep in mind the following:

- Height – your child should be able to use the top shelf of the play rack or bookshelf without having to constantly ask for your help.
- Weight – he or she should be able to open drawers on his or her own, pick up a basket or open the wardrobe door. If furniture is too heavy, it will discourage a child from using it.
- Convenience of use – buy a chair where the child can rest its feet on the floor, or a bed in which it will feel safe.
- Materials – let your child experience a variety of natural materials: wicker, wood, stone, cotton, linen, glass, ceramic and wool to name a few. Objects made of artificial materials should be a last resort.
- Quality and style – you may choose to have your child experience good-quality things, which are pretty and stylish, as opposed to cheap and plastic. This could teach them respect for possessions, and how to handle objects in a safe way, as well as building up an eye for aesthetics.
- Keep clean – allow your child to experience his or her room without constantly worrying about keeping it tidy. Pay attention to materials that don't get dirty easily and have washable surfaces. Have colours and patterns that are not only bright, but also don't show up dirt, so you can relax and enjoy your child's room too.

Properly selected furniture in a child's room will make it feel 'at home', safe and free. He or she shouldn't have to hear constantly: "don't move it," "watch out or you'll fall," or "don't touch or you'll get dirty." Remember: a relaxed child is a child who explores, develops well and is happy.

Colours, decorations, accessories... Toys, clothes, books or plastic materials – you will get a feeling for how much visual stimulation these things offer your child. So think about the number and type of decorations you use in their room. The room shouldn't be overpowering (▶ II – 61). Too much visual stimulation causes children to become tired faster, making them irritable and sometimes overwhelmed, so they find it difficult to make choices. It can even make them reluctant to go into their room.

- The colour of the walls. As they get older, children may spend an increasing amount of time in their rooms doing various things, so it's worth choosing a wall colour that will support these activities – neither too intense nor too dark, nor in fact too light. A well-chosen colour harmonizes with the natural light in the room – for example brightening hidden spaces. On the other hand, darker colours can fit nicely in rooms that are well-lit by daylight. Remember, though, that the sensation of a colourful room can also be achieved by selecting the right accessories. There is a lot of research and inspiration on the influence of colour on our health and wellbeing, and I encourage you to explore this topic.
- Wallpaper. For wallpaper, choose an area of the room away from the peaceful zones where the child needs less visual stimulation, such as the sleep or work zone. Find an area of the wall where wallpaper can be used as a decoration.
- Accessories. The devil is in the details here :). Things such as pillows, curtains, pots, rugs or stickers on the wardrobe can add a nice touch. The most important thing is that they should be stylish, coherent and introduce a variety of materials (preferably only natural), for example a wicker pot next to a ceramic one, a woollen drape next to a linen curtain or a metal lamp. Avoid plastic not only because it harms the environment, but also because there's little pleasure in touching it.
- Flowers. Plants and flowers have a positive effect on our health and well-being. Having them at home can sooth nerves, and they provide an excellent opportunity to learn about the laws of nature. They can be a great lesson in attention and responsibility. If you are worried that your child may eat plants, then choose non-poisonous species or hang them in the window, put them on shelves or on high cabinets. There are many possibilities – it's really worth it!

- Toys. Sometimes it can feel like the whole purpose of a baby's room is to store an increasing amount of toys. This is entirely wrong! Excess toys are not conducive to a child's development. All you have to do is stick to the rule that the only toys in a child's room are those which he or she is currently playing with. Rotation is a good way to give toys a second life.

How to arrange everything in a small room?
- Furniture – including each of the zones doesn't mean you need a lot of furniture. Take the music zone, for example. It's enough just to have a small number of instruments in a basket – and there you have it, your music zone.
- Shared areas – if your child's room is separate but quite small, choose things that you can move from the room to other parts of the house – for example if you have a walk-in wardrobe in your room. You can create a space in it for the child's dressing area.
- Connect sibling zones – if brothers or sisters live in the same room, you can connect their selected zones in one place, for example organizing one cabinet or wardrobe with two doors, one for each child.

A corner instead of a room? A separate child's room is a kind of luxury, an opportunity to improve the comfort of everyday life. Often, however, the youngest person in the family is not able to have a separate room. Is this a problem? Absolutely not! However, it does require a certain reorganisation of space in order to adjust to the needs and capabilities of the smallest household members. Here a division into different activity zones can really make a difference.
- Play area – designate a corner in the lounge for your child's toys, with the right furniture in place to play safely and comfortably.
- Dressing area – use the lower part of your wardrobe for your child's clothes, arranged so that they can access them freely.
- Work area – at the dining or coffee table, create a part that your child will always be able to use without feeling that it interferes with the functionality of the table.
- Reading zone – create a space next to the child's bed for his or her books so that he or she can use them comfortably in bed.

- Sleep/relax zone – if your child sleeps with you, you have a common zone. However, if he or she has a separate cot, you can place it next to your bed so that you have a common sleeping area too.
- Sports zone – why not hang a swing or jumper on the doorframe and without taking up space you've got a little bit of movement at home!
- Music zone – connect it to your zone: let your child's instruments be accompanied by your CDs, your music player, so that you can enjoy listening to music together!

Remember that:
- Don't make the room for yourself – make it for your child.
- From time to time, think about whether the room or corner is still suitable for your child.
- Watch your child – each baby or toddler's room will be different depending on their interests, character, needs and abilities.

Above all, engage your child! Arranging furniture, planting flowers, hanging pictures – these activities will make your child even more comfortable in his or her room. ◆

Dominica – mother of a daughter, caregiver for 4 animals and a bunch of plants. Owns and runs a company which assists and advises on the arrangement of space in the home with a child's development uppermost in mind.

11. Making your home safe for your baby

Your average apartment is not designed or furnished for the needs of a small child. But the comfort and safety of the youngest members of your household is a priority. Household accidents are the main cause of death or disability of children in all EU countries. Each year, there are 10 million reports of accidents involving children at home and tragically 40,000 of them result in death [1]. Experts estimate that 90% of accidents at home are preventable – and whose responsibility is this if not the parents? On the other hand, experience shows that protecting the child from every bruise and scratch is, on the one hand, impossible, and, on the other hand, harmful to a child's upbringing. You can't wrap a child in cotton wool. I propose a common sense approach.

Here's a list of things you need to do:
- Make sure the sleeping environment is safe. There should be no objects, soft toys, pillows, blankets (▶ II – 32).
- Secure the stairs, fireplace and other hazardous areas with gates (you can have, for instance, a baby gate at the entrance of the kitchen). Always pay attention to the manufacturer's recommendations.
- Try to eliminate gaps larger than 7 cm. They are dangerous because your toddler may try to squeeze its feet through them – or get its head stuck. Places you can often find them: between the cot and – for example – a chest of drawers with a changing table, between the rungs of any railings, between the safety gate and the floor, etc.
- Attach all furniture to the walls. Not just the pieces which are tall and narrow. Also fasten the TV and secure the cables of devices that are at the height of your countertop or above – equipment can fall when cables are pulled.
- Secure the windows. Having a short lock on the opening width of the window can be convenient so you can safely ventilate the apartment. Remember that bars or mosquito nets will not protect your child from falling out.

- Plan where you will keep your medical supplies, detergents and other potentially toxic substances. Store them in a place that is out of sight and inaccessible to children, preferably high (above tabletop level) and in a locked cabinet. Be consistent – dangerous substances should be put back immediately after each use.
- Look through your entire place for small objects which your child could choke on. Use your imagination – some objects don't look dangerous, but they can break into small pieces. Pay the greatest attention to small button batteries, for example in clocks or LED lights, they not only cause choking but also serious chemical burns (especially if they get stuck in the oesophagus.
- Check electrical installations. Injuries from electricity are rare, but you can't disregard them. Hide cables and replace sockets with ones with child locks (which work better than socket plugs).
- Remove all cords and wires that could form a loop which your child could put around his or her neck. This applies primarily to all roller blinds and shutters, but don't forget thin cables (for example from a phone charger) and lantern-type decorations and pendants. If you can't keep them out of your child's way – and sight – try to permanently roll the cables up so that they don't hang freely.
- Equip each bedroom and kitchen with fire detectors. Check them every 6 months and teach your household how the alarm sounds and what to do if it goes off (you should leave the house without stopping to pack things, and notify the fire department). It is worth practicing fire alarm drills with the whole family from time to time.
- Get rid of poisonous potted plants (and balcony and garden plants). Popular ones include Dieffenbachia, Croton, Dracaena, Fig trees, Philodendron, Anthurium, Blacksmith and Potted ivy. It's hard to make a complete list so it's best to just check all the plants you have at home.

Finally, a few words about the safeguards which work and those that don't. I would advise against locks that attract a child's attention – those which are colourful or have a 'childish' design. Avoid solutions which are trivial, such as those with a single button or Velcro. Better are those that have two unlock points to be pressed simultaneously or require considerable physical strength. Unfortunately, it is generally the case that the safety features are either one or the other – either safe, or comfortable to use. It's difficult to find ones that meet both criteria.

As parents, you need to approach your child's safety comprehensively and choose an educational approach that is most convenient for you. A rule of thumb is that the less protection there is, the more carefully you should supervise your child. Reports show that children's accidents happen as a result of a temporary break in active supervision – the parent went to open the door for the courier, answered the phone or went to the bathroom. In practice, it's not possible to keep a constant vigilance, and you have to accept this. As Joanna writes: "It's better to have everything installed and ready than to watch the knife drawer around the clock. Unfortunately, even the best security features do not relieve you from supervision – they are designed in such a way as to give you some more time to react. That's it." ♦

Agnes – child-proofer, an expert in child safety whose mission is to create child-friendly homes.

12. Baby essentials — do we have it easier than our mums?

When a mother discovers she's pregnant, she often goes through the so-called nesting instinct – she's thinking of a beautiful room, colourful clothes and pushing the latest stroller. And then, with each subsequent year, things start to accumulate. Nowadays you can get everything at your fingertips – which on the one hand is convenient, but on the other hand it's easy to get lost in a shopping frenzy.

How not to go crazy. The first time we have a child, we're often under the impression that everything will come in handy. Only after a while do we see the heap of clothes and toys growing incredibly fast, especially as family and friends come bearing gifts.

A good way to get your baby essentials together is to take a cool approach. Wait a while and when the initial emotions subside, think carefully about what you really need.

In the first trimester you may not feel very well, but it's best not to wait until the 9th month because you may not have the strength to run around the stores then. The optimal time to buy baby things seems to be between the 4th and 7th month of pregnancy.

HOW TO GET ON WITH IT

The list. Make a list of necessary things (clothes, cosmetics, accessories, equipment).

The budget. Think about how much you can and want to spend on all your baby things (▶ I -13). You can divide it into two: things you need before the birth and those you can hold back on (and even add to your wish list (e.g. for a baby shower).

Other sources of supply ;). Maybe you have a sister or a close friend who had a baby some time ago who could give you clothes or accessories? Or maybe it is worth going 'second hand'? In this way you can save money and be environmentally friendly (▶ II – 150).

The gender. Will you be finding out in advance? If not, don't worry if you're not sure about buying pink or blue. The range of clothes and accessories is so wide that you can easily find beautiful products in universal colours.

Finally, one more thing: who are you really buying for? Let's be honest – for a baby it really doesn't matter what he or she is dressed in (as long as it's warm and dry!) or what colour the carpet in his or her room is. We buy what we like. And that's ok! This is supposed to be fun for you too! Just try not to go to extremes, especially if you have a limited budget. ♦

Eve – Emily, Sebastian and Rosa's mother.

13. Baby essentials — putting it all together sensibly

Buying baby items can cost a lot of money. As Agatha says: "Children can be a bottomless piggy bank, but in a good way. Sometimes parents think their children need a super swanky pram and designer clothing. In fact, this is only in their imagination. What the child is wearing or riding in, is of very little interest to them at all.

Baby things can be bought economically, although opinions on whether it is right to save money are (as usual!) divided. Some people think that you shouldn't save money on a child, others think the opposite. Alice sums it up well: "I think a child costs as much as their parents want to spend." I agree with her, because it's up to us how much we want to spend – and what we can afford.

Make a list of all the things you need! At the very beginning, think about what you really need, because over time many products turn out to be unnecessary. You don't have to buy everything before the birth, some things, like pacifiers or breast pumps, can be bought only when you really need them. In the age of online shopping, this is fast and simple. When it comes to clothes, don't buy early – you don't know how big the baby will be when it's born, nor how fast it will grow. Ursula writes:"With my first child I wanted to be as prepared as possible by predicting every possible situation. As a result, I bought a lot of unnecessary things, and had far too many of them."

Once you have put together a list of necessary items, divide it into those that absolutely should be bought as new (e.g. car seat, mattress, pacifiers), those that you would like to buy as new (e.g. a beautiful blanket) and those that can be bought second hand (e.g. stroller, furniture, clothes).

Where to buy second-hand items?
- **Family and friends.** Maybe your sister's or friend's child has grown up a bit and no longer needs some of their baby clothes or accessories? You can offer to buy them for a small amount or they might be given to you for free, and when your baby has outgrown them, you'll pass them on!

- **Neighbours and the local community.** Local garage sales are fashionable again, and so-called 'baby swaps' are becoming increasingly popular. These are events where parents exchange or sell children's clothes, accessories or toys cheaply. There are also local selling groups and "mums groups" on Facebook – check which ones are around your area. Maybe you'll make some new friends at the same time?
Still popular and not "embarrassing" at all, since even celebrities buy from them ;) are thrift shops (some even catering exclusively to children) and street markets (where you can find strollers, furniture and accessories). You may also get lucky and find completely new or designer products in them.
- **The all-powerful Internet.** The possibilities here are endless – from sales platforms like eBay and Amazon, where you can filter "used" items, through to online second hand forums where mums sell their stuff.

How to buy new things.
- **Hunt for promotions and sales.** In store and online. They go on practically all year round and prices can fall anywhere between 30-90% at the end of each season.
- **Last season's models.** Manufacturers sometimes only change the smallest detail in the product to introduce their "new collection" and products from the previous one are usually a lot cheaper.
- **Outlets.** Physical and online. They regularly have new products with small, often-invisible minor faults.
- **Price comparison websites.** If you are a fan of online shopping, you know for sure that the price of one product can vary greatly between retailers.

What else can you do? Look for multifunctional products (e.g. a baby sling which can also be used as a blanket or hammock), buy reusable products (e.g. diapers, baby wipes, breast pads, changing pads) which are initially more expensive but cheaper in the long run, and in the case of cosmetics and cleaning products, look for natural substitutes which are cheaper, healthier and more environmentally friendly (▶ II – 25, 29).

If you do all these things you can save a substantial amount of money, and what you choose to spend it on is up to you. Maybe it's worth thinking about travelling together, just the two of you? ◆

Eve – Emily, Sebastian and Rosa's mother.

14. Baby essentials — clothes

There will come the long-awaited moment when you want to buy your first tiny little outfits. There are so many choices that sometimes you don't know what to do. I suggest some universal rules to follow, then I'll leave the rest in your hands!

Which size? You never know exactly how big your baby will be until it's born. Usually mums start by buying newborn size (0000). If the doctor thinks – based on the ultrasound – that your baby will be on the large side, you can buy a size 0-3 months (000). In any case it won't be bothered if its clothes are a bit big. And newborns grow really fast! For the same reason, it is not worth bulk buying. Buy a winter outfit just before winter, not during the spring sale.

Natural materials. For clothes, try to choose only natural fabrics (e.g. cotton, wool, linen or silk), because they are best for your child's delicate skin and are the least allergenic. Artificial materials often do not let air through and can be uncomfortable.

Safety and comfort. Certain elements in clothes are worth avoiding. These include cords and ribbons around the neck – babies like to play with them and can end up wrapping them around their neck or putting them in their mouth). Avoid things that are easy to tear off, such as beads, buttons, patches or velcro – they can be torn off or swallowed.

Easy to put on. If you've never dressed a baby, you may not have experienced trying to pull a tight bodysuit over your baby's head...

Your little one will wail, cry and kick with its feet when you're trying to dress it. So when you're buying baby clothes, it's worth considering whether they're easy to put on, especially in the first weeks of life when they're small and delicate, and you've not had much practice yet.

As a rule, full-length baby outfits with zips or poppers, which do not have to go over the head, work better.

Keep the wash simple. In a nutshell – only buy clothes that are machine-washable, and are unlikely to bleed in the wash. Unless, of course, you don't mind washing by hand. There will, for sure, be plenty of laundry!

New or used? Apart from the economic and environmental impact, there is one more thing you should be aware of. New clothes come into contact with a huge amount of chemicals during the production process and they're only removed after a few dozen washes. A small child has very sensitive skin, which is irritated easily. For this reason, a real advantage of used clothes is that they've already been washed many times. As Anna says: "Second-hand clothes are super – they're cheap, soft and the chemicals have been washed out of them."

Pink or blue? Or maybe just universal colours? This way, they will come in handy with the next possible child, even if it is a different gender. This is what Maggie advises: "My method is to choose outfits with very similar colours – and preferably without frills, bows, etc." This way everything can go in one washing machine at the same temperature, the colours don't mix and nothing falls off. And everything fits together, even when Dad dresses the baby!

Elegant or practical? If possible, go for practical clothes for everyday use, for example in colours where stains are not visible, and then buy a few extra outfits for "special occasions".

What exactly? For the first few months of its life, a baby doesn't need many things because they don't get dirty that often. 7 to 10 sets of clothes should be enough. Things change when food becomes more varied and your baby starts to crawl. Here is a basic list of season-independent clothes.
- 5 baby grows, sleepsuits or long-sleeve vests,

- 5 cardigans or long-sleeve jumpers,
- 5 short-sleeve vests,
- 5 pyjamas,
- 3-5 pairs of socks,
- 2-3 cotton beanies (generally only for the first weeks, mainly after bathtime),
- 2 blouses or sweatshirts.

Depending on the time of year, you might need to buy more or fewer long-sleeve or short-sleeve clothes.

Seasonal clothing
- Spring/Summer: 2 thin caps, head scarves or hats (to protect against the sun); lightweight outfit for spring.
- Autumn/Winter: warm outfit, winter hat, scarf or neckerchief, gloves.

What not to buy
- Shoes – I know, they're cute, but as long as your baby doesn't walk, they don't really have any use. If you want them for aesthetics however, make sure you get soft, flexible and comfortable shoes.
- Baby mittens – little gloves which new mothers are advised to buy newborns so the baby doesn't scratch itself. Eve, a midwife, advises against this: "A baby gets to know his or her body – where it ends and where the world begins. Mittens make it difficult for the child to touch its mouth, depriving it of the opportunity to experience an important stage of development."
- Pyjamas – you can, but you don't have to. Your baby can sleep in a sleepsuit.

Getting the clothes ready for your baby to wear. After buying your clothes, they should be washed (in a delicate detergent – check the label!) sometimes several times (especially new ones) to remove chemicals used in their production. It's not a bad idea to do an extra rinse in order to remove the washing agents. And then – to really kill the germs and bacteria – you might like to iron them for good measure.

Wishing you a successful and pleasant shopping experience :) ! ♦

Eve – Emily, Sebastian and Rosa's mother.

15. Baby essentials — cosmetics. The basics of baby care

You are standing in front of a shelf in a pharmacy, buckling under a huge range of baby cosmetics, seasonal cosmetics and 'specialised' products. There are so many of them that you don't know which to choose. Manufacturers make sure that each of these cosmetics is 'a must have' — but once your baby is born, you'll soon see how many of them are not necessary.

Necessary cosmetics. In fact, only two are essential: bath wash and nappy cream. The first one is for bathing and washing your baby's hair. Pour no more than the amount specified by the label into the bath, froth slightly and wash your baby. The second is an oily cream for everyday use (if it contains zinc, it may dry the skin a bit, but not always), which is supposed to create a barrier between the baby's skin and a wet diaper, protecting it from bacteria, urine and poo.

Cosmetics useful under 'special' conditions. Here I include moisturiser and a soothing cream for nappy rash. If your baby's skin is dry, you can use a moisturiser or balm to oil it. If your nappy cream does not contain zinc, it will also work as a moisturiser. Use a nappy soothing cream only after the first redness has appeared. Moisturise reddened areas with a thick layer. Do not moisturise the interior of intimate parts. In addition to protecting damaged skin from urine, the cream also has astringent and disinfectant properties.

Seasonal cosmetics.
- Wind and frost cream to protect your baby's delicate skin — it should be thick, preferably without water in the composition.
- Sunscreen (must be SPF 50 in summer, other seasons like winter, autumn and early spring may be SPF 30) to protect against sunburn — it's a must have for the whole family. Use it all year round, every time you leave the house and while you are outdoors, topping up every 2-3 hours. For babies it is better to choose mineral filters, because — although they give less protection than chemical ones — they're less sensitive. Don't worry about the high filter interfering with vitamin D absorption. With proper use and

healthy skin, creams do not block the absorption of vitamin D3. A proviso here, however: some experts (including the US Food & Drug administration, for example) recommend not using sunscreen on babies of 6 months or younger. Consult your pediatrician before using any sunscreen products on your baby.

Cosmetics that make life easier, but are not essential.
- Wet wipes. It's not a must have product, but it does make life much easier. Instead of wet wipes to wipe your baby's bottom, you can use single-use or reusable cotton swabs soaked in water – or just a regular wipe.

Once you know what you need, find the best possible ones.

The most important thing is what's inside! It might say 'for children' on the packaging, and show a beautiful chubby baby, but that doesn't mean anything. A beautiful package can contain a nasty interior. Don't be fooled by the smiling baby!
- Look for a short list of ingredients. The fewer the ingredients, the smaller the chance of an allergic reaction.
- Avoid potentially harmful ingredients. Besides causing allergies, some cosmetic ingredients are suspected of containing carcinogens, such as polyacrylamide [1]. Others show estrogenic activity, like butylparaben. These ingredients are approved for use in a limited concentration only. However, the question is, what is a safe dose for a newborn?
- Avoid strong detergents and irritants like SLS and SLES (Sodium Lauryl Sulfate, Sodium Laureth Sulfate). They dehydrate the skin and strip it of its protective oily coating. After using such agents, a lotion should be applied to help the skin regenerate.
- Avoid fragrances and essential oils. Scented or perfumed substances are very often the cause of allergies. Don't take any risks – start with fragrance-free cosmetics for your little one.

Natural cosmetics. First of all, choose cosmetics made of refined ingredients – they might be less natural, but are less likely to go off.

What about emollients? Emollients (included in emollient cosmetics) help to maintain proper hydration and moisturisation of the baby's delicate skin. Emollient cosmetics, whether needed or not, are widely advertised, recommended and constantly thrust on mothers at every step. If you decide to use them at all, it is worth following what I wrote above – the most important thing is what's inside. If your child does not suffer from atopic dermatitis (AD) or eczema, think about whether there's any sense in using them.

Keep in mind that cosmetics, no matter how good their ingredients, are still 'just cosmetics'. They don't cure the skin of ailments or diseases (and unsuitable cosmetics can even make a skin condition worse). If you see something which worries you, contact your pediatrician or dermatologist. Remember that the manufacturer's role is to sell, so shop with your head, not your emotions. Imagine using all the cosmetics on your newborn baby suggested by the manufacturers: hair shampoo, bath wash, face cream, body lotion, nappy cream, moisturised wipes, moisturisers... Each one of them contains at least 10 ingredients, so every day your baby's skin would be bombarded with about 70 substances alien to its body. Is that really a good idea? ◆

Anita – mum of two and chemistry graduate. She scrutinizes cosmetics and thoroughly analyzes their ingredients.

16. Baby essentials — vegan cosmetics

Vegetarian and vegan parents likely pay close attention to the ethical issues behind their cosmetics: whether the ingredients have been tested on animals or whether any of the ingredients contain zoonotic diseases (diseases which can be transmitted from animals to humans). Despite the total ban on animal testing connected to cosmetics and their ingredients throughout the European Union, and the declaration by companies not to carry out tests, it appears that this applies mainly to European companies selling their products in the EU alone. Yet most well-known companies also sell outside the EU. So how can you make sure that a company is really cruelty-free? Well, a good place to go is logicalharmony.net. The most common products in children's cosmetics which contain animal extracts are lanolin, beeswax or carmine. ◆

Joanna – Kazik's mother, Panda's partner, caretaker of two dogs and a cat. She likes to parent closely, in the here and now – and loves wraps.

17. Baby essentials — first aid kid

In addition to buying obvious accessories such as a car seat or a stroller, you also need to have a first aid kit. Children and their needs are different, but one thing is for certain: there are some items that should be in the first aid kit of every home with kids. I know there are plenty available, but believe me, you don't need all of them, especially when there is a pharmacy on almost every corner and at least one open around the clock.

Vitamin D. The beneficial effects of vitamin D3 on your body can be discussed for hours. Its beneficial effect is particularly important in newborns, infants and small children (▶ II – 10). Vitamin D helps to maintain healthy bones and teeth, strengthens immunity, reduces the risk of respiratory diseases and has an anti-inflammatory effect.

According to current guidelines, the following prophylactic doses should be used:
- newborn infants born prematurely (before 37 week): before or in week 32 – 800 IU, between weeks 33-36 - 400 IU,
- babies up to 6 months old: 400 IU,
- infants 6-12 months: 400-600 IU,
- children 1-18 years old: 600-1,000 IU.

Which product should you choose? You can opt for a food supplement in the form of: *twist-off* capsules (or tablets), oral drops (glass bottle with a dropper) or oral sprays; can all be bought without a prescription or with a doctor's prescription). Remember that these are prophylactic doses. When a deficiency is diagnosed, you may need to increase your dosage after a consultation with your paediatrician.

If you are feeding your baby modified milk (enriched with vitamin D), check how many units of the vitamin it contains, and only supplement the difference.

Probiotics. This is the second supplement worth considering for newborns and infants up to six months, especially if you're not breastfeeding your baby. The "good" bacteria they contain are extremely helpful in dealing with gastrointestinal problems such as colic, flatulence, diarrhoea and constipation, as well as protecting its small body from infection.
Which kind to choose? There are currently hundreds of probiotic products on the market. However, there are only a few tested ones that have a proven positive effect on newborns. These include, above all:
- *Lactobacillus rhamnosus GG* (ATCC 53103) – reduces the frequency and intensity of abdominal pain in children, shortens the time of infectious diarrhoea and reduces upper respiratory tract infections.
- *Lactobacillus reuteri Protectis* (DSM 17938) – a popular type, used against gastrointestinal problems in the very youngest. It significantly reduces colic symptoms in newborns and breastfed babies; not recommended for babies fed with formula as it may exacerbate symptoms of colic.

DHA acids. If you breastfeed and take DHA supplements (Omega 3 fatty acids, 500-600 mg per day) or eat fatty fish 2 or 3 times a week, there is no need to supplement DHA for your child. The same goes if your baby is fed formula enriched with these fatty acids. The need for DHA in children aged 6-36 months is 100-200 mg daily. Consider feeding your baby oily fish twice a week, or get DHA supplements from a pharmacy.

Physiological saline solution, specifically 0.9% NaCl in 5 ml ampoules. This is recommended for newborns, babies and small children. Its primary purpose is to wash your baby's eyes, but it can also be used for a runny nose. Saline solution can also be inhaled, for example to moisten the respiratory tract or liquefy nasal mucus and relieve stuffy noses.

Umbilical cord stump (tummy button) care. According to the latest WHO recommendations, the so-called 'dry umbilical cord stump' care should be carefully followed (more information can be found in Volume II of the book "Mums to Mums"). However, I know from experience that parents very often insist on using some kind of disinfectant, in which case I recommend – and only for short-term use – an octenidine spray. This is currently the only commonly available antiseptic for use on newborns. Always try to keep the belly button clean and dry after treatment. Do not use: hydrogen peroxide (it is ineffective), miodine (it will stain the navel violet or brown and you won't see if it heals well), alcohol or salicylic acid (they can cause severe skin irritation).

Nappy creams. There are a whole bunch of nappy lotions. You may ask: "Why use them at all?" but I think it's worth it. The skin of a baby is so sensitive that contact with urine can cause redness, rashes, burns and even erosions (▶ II – 15). The fact that disposable nappies (although comfortable) are partly made of plastic, can cause the skin on the bottom to "become loose". That's why it's so important to use preventative measures to protect the bottom against irritation every time you change the nappy, which should be at least every 3 hours.

Then what? First of all, there are two types of ointments and creams for the bottom:

- daily – the main ingredients are dexpanthenol, allantoin, vitamin F, lanolin, vitamins A + E. They are safe for newborns, including premature babies. The aim is to protect the delicate skin of infants from irritation while also helps with hydration and regeneration.
- for burns – if the cream you use every day no longer helps, and your child's skin is getting reddish, warm – sometimes even hot, and swelling or sores start to appear, then you will need to change course. Until the bottom heals, use creams with a drying, astringent and anti-inflammatory effect, then – when things have improved – you can go back to "everyday" creams. Nappy rash creams mainly contain: zinc oxide (it is important to apply a thin layer of cream so as not to dry the skin excessively), liquid extract from rhizome of cinnabar rhizome, 1% borax (additionally works as an antimicrobial agent in very extreme cases, as little as possible).

Before using any creams on your baby, I would recommend doing a tiny skin test on the cheek or behind the ear to make sure your baby is not allergic to the product and you are comfortable to use it.

Painkillers and antipyretics. The choice here is clear – paracetamol. Although it does not have an anti-inflammatory effect, it can be used from day 1. It is best to use an oral suspension (syrup) or you can buy suppositories (start with a dose of 50 mg; suppositories are single-dose drugs so they cannot be divided). Ibuprofen can be administered only after the baby is 3 months – its advantage is that it has an antipyretic, analgesic and anti-inflammatory effect (▶ II – 14).

Isotonic seawater nasal spray. Its use is similar to saline. Seawater sprays cleanse and detoxify a blocked nose. Make sure you choose the ones intended for children, because they have special nozzles which spray into the nasal cavity more gently.

Thermometer. A higher temperature of 36.5-37.5°C in a newborn baby is natural, as its thermoregulation is still adjusting. However, a fever (above 38.5°C), perhaps as a result of vaccination or infection, should definitely be a cause for concern for parents. You should definitely have a thermometer. But which one? I recommend infra-red electronic thermometers, because they are precise, hygienic, fast (the measurement only takes 1-2 seconds, so the child will not get upset) and can be used not only to measure body temperature, but also food, water and air temperature. There is one disadvantage, however – the PRICE.
I do not recommend the following types of thermometer:
- electronic – they're inaccurate,
- ear thermometers – they are only suitable for use over the age of 6 months, nor will they work if your baby has an ear infection, as you will not be able to use it; they are also not hygienic and each household member would need a separate tip,
- mercury – although the most accurate, unfortunately they are made of glass and contain toxicmercury (never put it in a child's bottom or mouth),
- mercury-free – they look like mercury ones, but contain liquid metal from gallium, indium and tin. Although it is equally accurate as mercury, the measurement takes 10 minutes and it is made from glass (never put them in the bottom or mouth).

Hygiene supplies. You can be sure that you'll need a non-woven compress or bandage (sterile and non sterile) and cotton pads in large quantities, for example when washing the face, eyes and ears of a newborn baby or for umbilical cord stump care. You will also need disposable or reusable hygienic pads when changing diapers and while airing the baby's bottom. Cotton buds are ideal for cleaning and drying the umbilical cord at the base, but get the adult ones, not the child ones. They will best reach all nooks and crannies around the umbilical cord stump.

Ticks and mosquitoes. Above all, it's worth protecting your kids from insect bites. You have a few options for protecting your child from mosquitoes, ticks and other bugs, depending on their age:
- Newborns and babies under 2 months old – don't use any repellents AT ALL. The only protection you can use is a tightly fitted, fine-mesh mosquito net.
- Babies (2- 12 months old) – use a mosquito net wherever possible (on your pushchair, crib, playpen, car seat) or, if necessary, use a natural repellent with high quality ingredients, made for young babies, and reapply every hour.
- Toddlers over 1 year old – depending on how many mosquitoes, ticks and bugs there are, use the organic chemical compound IR 3535 or natural repellents with high quality ingredients (these are less effective and work for a shorter time period).
- Children over 2 years old – my first choice would be repellents with 20% icaridin (also known as picaridin.) It is safe, effective with no known side effects. My second choice would be IR 3535, as it is less effective than icaridin. You can also use repellents made with high quality essential oils, but they are considerably less effective and work for shorter periods (30-60 mins), especially for ticks.

Accessories. Consider buying a heat pack or wheat bag (a bag filled with wheat which you can heat in a microwave or keep in the freezer for pain relief), a nasal aspirator and an inhaler. However, these are not things that will come in handy right after childbirth, so you can buy them a little later.

Emergency first aid kit. In addition to a regular first-aid kit, it is worth having a separate one with specialist first aid equipment (▶ II – 41).When looking at the list for your newborn baby, try to choose products that are marked for children from day one. Remember to follow the paediatrician's instructions and treat the first aid kit as an emergency aid. ◆

Anna — Pharmacy M.A., mother of Antonia and Misha, blogger on the proper use of medicines in children, pregnant women and breastfeeding mothers.

18. Baby essentials — equipment. Things you didn't even know existed!

The topic of what equipment your child needs from the very beginning is not such an easy topic, because — as Kate (one of the co-creators of this book) sums up perfectly: "What's great and what's not, is a very subjective matter, because every child is different." What for some of us are "must haves", aren't necessary at all for others. Since our mums were not unanimous on any subject at all, I'm presenting below the various options to choose from when putting together your baby list.

SLEEPING AREA
- A cot and some alternatives. The first thing you need to do is to make the sleeping arrangements for your child, and there are many options here. A popular choice is a classic cot of around 60 × 120 cms.
  Then it's a matter of its different elements, for example: a height-adjustable base, removable rungs, a drawer. Alternatively you can opt for: a bassinet (possibly on wheels or with a rocking element), an extra cot attached to your bed (a cot with one side removed), a Moses basket, a so-called *baby box* (a cardboard box with mattress; popular in Finland) or a *floor bed* (simply a mattress placed on the floor), or you may not choose to buy anything if your child will be sleeping with you (▶ II – 31). In the last case, prepare your bed so that your baby can't fall out (for example by attaching special rails). In addition, a travel cot may come in handy if you intend to travel frequently, although most guesthouses or hotels are equipped with them.
- The mattress — this is important, because the delicate body of a baby needs adequate support. Besides, I'm sure you want your baby to sleep

well ;). The mattress should be absolutely new, completely flat (without quilting, etc.), necessarily resilient and medium-hard (so that a compression doesn't form under the child). The material it is made from should be flexible (elastic foam, latex) and air-permeable. The mattress should be precisely adjusted to the size of the cot, so that there is no space for the child to fall into. The mattress needs special attention because germs and sometimes even insects can accumulate in it! Air it often, wash the cover and put in a waterproof underlay (because the contents of nappies like to leak!). Choose a good quality mattress (with approvals, certificates, etc.).

- **Bedding and sleeping.** Children under two should not sleep on a pillow, even if it's flat (their spine is of a different build than that of an adult and a pillow can cause the baby's head and spine not to be in a straight line). You can choose from: a duvet, a blanket or a baby sleeping bag (there are summer and winter versions), which work well for children who push their blankets off. It is also a good solution for parents who are worried that their child will cover his or her face with the cover (for the first months of its life a child is not able to keep his or her face free on its own). You'll need to buy a few sheets as well (made of natural materials, preferably with an elastic band). Attention! If your child has a problem with a flattened head, you should refer to a doctor.
- **Blankets.** They can be taken when you go for a walk or used when you put the baby on the floor. Choose those from natural materials.
- **A baby sleep wrap.** A bigger blanket can do the same job, but it needs to be stiffened a bit. Ideal for people with less experience in swaddling or carrying a baby because it provides more stability for the newborn.
- **Swaddles.** These are blankets made of thin material like cotton or bamboo, sometimes in the form of little outfits. The child is wrapped in it (quite tightly) and it's said to have a calming effect. Use them with care (▶ II – 34).
- **Night light.** This is useful for night time wakes and feeding.
  It shouldn't be left on all night as it can disturb a baby's sleep. It is important that the light gives off a very gentle and warm light so as not to wake the baby (▶ II – 34). A salt or dark lamp may be a good solution.
- **Electronic nanny and breathing monitor.** These are inventions of our time! An electronic nanny consists of a base (which you place on the crib) and headphones (which you take with you so you can hear the baby crying).

There are those which only eavesdrop, and those with accessories such as a camera or thermometer. A breathing monitor, placed in the cot, monitors your baby's breathing and sets off an alarm if it's not detected, potentially reducing the risk of sudden infant death syndrome (SIDS, ► II – 32). The monitor can be connected to an electronic nanny or be a separate device.
- **Air humidifier and hygrometer.** Optimal air humidity (which has a positive effect on the quality of sleep) is about 50% (40-60%) and without the help of a humidifier, it is often difficult to achieve this, especially during hot periods.
- **White noise.** Apparently, white noise or the noise of various devices calms many babies because it reminds them of their mother's womb. In our case the dryer proved its worth, but a vacuum cleaner – or even a special teddy – could do the job. The device must not be too loud however, up to 50 decibels only.

FEEDING
- **Feeding pillow.** This is most often shaped like a croissant, on which you can rest your baby and your arm during feeding. A lot of mums recommend it, but it could equally be replaced by a rolled-up blanket, for example.
- **Breast pump.** Can be very useful for breastfeeding. This allows you to pump milk and so leave your baby in the care of someone else. For more frequent use, it's worth investing in an electric one (it's faster and more comfortable), with the manual one there in case of an emergency. Some mums buy it in advance while others prefer to wait until it is really needed.
- **Containers for freezing breastmilk.** They'll come in handy if you've pumped a lot of milk or you want to stockpile for an emergency situation (like when you know you're going to have to leave the baby in its Dad's care for a couple of days). Frozen breast milk can be stored in a refrigerator or in a freezer (temperature -14 or lower) for several weeks [1].

If you're feeding with formula, it's a good idea to buy the right equipment for this. Think about some of the things in this list:
- **The bottles.** 2-3 bottles, each with a teat suitable for your baby, should be enough. Consider buying accessories to help you clean your bottles, like brushes, or possibly a sterilizer or a steamer. But boiling bottles in a saucepan of water is also sufficient. If you are going to breastfeed, you can choose a special milk cup instead of a bottle, which is particularly

suitable for newborn babies as there is no risk of it interfering with the breast sucking reflex. This gadget can be useful when you might not be able to breastfeed, for example due to ill health or when your baby is being cared for by others.
- Thermos, thermo-packaging or thermal bottle – for when you need warm water to make a bottle, like when you go out in the evening.
- Bottle warmer – helps to keep the milk – mother's or formula – warm. You can also heat a bottle in a pot of hot water.

BATH TIME

First, think about where you're going to bathe your baby, and then what you'll need.
- A bathtub and a stand – my advice is to first think where you'll put it, because if there is no space available you will need a special bath. It's important that the bath is at a suitable height, as it's not easy to bend down continuously.
- Bath bucket. Can be an alternative to a bathtub, especially for children who don't like bathing in a larger tub.
- Bath towels. At least two, sufficiently large, of natural materials. They can be with a hood, but this is not necessary.
- Newborn cosmetics. There are two main principles: The less, the better (▶ I – 15), the more natural, the better (▶ II -24).
- Bathing seat or bed. Slightly controversial gadgets. Some are useful, others lie unused. If you decide on these accessories, keep them clean, because they can get mouldy.
- Bathing accessories: water thermometer (may come in handy at first, but you will soon know how to check the water temperature by hand), hair brush (with soft bristles), nail clippers or rounded nail scissors and sterile compresses, swabs, saline solution, etc. (▶ I – 17).

OTHER

- Clothes. Most mums love to buy them, but it's worth using your head and not buying anything on a whim (▶ I – 14).
- Washing powders and cleaning products. On the one hand it is good to keep things clean, but on the other, chemical cleaning products can be harmful

(▶ II – 20). And just because a particular washing powder says it's suitable for children doesn't necessarily mean anything – always read the label!

- **Nappies.** They can be disposable (pay attention to their composition!) or reusable (▶ I – 21). First, buy them in the smallest sizes, but don't buy a wholesale supply, because your baby will move through the sizes quickly. Or maybe you will give them up completely, because you decide on the so-called natural baby hygiene (▶ II – 27)?
- **Nappy bin.** There are indeed such things! They have special bags and can be closed so the smell doesn't waft around the house. You'll appreciate it when you start extending your baby's diet ;).
- **Wipe warmers.** And yes, it does exist! Generally speaking, the concept is good, because not every baby stoically endures you putting a cold, wet wipe on its warm body. Here's an economical (and natural) version: hot water kept in a thermos combined with reusable baby wipes.
- **Change table.** It'll come in handy when changing the baby. When at a suitable height, it will also take care of your back. Buy 3-4 covers for it.
- **Stroller and accessories.** In most cases, a stroller is very useful (▶ I – 19), although there are some children who do not like prams very much. You can also add a sleeping bag, rain cover, mosquito net, cup holder or muff (that keeps your hands warm in the winter) to your stroller.
- **Baby bag (for the stroller).** It should be roomy, comfortable, with many pockets, and indestructible (with resistant materials).
- **Car seat.** Must be brand new! (▶ I – 20)
- **Dresser / wardrobe / cupboard for baby's clothes.** Before you buy any furniture, read the chapter "An oasis of peace and development, or how to arrange your baby's room" (▶ I – 10), where you will find valuable tips on this subject.
- **High chair (for feeding)** – only if your baby is able to sit up by themselves! It will only be useful once your baby starts eating solid foods or purees.
- **A baby sling or ergonomic carrier** – saved many parents their arms and backs (▶ II – 36), especially good for children who do not like strollers.
- **Muslin cloths.** Perfect as a changing mat, covering the parent's shoulder from the baby's spit up, while bathing, swaddling and instead of a blanket on hot days.

- Playmat – a blanket or mat with arches, on which toys can be hung. It has supporters and opponents, as usual. It can be replaced by an ordinary blanket and toy stand, perhaps hand-made by a parent.
- Rocker/bouncer – a controversial matter. On the one hand, it's a great idea, because you can take your child with you to the kitchen, for example, and a baby placed in a semi-vertical position is happy to see something more than the ceiling. On the other hand the rocker or bouncer cannot be used too often because the child has limited movements, which is not good from a physiotherapeutic point of view. If you want one for your baby, the choice is huge (colourful, with gadgets, and even self-rocking). Use it sensibly!
- Soother, dummy, pacifier. Haha, I left this gem for last! They have as many opponents as they have supporters, so you have to make your own decision (► II – 18).

What not to buy? There are a few things you just shouldn't use.
- Cushion wedge. Popular among parents whose baby spits up a lot. There is no scientific evidence that its use helps, however, and additionally, it is inadvisable from a physiotherapeutic point of view (for the same reasons as the normal pillow discussed earlier).
- Butterfly cushion (or 'wings') for a stroller, car seat, or when traveling. This is a discussion point. On the one hand, the plus is that it reduces head shocks. On the other hand, it may adversely affect the shape of the baby's spine, and by limiting the movements of the child's head, it may prevent it from breathing freely (if the head is turned to the side).
- Cot bumper / cot protector. The general rule is that there should be as few items as possible in a cot, so the air can circulate freely which reduces the risk of SIDS. So the rung protector or cot bumper is out of the question and good thing too, because children really don't need it, especially when they are tiny, as they don't move around in bed by themselves yet. P.S. In some countries their sale is prohibited.
- Canopy for the cot. As above. They restrict the free flow of air and do not perform any function other than looking good (appreciated only by some people).
- Sleeping cocoons. Some people recommend them for those who want to sleep with their child, as a protection against accidental crushing. They're

controversial for the same reason as canopies and cot bumpers. They are also soft and can make it difficult for the child to turn its head freely, which can make breathing difficult.

Faced with an abundance of colourful advertisements and companies outdoing each other in the production of newer and newer inventions, you can quickly get lost in the maze of gadgets offered to future mums, and not all of them may be a hit. So, before you buy a new, great baby invention, think twice about whether you need it or not. ◆

Violet – Antonine's mum.

19. Baby essentials — prams. Your child's first 4 wheels

The pram is one of the basic elements of your baby list. Unfortunately, it's often the case that buying your baby's first pram or stroller is a missed hit. Why? Because young parents rarely know what they need from a pram and try to buy an ideal model. But a perfect model simply does not exist, despite the assurances of manufacturers and "specialists" on internet forums. Besides, there is no universal pram or stroller – each of us has different needs and requirements, depending on where and how we live. So it's worth thinking carefully about which pram or stroller will be best for you.

There are a few basic types of strollers: the bassinet (carry cot) is for a baby until it can sit up by itself, the stroller is for a sitting child, the umbrella stroller (or yoyo) is a lightweight and handy stroller for short distance walkers, double strollers – for twins or children 1 year or older, and running strollers (2 back wheels, 1 front wheel).

What should you think about before buying a pram?
- ◆ What kind of ground will the pram used on? Will it be pushed on pavements in the city, or on bumpy roads in the countryside or in the forest? This is the biggest factor in choice of shock absorption and wheels.

- Will you have to carry it often (down the stairs, in the car)? If so, then you need to pay special attention to weight and ease of folding.
- Where will it be stored and will you need to put it in the car often? In this case, the size of the pram – folded and unfolded – will be important, as well as ease of folding.
- Budget and condition – will it be new or used?
- Is there one pram for the whole early period (2 in 1) or 2 prams (first the bassinet itself and then the stroller)?

Important issues when deciding on a pram. 3-in-1, 2-in-1 or the bassinet by itself? Prams which only have the bassinet are usually retro models on large wheels. The 2-in-1 stroller gives you the opportunity to buy a bassinet and stroller that can be attached to a single frame, while the 3-in-1 is an extension of this option with a car carrier or capsule. Unfortunately, car carriers attached to strollers usually do not have the appropriate safety standard and ADAC crash test results, and they are often not suitable for a particular vehicle or child, so this option is best avoided. "Here the saying that 'if something is for everything, it's for nothing' applies," summarises Anna about the 3-in-1 option.

Safety. The pram is fit for sale if the following approvals are in place: Certificate of the National Institute of Hygiene, Certificate of the National Dermatological Society, Certificate and positive opinion of the Mother and Child Institute. It is worth checking whether the pram meets global or EU safety standards for the materials used and whether it has any additional approvals. Another point of safety is the belts in the pram: three-point or five-point. The latter are safer and more comfortable. Besides that, pay attention to whether they are wide enough, if they have comfortable shoulder cushions, how much they can be adjusted and whether the clasp is comfortable for the parent and not easy enough for the child to unfasten. A safety belt is also useful in a stroller, preferably one that can detach on both sides. When choosing the stroller, also pay attention to the solidity of the frames and fastenings. The type of brake is also important – it should be comfortable to use and include at least two parking brakes, one on each of the rear wheels.

Cushioning. There is a distinction between hard and soft suspensions, the latter cushions have uneven surfaces, which is particularly important when transporting children up to the age of 1. The strollers are fitted with 3 types of shock absorbers – wishbones, springs and belts. In addition, the cushioning also depends on the type of wheels – the rubber air pump wheels are better than the foam ones.

Handling. Pushing with ease. Some prams can be pushed with one hand, almost completely without any exertion. The handling of a stroller can be tested when the front wheels are higher than the rear ones in order to climb the kerb for example. It is worth checking how much strength the loaded stroller needs to lift the front wheels by pressing down on the handle.

Weight. The average weight of a pram can vary from 10 to 25 kg. Strollers are usually lighter. Those that are too heavy can be problematic not only when bringing a pram into a building or packing it into the boot of a car, but are also less manoeuvrable and not easy to push. The weight of the pram or stroller is influenced by its size, the material from which the frame is made, suspension and the type of wheels (pumped tyres are heavier than foam or plastic).

Size. The size of the pram before and after folding is important when transporting it (you should always check if it fits in the boot), when storing it in the house, as well as when pushing it into narrow doors or between checkout barriers in the shop. It's helpful if the wheels detach easily. It is also worth checking if it's easy and intuitive to fold, if it can be placed in a vertical position after folding, whether it can fold with or without a pram attached to the frame, and if there's a lock after folding.

Bassinet. The size of the bassinet is important – the bigger the better. The problem is when a child is unable to sit up by itself (therefore not yet ready for a stroller), but the bassinet is already too short for it. In addition, in winter it has to fit a child in a winter outfit and a sleeping bag, which takes up a lot of space. If the baby is born in winter, it is also important that the bottom of the pram or stroller is made of well-insulated materials. A bottom made of plastic or plywood is thinner, however, a wooden bottom provides better protection against the cold. In summer, the pram needs to have adequate ventilation such as a little window with mesh to avoid the baby getting too hot. Strollers with a bassinet have also appeared on the market, the underside of which can be slightly lifted, allowing the baby, who is not yet sitting, but is already interested in the environment, to increase its field of vision. Some manufacturers offer the so-called soft bassinets, which are placed on an unfolded stroller – in this case the basic purchase is a stroller, and the soft bassinet is complementary.

A stroller. When choosing a pram with a stroller, you need to pay attention to the size and type of seat: classic, bucket or hammock. In the case of a classic seat, pay attention to the degree of incline of the backrest and whether the seat is let down to the point of being horizontal. As we all know, children often fall asleep on walks, so it can be very useful to let it back until it's horizontal. The size of the seat is also important as it affects the comfort of the child in winter, when it takes up a lot of space in its jacket and sleeping bag. An adjustable footrest, which can be adjusted to the baby's height, is useful, so that the legs will not hang inertly. It is also worth noting the type of buckle (3 or 5 point), its width, adjustment and the material from which the seat belt is made, as well as whether the belt is detachable and the buckle is comfortable.

Some prams have the option of mounting the seat in two ways – forwards or backwards (where the child is facing the parent). On other models, this function is made possible by the moveable handle on the stroller.

The canopy. When choosing a stroller, pay attention to the size of the canopy – whether it will protect your baby from wind, rain and sun, and whether it protects the sides of your child in winter. You might want to have a window in the canopy so you can see your child, facing the direction in which you are traveling. In the summer it is important that the stroller has a detachable ventilation part to protect against the sun, while still providing ventilation and not allowing too high a temperature. Also, it's worth paying attention to the material – whether it's waterproof and whether it has the right filters to protect against UV rays.

Handle. If the stroller is to be used by parents who differ in height, you need to pay attention to the adjustable height of the handle. You also need to "try out" the stroller to make sure that the distance between the handle and the stroller is not too short so it's uncomfortable to walk. An adjustable handle can also be useful if you want to quickly change the baby's position to protect it from the wind or the sun. Keep in mind that the stroller and bassinet can be positioned in both directions. It has the same effect as changing the handle and the difference in the size of the wheels does not matter. Repositioning it with a child inside, however, can be difficult. Regardless of what you go for, it's good to have a stroller with the choice of whether the child faces the parent or the direction of travel. In the early stages the child tends to want to see the parent at all times but soon starts to be more interested in where it's going.

The brake. There are two types: hand and foot brakes, which can be applied to one wheel or more. Pram brakes have two functions: to stop the pram and to slow it down on sloping surfaces. Some strollers only have a parking brake, while others also have a release and sometimes an additional brake which allows you to rock it.

Wheels. There are 3 and 4 wheeled prams on the market. The latter are more stable, the former are more agile. Furthermore, the pram can have front swivel wheels or not. There are now also models with swivel wheels which can be locked to only allow the pram to go straight ahead and not swivel. The diameter of the wheels is also important when it comes to shock absorption. Pram wheels can be foam filled, plastic pumped or rubber. When choosing a pram, you need to think about which terrain you intend to use it on most often. In difficult terrain, pumped wheels are best. In urban areas, foam filled wheels are sufficient – they are much lighter and you don't have the risk of puncturing the inner tube. Plastic wheels are only suitable for flat surfaces. Rubber wheels (also called polyurethane wheels), which combine the properties of foam and pumped wheels, are becoming increasingly popular.

Adapters. When buying a stroller, consider buying a car seat at the same time. Most approved car seats are equipped with adapters that allow you to mount it on a stroller. It is worth checking whether the selected stroller is compatible with the adapters of the selected car seat.

The basket. Pay attention to the capacity of the basket underneath the pram, as well as its accessibility when the bassinet or stroller is in position, and to the lightness of the pram when the basket is loaded. It is also important that the basket is made of waterproof material, has a solid bottom and high sides.

Fabric. It is important that it is made of durable, safe materials, with the option of taking it off to wash.

Extras. Some prams come with accessories such as: mosquito net, bag, rain cover, cup holder, sun canopy, sunshade, umbrella, sleeping bag, foot muff. Usually these items are designed for a specific model of stroller and even if they are not included in the set, you can add them by buying them later. Before buying a pram, it's a good idea to find out how many extras you think will be necessary.

Unusual prams. Models of 'running prams' for active parents have appeared on the market. Double strollers are also available for parents of twins or children with an age difference within two years. For these strollers, it is also worth considering the positioning of the seats – two seats arranged side by side, or one in front of the other, as well as checking the weight, size (so that the stroller fits in the elevator, house door or between checkouts in the shop) and the possibility of folding the frame to reduce it from a double to a single stroller.

New or used? Each has its pros and cons. When buying a second-hand pram, the plus point is undoubtedly the price. New strollers can be extremely pricey. By buying a used pram you can save 30-50% of the cost and get really good accessories. However, it won't then be subject to warranty, and some defects or damages may not be visible at first sight.

When buying a used pram, pay attention to – among other things: the condition of the fabric (stains, holes, abrasions), the condition of the wheels (tension, tread, and above all, whether the stroller leans to one side, which can happen after impact with a kerb, or the stroller does not rattle or clatter. Check that the following work without flaws: belts, brakes, folding system, backrest and handle adjustment. It is also good to know where and under what conditions the stroller was stored (whether it's damp or the owner's cats used it as a bed, or whether cigarettes were smoked in its proximity).

When buying a pram on the internet, pay attention to whether the seller is based in your country. If there's a problem with the pram or problems with the complaints procedure, a complaints officer can only provide support in negotiations with companies which have a branch in their country. Cases with foreign entities have to be dealt with through the European Consumer Centre or similar entities which are much more cumbersome. If you have the opportunity, physically inspect and test the pram before buying it. Also read the shop's regulation concerning its repair – how many service points are there are in your country, how long does it take to deliver the parts from the seller to the service point, who bears the costs associated with this, is it possible to obtain a replacement stroller in the meantime, how long is the warranty or guarantee period and what does it cover? After considering the above issues, your choice of stroller should turn out to be a perfect investment for you and your little one. ♦

Anna – happy and fulfilled mum.

20. Baby essentials — the car seat

Every parent wants to keep their child safe. Even before the birth, you prepare the baby list, and this includes a car seat. Some people don't care about the price and choose the most expensive model available on the market (perhaps endorsed by celebrities on TV), others buy a new car seat as part of a package with a pram and a stroller (the latter are not subject to any crash tests), while others receive a car seat inherited from family or friends. Some hospitals require parents to show the car seat in which the little one will go home when discharging the newborn. Unfortunately, the question of choosing this single, correct and safe seat is not so obvious.

The classification of car seats according to the weight of the child they carry is as follows:
- group 0 is intended for infants not exceeding 10 kg,
- group 0+ for infants not exceeding 13 kg,
- group I for children between 9-18 kg,
- group II for children between 15-25 kg,
- group III for children between 22 and 36 kg.

Why should a child sit facing backwards? If the car brakes suddenly, your body jerks forward because the body continues to move in the original direction. The same thing happens when there is a rear impact – in this case the body moves violently, but towards the rear seat. Front collisions are most often at higher speeds, while rear collisions generally occur when the vehicle is moving at a lower speed or is not moving at all. A jerk forward is usually felt more than a jerk backwards. Therefore position the child seat backwards for as long as possible. Your baby's body is very different to yours: its head is disproportionately large compared to its body, so the force on its head will be greater in an accident. The critical point is the cervical section of the spine, which can suffer most in a frontal collision. So for newborns and infants, back-facing seats are used to minimise the risk of injury to the cervical section of the spine.

Tests. When choosing a car seat, make sure that it protects the cervical section of the spine properly. The Swedish Plus Test for car seats can help you with this. This is done in two categories: 18 kg and 25 kg. The Plus Test is carried out for a vehicle travelling at 56 km/h.

Another important test is the German ADAC test, which assesses the seat on the basis of five criteria: safety, handling (whether or not it is too complicated), ergonomics, presence of harmful substances and ease of maintenance.

What are the most important aspects when buying a car seat that you should pay attention to?
- Check what's available on the market or consult a professional salesperson, but always exercise a healthy scepticism when dealing with salespeople. If they promote seats that do not have the appropriate tests or forward-facing seats for toddlers under 3 years of age, it means that they have not

been properly trained and do not fully understand what the safest seats for children are.
- ♦ Check that the seat you have chosen has passed the appropriate tests[5] and what place it has in the rankings. If a model has not passed any test which simulates a frontal or rear collision, you can't be sure if it will do its job in a real accident.
- ♦ Buy a new seat. Remember, it's like with shoes or fountain pens – it's better not to use them after somebody else. Every car seat has an expiry date – in other words, a shelf life. After the date has passed, it shouldn't be used. For example, plastics are used in the production of a seat, and plastic ages and wears out. You should immediately stop using a baby seat if the car is involved in an accident, however minor, and even if the child was not in the seat at the time. Micro cracks may cause it to break apart during the next impact. When writing a report after an accident, it is worth mentioning the seat that was in the vehicle, so that you can claim compensation for the damaged seat.
- ♦ Don't buy a seat from a supermarket, even if the most beautiful fairy tale characters are smiling from it or it has the most beautiful and colourful upholstery. These types of seats do not pass crash tests. They will protect you from a fine, but they will not save your child's health or life during an accident. Not even the superhero whose image adorns the seat's backrest will help.
- ♦ When purchasing the seat, ask the shop assistant to instruct you on its correct installation and use. The seat must be securely mounted and the child must be properly secured in place.
- ♦ Pay attention to the type of attachment of the seat in the car. Seats can be secured by a seat belt or the ISOFIX system. Convenient options are models clipped into a special base which is attached using the ISOFIX system. Before buying, make sure that the car has suitable anchorage points for mounting this type of seat or base. ISOFIX car seats and bases have three anchorage points: two anchors and a top tether[6] or stabilising leg.[7]

---

[5] Tests as: ADAC – German test, OEAMTC – Austrian test, AA – British test, NHTSA – American test, Plus Test – Swedish test.
[6] The fastening for this belt is on the floor of the boot or on the back of the back seat base. If the seat is equipped with this belt, it must be clipped-on properly.
[7] When installing a seat with a stabilising leg, make sure that there is storage space in the floor. If there is one, you need to know what conditions must be met to install the car seat in this position.

When to change to a larger seat? Until recently it was thought that the first seat or "newborn capsule" should be used as long as possible because it is the safest one for the child. However, you must change to the next size up when your child's weight exceeds the standards set for that particular seat. This is because the child's head is above the upper edge of the seat's backrest. It's also time to change when the seat belts become too short to be properly fastened. A completely different criterion is the age of your child. While a newborn baby is not disturbed by a reclined position and limited field of vision, a 10-month-old baby wants to see the world around it. This is when the rear way facing (RFW) child safety seat (▶ II – 38) comes into play, which is as safe as the "newborn capsule" but gives much more comfort to the child, who can see the world go by through the rear or side windows.

"The purchase of a seat is one of the most important elements of your baby list. It is not worth saving on it, because the child's life and health is priceless," stresses Madelaine. In a nutshell, this is the recommended advice given in this chapter. ◆

Magdalene – privately the mother of Lucia and Nikodem, professionally a physicist and musician in one.

21. Reusable nappies. Back to the past or a modern solution?

Modern reusable nappies are no longer cooked in a large pot and fastened with pins which are unsafe for the child. More and more parents are choosing the reusable option again, convinced by the health, ecological and economic arguments, as well as the ease of use comparable to disposable diapers.

Why use reusable nappies?
- The parents decide for themselves what materials and substances the baby's delicate skin comes into contact with. In the case of "reusable" nappies the composition is known – they are certified, safe and gentle

materials for the baby's skin. With disposable nappies, the environment in the warehouse is unknown.
- Thanks to the multitude of materials, cutters and systems, every family will find a reusable solution which works for them.
- Disposable nappies consumed by 1 child equal about a ton of rubbish, taking over 500 years to decompose [1].
- Over 2 years, a reasonably selected set of reusable diapers will – together with the laundry, amount to a cheaper alternative than the cost of disposables [2].
- Reusables are patterned, colourful and stylishly complement the baby's outfit.
- Reusable nappies are often sewn by small, family businesses, many of which started out by honing their products on their own children.

There are perhaps 3 disadvantages of reusables compared to disposables: they get wet through more quickly (depending on the type of reusable nappy used), they require extra washing roughly every 2 days, and time spent every 2 or 3 days folding the nappies.

What do modern reusable nappies look like? The advantages of reusables may convince you that it is worth checking them out, but it might be hard for you to imagine what such a nappy really looks like. Today's "reusables" consist of two layers: a waterproof but air-permeable layer made of, for example, PUL material or wool, whose task is to retain moisture inside and protect clothes from getting wet, and an absorbent insert made of a material such as cotton or bamboo which, as the name suggests, absorbs the urine.

They are fastened with snap fasteners or Velcro, which also makes it possible to adjust the nappy according to waist size. They also often have two or three rows of snaps along the nappy, which allows you to adjust the size of the nappy to match the size of the baby. Thanks to this, the same nappy can be worn by a 5 or 12 kg infant. There are also size-appropriate nappies for premature and newborn babies all the way up to XL.

Types of reusables
- Pocket – in which the absorbent pad is put in a special pocket placed in the nappy. The baby's skin has no direct contact with the pad, only with the pocket material. When changing, the whole thing (pad and pocket) goes into the wash.
  Advantages: It's easy to put on, even a child who is wiggling or trying to escape. The absorbent pad can be selected freely, adjusting the absorbency to your current needs.
  Disadvantages: Pulling out a wet pad can be unpleasant and it can be tedious to place the pad in a pocket. When nappying mainly with pockets, you need a lot of pockets because you put a new one on every time you change the nappy.
- A nappy wrap – a nappy consisting only of a waterproof layer. You can insert any absorbent pad, fitted nappy, prefold or even a cloth or terry square. If the wrap does not get dirty with a 'number 2', you can put it aside for ventilation when changing the nappy and use it again the next time, until it needs a wash.
  Advantages: The most economical system of nappying, as only a few (about 4-8 pieces) and 18-35 inserts are needed. Great freedom – you can put anything absorbent into the nappy and the inserts can be folded in many ways. There is no need to touch the wet nappy pad – just "pour it out" from the wrapper into the wet diaper basket/bag. It dries quickly.
  The downside: It is harder to fit on a very wriggly baby, the pad inside can move while you're chasing the baby. It is harder to put it on while you're holding the baby standing up.
- SIO ("Snap-in-One") – a wrap with snaps inside, to which the absorbent pads are clipped (also with snaps). Thanks to the snaps, the inserts will not slip or move. The child's skin comes into contact with the pad material. The SIO can also be used as a regular wrapper, filling the center with any absorbent pad.
  Advantages: More economical system than pockets. The SIO can be used repeatedly, just like the wrapper, by changing the absorbent pad. Easy to put on to a wriggling child. You don't have to think about which pad to choose because they are already set for you.
  Disadvantages: By having set pads, you cannot easily control the absorbency.

- AIO ("All-in-One") – called by some "multiple pampers" because, unlike other systems, the waterproof layer is sewn here with an absorbent layer. When changing nappies it all goes to the wash. The baby's skin comes into contact with the material inside the diaper.
Advantages: The simplest system: you don't have to clip or insert anything, nor look for the right cartridge in the wash – everything is in place and can go straight onto the bottom after drying.
Disadvantages: Cost similar to a pocket with insert pads, because you need as many nappies as changes. Limited ability to control absorbency. May take a long time to dry.
- Fitted nappies – a type of reusable insert. It has the shape of a nappy, but consists entirely of an absorbent layer. Popular for newborns during the night and for toddlers who pee a lot. It can have a pocket for absorbent pads (freely selectable) or a clip-on insert (already included). Requires a swaddle.
Advantages: Usually highly absorbent. It stops the poo (even the liquid, milky ones), without contaminating the swaddle.
Disadvantages: Doesn't have as much freedom of movement as other systems. It can take a long time to dry. It has the most expensive insert pads.
- Other types of pads include folding pads, long, pre-fold or a tethered nappy. They differ in the material from which they are made (for example bamboo, cotton, hemp, flax), size and shape (square, rectangular, lengthways) and the way they are folded – all these factors influence their absorbency and convenience of use.

Types of material from which reusable nappies are made.
- External materials (wrappers, pockets) which are not supposed to let moisture out are wool, PUL, TPU, nylon, fleece, laminated cotton.
- Internal materials (absorbent pads, cloths) which are designed to absorb moisture: bamboo, cotton, cotton velour, hemp, soybean, microfibre. Sometimes the nappies are additionally sewn on from the inside with materials that give a feeling of dryness (microfleece, synthetic velour) or freshness (coolmax, thermo, maya).

How to store and wash? Nappies can wait up to three days for laundry. During this time they can be kept in a large laundry bag (the whole open bag is then thrown into the washing machine and the nappies fall out of the bag during washing) or in a bucket. Of course, the fecal matter (often known as 'no. 2), should be disposed of in the toilet. Some parents choose one with a tight lid, others keep it open. The nappies in the sack and the open bucket get more air, so there is less bacterial growth. You can unfasten the mesh sack in the bucket, which can also be flipped open into the washing machine – this saves you time and does not require you to put wet nappies in the bucket. To mask the smell, essential oils can be poured in.

A common question is the issue of cleanliness and hygiene of reusables. There are two ways to approach this. You can add a special, biodegradable disinfectant to the wash (works from 40oC), which removes bacteria from diapers, or wash them at 60oC (after 20 minutes of washing at this temperature, E-coli bacteria die). Before washing, it is good to set the washing machine to rinse and spin to remove some of the dirt from the nappies.

How many nappies do you need? When planning your shopping, you need to take into account the number of nappy changes, frequency of washing and drying time. It all depends on how often you want to wash them, how quickly everything will dry and how big your baby is. If you plan to do your laundry every day and you have a tumble dryer, you need fewer nappies than if you choose to wash every 3 days and air dry. With a newborn baby you sometimes need a dozen (10-15) changes a day, and with a large, walking baby you need several (about 6). If there is no poo, the nappy can be changed every 2-3 hours during the day, although some parents change after each pee. At night you can change it several times, but if your baby doesn't mind and sleeps through the night, you can choose an appropriately absorbant pad for the whole night.

How to start? It seems that the whole reusable thing is worth doing, but it can also seem like a complete mystery. Fortunately, many places have workshops where you can learn everything and talk to users. There is also a kind of 'nappy network' in some countries where you can borrow nappies after paying a returnable deposit and test them before purchase, enabling you to try them out and pick the solution which works best for you. You can also ask for advice on Facebook – nappy groups are very active there and members are happy to advise and support.

Where can you buy them? In large cities you will find reusable nappies in local stores with organic children's items, and online shops. Most manufacturers also have their own online shops. You can also look for used nappies on nappy buy-and-sell groups on Facebook. Some parents with a small budget go for Chinese nappies, however, for ethical and quality reasons (hard, strongly pressing rubber bands, rigid, unpleasant to the touch PUL, low absorbent pads) and lack of certificates confirming the lack of contamination in the materials, this is not a recommended choice. However, Chinese reusables are more ecological and healthier than most disposables.

Can you make nappies yourself? Yes! There are nappy shops where you can find everything you need and many helpful Facebook groups. ♦

Mary – promoter of reusable nappies.

22. Help! Twins!

You took the pregnancy test and discovered that you were expecting a baby. You made an appointment for your first visit to the doctor or gynecologist. However, you were definitely not prepared for what you saw and heard during the ultrasound! The doctor congratulated you on your multiple pregnancy with a smile on her face. Your world turned upside down. You were probably anxious about what it would be like with one baby, and now you are suddenly expecting two. Does it help just to scream: "Help! Twins!"?

Expecting twins – a few words about multiple pregnancy. Having a 1-year-old son, my husband and I decided to try for another child. Entering the doctor's office, I jokingly told the doctor that I was sure I was pregnant (I had high test results for beta-HCG) and that I was there to count how many babies there were. We started to laugh, and then the doctor did an ultrasound. But then my doctor's eyes started widening. I immediately worried that something was wrong. When I saw one and then the other heart, I was shocked. I wasn't expecting the twins to be connected in such a way. I asked for a printout with comments, because I didn't know how to tell my husband and family. I knew it would be hard for them to believe it. It took us a long time to get used to the idea of two babies growing inside of me. As it turns out, it wasn't just me who was shocked by the news: "My experience was full of bumpy roads, I wasn't prepared for twins and I was shocked at first," writes Alice, mother of 2 sons.

The pregnancy itself ran smoothly. However, it is often like Anna, the mother of a daughter and a son, says: "The two of them were a total surprise. Pregnancy, like most with twins, was not the easiest." I was under intensive care because my sons shared a placenta. There were standard inconveniences common to a pregnant woman, such as heartburn, stretch marks, fatigue and later problems with falling asleep, mood swings or cravings – in my case, herrings and greens :). I was active until the birth that took place via cesarean section in week 37.

Essential equipment for twins. We started to prepare the nursery for the children as early as week 22. At the beginning there were more questions and doubts than solutions, despite the fact we had the experience of our older son. Now, though, we had to meet the needs of 2. With the twins the following worked well:

- A breast pump – we had an electric one. It worked for us to start lactation at the very beginning of feeding. It allowed me to provide milk to one of my sons, who was too weak for breastfeeding and had to be in an incubator right after the birth. Later on, I pumped milk so that my partner could take part in the feeding process and I could leave the house without the babies.
- Feeding bottles – so that the father could also feed the children; also worked well during hospital stays and for longer trips outside the house.
- A large feeding pillow – thanks to this I was able to feed the little ones at the same time. Well made, it helped with many activities like having an extra pair of hands. Sometimes, when I had to reach for something that was further away from my child, the pillow allowed me to restrict the little one's movements.
- The twins' pram is the piece of equipment we took the longest to choose. There are several models: side by side, one behind the other, and in the smallest models they sit one above the other. We chose the lightest one, easy to assemble and made of an easy-to-clean material. We decided against the side-by-side option because we might not fit through doors,

gates, lifts or on public transport. We opted for a multifunctional pram, the lightest on the market, with both bassinets and strollers and the possibility of using your car seat.
- The electric bouncer was most useful when one baby cried intensely and woke up the other one. Carrying both at the same time was practically impossible so we would place one in our mechanical helper.

Everything times two? There are a lot of gadgets for twins on the market and they tend to be very expensive. The only one we decided on was the pram. The rest of the stuff, like sledges, bikes, etc., we simply bought a duplicate. With two babies, we bought double quantities of clothes, baby blankets and disposable diapers. Cosmetics we bought for one child on an ongoing basis.

Breastfeeding twins. Already during pregnancy, due to the extended feeding of my first son, I was looking for information on breastfeeding two babies. Unfortunately, most of the information I came across was that with twins it does not work :-(. If you are at such a point, I want to assure you that breastfeeding twins is possible (▶ II – 43). But while breastfeeding even a single baby is a beautiful adventure, and has many benefits for the baby and the mother, it can also cause problems.

In my case, it worked well to feed the twins at the same time. The fact that I was breastfeeding my sons one by one meant that I fed them all day and we didn't have time for walks or rest. And for a long time I couldn't function like this. The most comfortable position for me was the one in which the babies were placed on a feeding pillow, their heads at the breast and body and legs under the armpit towards my back. We had a couple of crises during our two-year 'milky way', but each time a wise midwife or lactation counsellor always came to my aid.

Daily life with the twins. As a mother of 5-year-old twins, I can say that being their parent is a great adventure. Every day they surprise me with their actions, attitudes and perception of the world. The beginning was difficult and required a lot from our side as parents. We had to switch from taking care of one child to two – in fact three in total. In the first months our task was primarily to meet their needs, such as eating, sleeping or being close to us. It was important to establish fixed times for all the activities and to learn how to feed simultaneously. Most of the time I took care of the little ones on my own, so I had to be well-organised to meet the challenge. In the children's corner or nursery you MUST have everything at hand, not in the cupboard next door or in another room. With one toddler you can always go for something, holding him in your arms, with two it is very difficult. Until almost the 6th month the twins slept in one cot. Thanks to this, they had longer naps because they felt close, could cuddle and touch each other. The cot was also our changing table, which allowed me to keep an eye on the other baby at all times. When one started to cry, often the other one would start too (unfortunately, the film script turned out not to be fiction). At the beginning I panicked when my sons cried at the same time, because on the day of birth I didn't grow a second pair of hands, so very needed at times. However, I quickly found out that a calm approach not only solves a problem faster and more efficiently, but also calms the little ones themselves. An additional pair of hands was sometimes replaced by the electric bouncer, in which the boys liked to stay and often went to sleep in.

The biggest challenge was bathing and going for walks by myself. My boys loved to bathe together. However, if I bathed them myself, I would put the tub and everything I needed on the carpet in the children's room. Thanks to this, I could bathe one of them while the other one played in the cot or the rocker. When they became more mobile, leaving the room to explore the house, I used car seats. I put my sons in so-called capsules, then I could put them on the floor and rock them when they were unsettled. I had my eye on them and I was sure that they were safe. I also used them when I took them out for walks by myself in the stroller, so I wasn't afraid that I would put one in the stroller and the other one would do something to himself.

As time passed, differences in character began to be visible in my boys. Each of them had their own pace in developing their skills, or in passing developmental milestones. Caring for the two of them turned out to be easier than it was for our older son. The boys always played and still play with each other. Even when they quarrel, they always have each other's backs. They are inseparable and every time one of them gets something, he asks for a portion for the other. Their strong bond was already visible in the delivery room. When the doctor took one for examination, the other immediately looked for him with his hands and cried. As soon as he felt his brother close, he hugged him and silence reigned :-).

I guess you don't know what to expect when twins are born. You're afraid that you won't be able to manage, and that life after their birth will turn into an endless process of feeding, settling and putting them to sleep. It doesn't necessarily have to be like this! I guarantee you that what you will experience with twins, you will not experience with one child :). ♦

Kate – mum to John and twins Frank and Alex.

My story

I thought everything was lost...

I'm sitting in the waiting room. I'm looking around. Kettle, cups, coffee, tea, newspapers, TV – all at your fingertips. I rest my eyes on some stupid programme about people with imaginary problems. Lately, so many things seem small, unimportant and so insignificant. I feel the bleeding is slowly subsiding, but I still try to prepare for the worst. Another woman enters the waiting room. Her pregnant belly is leading the way, proudly presenting itself in all its glory. I sigh because I don't know if I can still talk about myself as pregnant. The nurse invites me into the doctor's office. I look inside and feel relieved. How good that the doctor is a young woman. With a warm gesture she points to the chair and scrupulously checks my records. Smiling, she asks questions. She wants to know if this is my first pregnancy and asks detailed questions. I'm answering in detail, step by step. Her brown eyes follow my lips and stare at me with seriousness and commitment. I have the impression that she is a good doctor.

I go to the couch, holding my breath for the doctor's words, "there's still hope you didn't miscarry." Unfortunately, they can't do an ultrasound today. They have too many patients. "Come back to us the day after tomorrow, first thing in the morning," says the doctor in a warm, calm voice. "The day after tomorrow, my husband and I are flying to Gran Canaria." I answer, not at all looking forward to the long-awaited vacation. We'll probably have to cancel it.

I go home and hide under a blanket. I don't feel like eating and I don't have the strength to move. I wasn't happy with the initial examination. "There's definitely a private clinic somewhere here," I think. I start looking. I found one! After a few minutes the gentle voice of the receptionist says that they can see me tomorrow at 6.30 p.m. A sigh of relief. At least we'll know where we stand. It's hard to tell how I feel. Fear? Emptiness? Grief? I guess we shared our good news with the world too quickly. We could have at least waited until 3 months.

I am pulled out of my heavy thoughts by the noise of the key in the door. It's Paul – my husband, my support. Right now I need him like never before. I look at his tired face, I can see the sadness in his eyes. He hugs me, as hard as he can. I don't have to explain anything to him. He knows me well. We huddle together under a blanket and consider every possible option. Tomorrow's visit to the gynaecologist will dispel all doubts and we'll wait for it like a desert needs rain.

It's morning. I'm awakened from my sleep by my morning sickness. I run to the bathroom and perform the daily ritual. It has been going on for a few weeks now and today I feel fortunate it's happening the same as before. There is hope...

At work, the day goes by quite quickly. Everyone wants something, I answer the phone every now and then. For a moment I forget I'm waiting for 6:30pm

On the way to the doctor's, Paul and I talk about everything and nothing – as in any good marriage.

We're getting there. My heart is beating like crazy. Quick registration and we wait. There's a slight delay and every minute feels like an hour.

Finally our turn. The doctor himself leads us to the office. He's older – his pigeon hair colour gives him away. He seems very reliable, and he's nice. He asks a few questions, weaves a few jokes into the conversation to lighten the atmosphere. He's fine with Paul being with me the whole time.

First the initial observation, then the ultrasound. I'm lying on my back, my legs bent at the knees. My heart's beating hard. I feel the foreign object wandering around me to find any sign of our child's life. The calculations show that it's only been 7 weeks, so if it's still there, it might still be too early to confirm anything. It's complete silence. I'm looking at the monitor, but all I see is some kind of black, moving spot. Paul is holding his breath. I guess I've never seen him so stressed out. Suddenly a little bean appears to our eyes. "Oh, there he is. Look." – says the doctor. – "You want to listen to his heart?" I'm nodding my head because I can't get a single word out of myself. Paul's eyes are glistening, and his smile reaches from ear to ear. Suddenly the office is filled with the most beautiful sound in the world – the sound of new life. The life that we two have created. "There is our little warrior," I speak in a squeaky voice, feeling tears flowing down my cheeks. "Is he a warrior? I don't know," says the doctor. He can't yet determine the sex of the child. "But wait, here's a question…" I'm euphoric about the intrigued voice of the gynecologist. Paul's pale. "Is something wrong?" I have a thousand thoughts in my head. Is the bearing unstuck? Is there some kind of mutation? What does he see there?

"Just a moment… you know… the question is, is there one embryo or are there two…?" asks the doctor with uncertainty. But what do you mean two? What? Paul nearly falls off the chair and stares in disbelief at the blurred image on the monitor. I don't think it's getting to him yet, he's not processing this information.

"Oh, I don't know if I can show two at once… look now! Congratulations, they're twins!"

The doctor's words rebound in my head with infinite echo. Neither of us expected that. More than once I told Paul that I have a feeling that my stomach is somehow strangely large for the 7th week of pregnancy. Friends have joked about twins more than once, but we've never, ever really taken that outcome seriously. When I finally understand the doctor's words, I start laughing loudly and tears are flowing down my cheeks. I smile like a fool, but Paul's face is getting more and more white. It's good that he's sitting on a chair, because otherwise he'd have fallen on the floor.

The gynaecologist hasn't stopped looking. The image on the monitor is in constant motion. I'm brought back to reality by Paul's comment, "Doctor… maybe that's enough already?!" Everyone laughs, and the gynaecologist explains that he is just checking to see if everything is alright. "At the moment, I don't see any danger. But remember, twin pregnancies aren't easy, and there may – or may not – be some complications. You should see your family doctor and they'll guide you through it," explains the doctor as he prints out the first picture of our children.

I can't stop smiling. I look at the ultrasound and still can't believe that our family will be a little bigger than we planned. Paul is still a little shocked, shaking his head every now and then, as if he doesn't know whether it's a joke, a dream, a conspiracy or reality. "We'll manage somehow!" – I pat him on the shoulder and we go home, where we can gather our thoughts and plan our lives – for the four of us. ◆

Annette – mum of Anthony and Frank.

MUM

A healthy and well-cared future mum

23. Under good care — how do I choose the right doctor to lead me through pregnancy?

The ideal doctor to lead you through pregnancy is a gynaecologist who specialises in obstetrics from the hospital where you plan to give birth. But how often does that happen in reality?

Who can lead a pregnancy? It's not only a gynecologist who can lead your pregnancy. In many countries, several appropriately-trained medical practitioners can, including an obstetrician-gynecologist (Ob-Gyn) and nurse practitioner. Not everyone knows this, but a midwife can also take care of a woman during pregnancy, as long as it is proceeding to plan. The midwife may issue a referral for tests (blood, urine), and must refer you to a gynaecologist for a consultation and ultrasound examination. All this is usually covered by the national or public health service, unless you decide to take private medical care. Remember that the first medical visit (or visit to the midwife) should take place by week 10.

What should the person leading your pregnancy be like? The person – or people – who are leading the pregnancy should examine and monitor you regularly, ensure that your baby is developing properly, explain things calmly so that you can be confident about yourself and your baby, be available for you and refer you to a specialist or hospital if necessary. He, she or they should answer all questions about your child's development throughout the course of the pregnancy, and should dispel any concerns you may have. If you have any doubts about your care, you can always change doctors or seek advice from another specialist.

Regular visits and examinations are the basis for proper communication between the mother-to-be and the doctor or midwife. Often a simple conversation during the visit can reveal potentially dangerous symptoms that you might otherwise not pay attention to. The doctor must be able to listen and catch the most important information. For this reason he or she must inspire confidence, and if this is not the case, then you need to find another one. If you have any unwanted symptoms (cramps, bleeding or pain), you need to be sure that you can talk to your doctor at any time of the day or night.

Therefore, good practice includes being provided with a phone number that you can call at any time with your concerns.

Do we know each other? If the doctor or midwife of your choice is someone new to you and has no idea of any past illnesses, treatments or attempts to get pregnant, I do advise you to write everything down before your first visit. You will get asked a lot of questions during your visits, especially your first one, so you need to have information on hand. Also remember to write down your doctor's recommendations. Take all previous test results with you for each subsequent visit. It is not a bad idea to keep them all together in one bag so that you can always grab it if you suddenly need to go to the hospital.

During your first visit you can also expect questions about the date of the first day of your last period, past pregnancies, miscarriages, gynaecological diseases, life situations, diseases (your and your family's), medications you are taking and even your work situation. Information will be collected about addictions (cigarettes, alcohol, other stimulants), problems related to nutrition or hereditary diseases – so-called 'environmental influences'. Especially in the case of unplanned pregnancies, you may not have any inkling of problems with thyroid or sugar levels. During the ultrasound examination a cyst or fibroid (benign tumour) may show up, and you probably won't have known anything about it before. Of course, it is best to see a doctor who has the equipment for such examinations so you don't have to make an appointment with another specialist.

Many women know the difference a gentle doctor and a less delicate one can make during a gynaecological examination, regardless of their gender. The choice of the gynaecologist is an individual matter for each woman.

Where do you work? It would be much easier if the attending doctor worked in the hospital where you plan to give birth. When you look for a doctor, consider if it's important to you. As Anna writes: "A lot depends on the hospital; my first attending physician worked in the hospital where I gave birth, but it didn't make any difference as I didn't meet him even once."

Some mums say that the most important decision a mother makes is the choice of midwife, because it is the midwife who is usually at the birth.

Distance from home. Another important issue is location. Not everyone can commute to a distant city for a monthly visit. Sometimes it just needs to be recalculated. Hopefully there is a good, recommended gynecologist in your area. During the visit, the doctor usually orders laboratory tests – not only basic morphology, but often also other tests such as hormonal ones. You may be referred to an endocrinologist, neurologist, dermatologist, dietician or even a dentist for a check up. Your doctor may also have prenatal tests done to determine the risk of genetic defects. Consider the distance between the doctor and your home, make sure that your laboratory performs the prescribed tests and confirm the times – usually in the morning and on an empty stomach).

Trust and chemistry. Trust between you and your doctor is essential. A patient who conceals bad test results can harm her own child – and herself. A doctor who, in case of an emergency, does not answer the phone or sends concerning results to another specialist without trying to find out the cause of the situation themselves, also endangers the child. There can be no question of trust in such cases. This relationship must be stopped immediately and a new doctor must be found. Remember – the doctor is for you, you are not for them.

A good gynaecologist is warm and kind, but this does not mean that his or her office is a place of confession and gossip. Try to answer the questions asked specifically and directly. If you don't understand something, ask. You have their phone number :). ◆

Margaret – mum of Anna, Matthew and Jacob. Owner of a family-friendly cafe.

24. Caution advised! What medical test should you avoid in pregnancy?

Diseases, accidents and various situations requiring medical interventions and diagnostic tests can happen to an expecting mother. While there are no doubts about the safety of the ultrasound and ECG, there are question marks over other tests and whether they can be performed during pregnancy.

In fact, the waters are a bit muddy here, because for ethical reasons there has been no research on whether diagnostic and imaging tests during pregnancy can be harmful. In principle the first-line ultrasound is a first-line examination of a pregnant woman, but the test is not always enough and other methods might need to be used. Some tests should be avoided during pregnancy, i.e. they should be delayed as long as possible after the birth, or performed as a last resort if the benefits of the test are greater than the risks involved.

Magnetic resonance imaging (MRI) with contrast. This is an imaging test that uses electromagnetic radiation. The camera itself emits very low intensity radiation in a standard MRI, which should not interfere with the functioning of the human body, including the developing baby. However, a contrast is often given for better imaging of tissue. And that's the problem. Well, in most contrast agents there is gadolinium – a metal which can penetrate the placenta and accumulate in the baby's body, adversely affecting its development. In the case of a contrast-free MRI, the pregnancy is not at risk, but it is not recommended to perform in the first trimester.

Computer tomography (CT). This is an imaging examination using an X-ray. This radiation shows significant interactions with living tissues. So far, no safe dose has been established, and in fact, any dose can lead to mutations in cells. Despite the development of technology, the radiation dose in a CT scan is much higher than that used in radiography. Often a contrast is required for examination.

X-ray test. Despite the minimum doses used in carrying it out, it is best to avoid X-rays during pregnancy, especially in the first trimester.

Myocardial perfusion scan. Imaging examination to assess organ function. The examination uses radioactive elements that emit gamma radiation. It is essential that this scan is not performed during pregnancy.

Cystography. X-ray imaging for bladder evaluation. This is done as a last resort.

Urography. X-ray examination with shading agent for urinary tract imaging. The procedure for pregnant women is the same – the examination is performed only in case of a life or health threat.

Medical procedures. All surgical procedures that are necessary to save life or health must take place. However, beauty or other surgical procedures that are not strictly necessary should be postponed. A frequent procedure is tooth extraction, often surgical. It's safe from the second trimester, but if you can wait, it is better to do it after the birth. Having said that, you must not leave a rotten tooth until the birth. Dental infections can lead to blood infections and can even result in preterm birth. In addition, a sore tooth weakens the whole body, leaving you more susceptible to infections. Whitening and implantations are discouraged during pregnancy, but you can have sundblasting.

A very important principle that you absolutely must follow when you're pregnant is to inform all kinds of specialists – doctors, dentists, nurses, beauticians or hairdressers – that you are pregnant. ◆

Agnes – Pola's mum and midwife.

25. Nausea, drowsiness and hypersensitivity to smells… How to deal with pregnancy ailments?

Pregnancy is a time of change in your body as it adapts to the needs of the developing baby. Many of us are plagued by various discomforts during this time, but with the right measures it is possible to live with them. There are symptoms that are so-called physiological ones, there are those that are worrying and require immediate consultation with a doctor, and then there are those that require hospitalisation, because they may endanger the life of the mother or child, such as unrestrained vomiting, cholestasis (see description below), listeria or preeclampsia.

Nausea and vomiting are the most common ailments suffered by pregnant women. They most often occur in the morning, so it is best to eat something like biscuits, nuts or almonds before getting out of bed. Eat little but often, choose low-glycemic products, avoid leaning forward, for example when brushing your teeth, suck mint lozenges or chew gum. Avoid intense smells as pregnancy hormones often cause hypersensitivity to odours, which can make nausea even worse. Ginger in tea or biscuits can help. Try acupressure on your wrist, and always carry a bottle of water, refreshing wipes and a plastic bag with you when you leave home, just in case ;).

Heartburn is a burning sensation in the esophagus. To reduce symptoms, eat small, easily digestible meals, and often. Avoid spicy, greasy and hot foods. Eat slowly in an upright position. Once heartburn appears, use ground cumin and marjoram (1 : 1), munch almonds, drink milk, yoghurt or mint tea before bedtime. Consult your doctor (perhaps an ENT (Ear, Nose and Throat specialist) or a physiotherapist if the heartburn is particularly painful (yes, he or she can also help with this ailment!). Don't discount the services of a speech and language therapist (SLT) either.

Pressure on the bladder is due to the exertion of the expanding uterus. Exercise the pelvic floor muscles (Kegel exercises are often performed here) (▸ II – 106) to prevent incontinence and prepare for natural delivery. Drink water, poo frequently and take care of your intimate hygiene. Wear comfortable clothes and airy underwear, and if going to the loo is accompanied by pain, discharge, or burning of the intimate area, it can mean urinary tract infections, so be sure to consult your doctor.

Drowsiness and fatigue is one of the first symptoms of pregnancy. Try to rest and get a good night's sleep, and if you can, take a regenerative nap during the day. Walk in the open air, avoid coffee, strong tea and sweets, as they can add to your symptoms.

Enlarging breasts and their tenderness. It is important to choose the correct size bra for your breasts, so that the material does not irritate or rub them, and at the same time supports them well. You can massage your breasts in the shower with a stream of water, but remember that massaging the nipples can cause the release of oxytocin, which is associated with cramps and preterm birth, so be aware of this.

Constipation and hemorrhoids. Constipation can lead to the formation of hemorrhoids, so drink plenty of water and water with lemon on an empty stomach, eat whole-grain products rich in fibre as well as apples, dried plums, raisins, apricots or figs. Avoid sitting for a long time or lying on your back (try to sleep on your side, preferably the left side, as this position does not cause pressure on the inferior vena cava vein, which can cause circulatory disorders). Try to be active (walk, swim), relax while using the loo, have a salt bath. If symptoms persist, consult your doctor.

Pain, dizziness or fainting is associated with a drop or increase in blood pressure. If it happens a lot, consult your doctor or cardiologist as soon as possible in order to rule out pregnancy hypertension. Any pressure above 140/90 mm Hg is treated as a pathological condition. Beware of suddenly getting up from a lying position as this can trigger such feelings.

Flatulence. You can prevent flatulence by avoiding food which is hard to digest, fizzy drinks and sweets. Eat little, but often and slowly, drink natural juices, eat products containing lactic acid bacteria, and try to be as active as possible.

Swellings are often brought on by salt in the diet, which retains water in the body. While resting, lift your legs a little higher and try soaking them in cold water. Round-the-clock swelling is often associated with hypertension or preeclampsia, so it is important to drink lots of water (2.5 l or more), control your blood pressure and monitor your urine. Consult your doctor if in doubt or if the swelling continues.

Itchy skin often accompanies a growing tummy or breasts, because the skin is most stretched in these places. Unfortunately, it can also be a sign of cholestasis which is dangerous for the mother and child (it most often appears in the third trimester of pregnancy). It is basically the impairment of bile production by the liver, showing itself by persistent itching of the whole body, especially the hands and soles of the feet. It is especially discomforting at night. If you experience extreme itching in late pregnancy, you must consult your doctor or visit the emergency room immediately.

Spinal pains are caused by an increase in body weight and a change in your centre of gravity. If possible, go to a pilates session for pregnant women, swim, walk, find relieving positions or have a massage designed for pregnant women. Remember to prevent back pain, wear comfortable shoes and sleep on a comfortable mattress. Consult your doctor in the case of very severe pain.

Varicose veins. First of all, avoid medical treatments. Do not cross your legs, avoid standing or sitting for long periods, avoid hot baths and prolonged exposure to the sun, which intensify the symptoms. Do appropriate circulatory exercises, walk indoors, wear comfortable shoes and clothing. Consult a doctor about wearing special tights for pregnant women.

Muscle spasms (mainly in the legs). Follow a diet rich in magnesium, potassium and calcium. Massage the affected area vigorously, use antithrombotic prophylactics and perform exercises that increase circulation. In case of strong and frequent contractions, consult your doctor. He or she may suggest a suitable supplement, or you may need a cardiac consultation.

Toothaches or bleeding gums can be the result of hormonal changes in a pregnant woman's body, causing the gums to loosen and change the composition of saliva, which in turn increases the risk of periodontal (gum) disease. There is a clear relationship between periodontal disease and low birth weight, premature birth or even miscarriage. For these reasons, at least two visits to the dentist are advisable during pregnancy. When brushing your teeth, use a soft bristle toothbrush and make sure you have a calcium-rich diet.

Every pregnancy is different, and not all of these conditions will happen to you. However, it is important to know how to act if they do. Remember that if anything worries you, do not hesitate to consult a doctor or go to the hospital. ◆

Agatha – mum to Simon and Jacob, physiotherapist.
Consultation: Agnes – a midwife.

26. Don't ignore them! Things you should be concerned about during pregnancy

Many of the unpleasant symptoms that occur during pregnancy do not indicate any abnormalities or risks. These include nausea, back pain and dizziness. However, there are some symptoms that require medical consultation, sometimes even very quick intervention and treatment. In this chapter you will find a list of the most common.

Stomach ache. Pregnancy is a period of intense change in the anatomy of your body. From the size of a small fist, your uterus increases to the size of a ripe watermelon. This is bound to affect your wellbeing. Your muscles stretch intensively, together with the ligaments supporting the genital organ. In addition, the intestines and other organs of the abdominal cavity move upwards. All this can cause a feeling of discomfort, pulling or stabbing in the groin. Such ailments are normal and should not worry you. Moreover, as early as 18-20 weeks, your uterus may feel tense several times a day. There may be a hardening of the abdomen, especially when you're tired, suddenly change position or after intercourse. These are the so-called Braxton-Hicks cramps, which are evidence that the uterus is growing and, figuratively speaking, "exercising before birth". You'll need to see a doctor if the abdominal pain is constant, resembles menstrual pains, or regular cramps appear, which can radiate into the spine or make the uterus feel like it is being pulled down, and also when it is accompanied by spotting or bleeding. If this happens, you should see your doctor as soon as possible or go to the hospital.

Bleeding / spotting. During pregnancy, the blood supply to the woman's reproductive organs increases, so that in some situations there may be slight bleeding. This isn't usually dangerous. In the first weeks, implantation bleeding can occur during menstruation and also after intercourse. However, in every situation where such symptoms occur, a doctor's consultation is necessary to rule out more serious problems. Bleeding may mean the risk of miscarriage or premature birth, placenta detachment or indicate cervical erosion. Upon a gynaecological examination and ultrasound, your doctor will tell you if urgent intervention is needed.

Vaginal discharge, itching, burning. These are the most common symptoms of intimate infections, which, unfortunately, appear readily during pregnancy due to the change of vaginal pH from acidic to alkaline. In such an environment, it is much easier for bacteria, viruses and fungi, which are the cause of infections, to survive. If you see that the vaginal discharge has changed its colour, texture or smell, or you feel itching or burning around the vagina, make an appointment to see your gynaecologist. These symptoms do not require an urgent consultation in the emergency room, but you should be examined within a few days by a doctor who will assess and recommend appropriate treatment. Untreated intimate infections can lead to an intrauterine infection of the baby, and sometimes (very rarely) make a natural birth not possible, as there is a risk of infecting the baby as it passes through the birth canal. According to the standards of perinatal care, active infection with human papillomavirus, or so-called genital warts does not need medical intervention. Nowadays, even with the HIV virus, a woman can give birth naturally if the viral load is small.

Lower limb swelling. This is a common problem for pregnant women, especially those whose third trimester falls during the summer heat. The uterus, as it gets bigger and heavier, presses on blood vessels reaching the legs, which reduces circulation to them. However, the excess fluid should ease if you rest your legs slightly higher than the rest of the body. If, after some time, the swelling still does not disappear, see a doctor. The accompanying pain in the legs, redness or flushing may indicate that a clot has formed in the veins which is hindering blood flow, caused by a disease called thrombotic vein inflammation. This disease requires rapid treatment, because otherwise it may lead to life-threatening illnesses such as a pulmonary embolism.

Lack of movement by the baby or a change in its nature. The majority of women who have had their first pregnancy begin to feel the baby's movements around week 18 (in subsequent pregnancies it may happen earlier). If you haven't felt your baby's movements by the end of week 20, it's best to report it to your doctor. A quick intervention may be needed if – after feeling regular movements several times a day – movement has subsided and does not appear for 24 hours. It may be that your baby has only changed his or her position or has taken a long nap, but you mustn't ignore this. It will need to be confirmed via ultrasound and KTG tests whether the baby is all right. On the other hand, it can happen that the baby moves intensively, thereby signaling a bad mood. If your baby exhibits unusual behaviour which does not go away after you've changed position, rested or drunk a glass of water, you should also seek medical consultation.

Premature fetal membrane rupture. This can happen even a few weeks before the due date. The amount of amniotic fluid coming out does not have to be large. Sometimes women only experience a non-substantial dampness on their underwear, which can initially be mistaken for abundant mucus secretion or discharge. It needs to be ascertained whether, instead of amniotic fluid, involuntary urination due to a stronger kick or pressure of the baby's head on the bladder wasn't the cause. In the course of the medical examination, a test (with a litmus strip) will be performed, which will help to distinguish amniotic fluid from other secretions. In the case of premature rupture of the fetal membranes, there is a risk of an intrauterine infection for the baby. An antibiotic administered early enough, however, will protect the child and give it more time for further development.

Itchy skin. In particular, itching in the palms of your hands or feet, which may get stronger at night, is a typical symptom of cholestasis of pregnancy, or liver condition that occurs during in pregnant women. This is an illness that should be treated quickly, as it is very dangerous for the unborn baby. Report this symptom to your doctor as soon as possible, who should order the appropriate tests and start treatment.

Other. Every woman experiences pregnancy differently. Some bloom or 'glow', while others would prefer to spend all their time in bed under a blanket. Periodic discomfort and fatigue can happen and simply requires rest. However, if you experience frequent or sudden severe headaches, fainting or darkness in front of your eyes, please report it. Such symptoms may indicate arterial hypertension, which should be treated and regularly checked. Frequent urination may be caused by the pressure of the growing uterus on the bladder, but it may also indicate an infection of the urinary system, especially if it is accompanied by abdominal pain, burning or pain during urination. Intense vomiting or diarrhoea can quickly lead to dehydration, and it is also worth seeing a doctor. The same applies to high fever, especially if it is accompanied by other symptoms such as chills.

The symptoms you've just read about are only some of the most common ones. If you notice anything that is causing you concern, don't wait – contact your doctor. Remember that pregnancy stress is definitely not recommended for both you and your baby, so any doubts need to be dispelled. ◆

Sylvia – midwife and mum to Lucia.

27. Sugar and spice... A few words about gestational diabetes

Pregnancy is a time of many changes in the female body. As a result of increased levels of hormones such as estrogen, progesterone or prolactin – your glucose and insulin metabolism deteriorates. The emerging glucose intolerance and hyperglycemic states (elevated blood glucose levels) may exceed accepted standards and should be diagnosed as *gestational diabetes mellitus* or GDM for short. However, we are only talking here about women who have never had such problems before and for whom this issue has only appeared for the first time during their pregnancy.

According to the epidemiological data, GDM is a problem which is increasing year by year [1]. Women who fall into the following categories are most predisposed to gestational diabetes:
- over 35 years old,
- overweight,
- previously gave birth to children with a high birth weight (over 4 kg),
- have a history of obstetric failure (miscarriages, intrauterine deaths, malformations),
- have a diagnosis of hypertension,
- expecting or have had multiple births,

- have polycystic ovary syndrome,
- have had diabetes after a previous pregnancy.

Changes in carbohydrate tolerance may carry some risk for both the mother and her child, therefore screening for GDM is carried out for every pregnant woman.

What complications can pregnancy diabetes have? If it develops in the first trimester, it unfortunately increases the risk of miscarriage or malformation in the baby. If it occurs after the first trimester, the greatest risk is posed by transmission of excessive glucose to the baby, which may lead to macrosomy (excessive growth of the baby's body). A high body weight in the baby creates the risk of perinatal injuries, fetal oxygen deficiency and even intrauterine death. Moreover, GDM may cause, among other things, the risk of respiratory disorders, excessive jaundice, hypoglycemia (reduced glycemic level) or various types of heart disorders in a child. Complications that may occur in the mother include:

- pregnancy-induced hypertension and preeclampsia,
- premature birth,
- a surgical birth,
- the need to induce a birth or perform a caesarean section,
- perinatal injuries (damage to the genital tract, perineum).

But let's remember that a diabetes pregnancy which is properly managed and normalised will not pose a threat to mother and child. The important thing is to detect it.

Diagnostics for gestational diabetes. The first test for diabetes in pregnancy is performed early in your pregnancy. On your first visit, your attending doctor will test your fasting glucose level or ask you to eat a normal breakfast before taking the test – it varies from country to country. The normal result should not exceed 92 mg/dl.

If you are at risk, your doctor will immediately refer you for an oral 75 g glucose load test (OGTT). If your fasting glucose score was fine, you will not undergo the test between weeks 24 and 28.

What is the glucose load test? This is a complex test that takes a little more time (about 2-3 hours) because it has three stages and includes a glucose test:
* on an empty stomach,
* one hour after drinking the aqueous glucose solution,
* two hours after drinking the solution.

It is important that the first fasting determination is done at a minimum 8-14 hours after the previous meal. In the days before the test, do not change your diet, so that the result is a reliable reflection of your diet. Eat as you always do and don't avoid sweets or other types of carbohydrates.

When going for the test, find out in advance whether the facility has its own glucose or whether you need to buy it at the pharmacy. Dissolve 75 g of glucose in 250-300 ml of water and drink within five minutes. If you are nauseous or just feel you may not be able to handle it, take a lemon with you and add a few drops of juice to the solution — most doctors agree that this does not affect the test result and may help. If you vomit, the test cannot be continued, the result will not be reliable and you will have to repeat it. Also remember that while waiting for the next step, you will have to sit, and not eat or drink. Walking is not recommended — physical effort will accelerate the glucose metabolism. It is best to take a good book or magazine with you. According to current standards, the following results are considered healthy:
* fasting: below 92 mg/dl,
* after 1 hour: below 180 mg/dl,
* after 2 hours: below 153 mg/dl.

If these standards are exceeded by up to 1 mg/dl, the doctor must diagnose gestational diabetes and introduce the appropriate procedures. The gynaecologist conducting the pregnancy may continue to guide you on his or her own or, if in doubt, refer you to a diabetes clinic. The basic treatment is the introduction of an appropriate diet adjusted to the mother's BMI, and if that is not enough, insulin will need to be added.

If it turns out that you have diabetes, you will first receive a glucometer — a device that you should keep with you permanently from now on. It is used several times a day to measure your blood glucose by examining a drop of blood taken from your fingertip. It is not painful and you get used to it quickly. Your doctor will let you know how often it needs to be done — usually 4-6 times a day, in the morning on an empty stomach and then after meals. It's also possible to place sensors on the back of the arm and check your glucose concentration using an app on your phone.

New diet. You will also receive recommendations for your diet. It will be important to have regular meals at fixed times, covering your current calorie needs and rich in appropriate ingredients. You can get help in composing your diet from a diabetologist or dietician, who will advise you on how you should put together your meals, what foods to avoid, and which should be permanently on your menu. This will help you to control your weight gain, which – in the case of gestational diabetes – will be constantly monitored.

Physical activity. If your pregnancy is proceeding without other complications, physical exercise is beneficial. This will help to reduce body fat and increase the burning of glucose, making it easier for you to take care of your glycemic level and ensure that you feel better.

Tests. Your doctor will probably recommend that you check your blood pressure and thyroid parameters more often (as the risk of hypothyroidism increases). Moreover, he or she will thoroughly evaluate your child's welfare in KTG and ultrasound tests, especially in the last weeks of pregnancy.

What kind of birth awaits you? Many women worry that, should they have gestational diabetes, their pregnancy will have to end with a caesarean section, but this is not true. This is only necessary in the case of a fetal macrosomia (with diabetes it weighs > 4,300 g, without diabetes > 4,500 g) or if the mother has a small pelvis bone (which increases the risk of of shoulder distortion if the child is wedged in the birth canal),or if there are other obstetric or extra-obstetrical indications. It is also possible to induce the birth earlier (earliest at week 37) if an excessive weight gain is suspected. A pregnancy that runs without complications may end in a fully natural birth, but an individual approach on the part of the staff and continuous thorough evaluation are important.

If you have any questions, concerns or doubts, talk to your doctor or midwife or go to a diabetes clinic. Knowledge and greater awareness of the problem will certainly reduce your anxiety and make you feel better, which also has a positive impact on the illness itself.

In the majority of women who have gestational diabetes, the condition passes during the postpartum period and glucose levels return to normal. After this period it is recommended to perform a second glucose load test. Later, due to the increased risk of type 2 diabetes, a woman should have a fasting glucose test at least once every 3 years. If you plan to have another baby, it is worth repeating the glucose load test earlier. And don't stop with the healthy eating habits and regular physical activity – this will help you maintain a healthy body weight. This is not only a healthy preventative measure for the future, but also a way to get in shape, return to shape and above all feel better. In the end it's healthy body, healthy mind! ◆

Sylvia – midwife and mum to Lucia.

28. A pregnant woman walks into a pharmacy... Basic principles of medicine use during pregnancy

How beautiful it would be to go through the whole pregnancy in perfect health and well-being, and give birth to a perfectly healthy baby... I know some such mothers. Pregnancy was the most beautiful time for them, they felt great, they did not suffer from spinal pain, anaemia, heartburn, cramps, allergies – yeah, they did not even get a cold. Unfortunately, such women are a minority.

A complete understanding of the safety of medicinal substances for future mums is still limited, but it is improving year by year. The number of clinical trials is increasing and we are better understanding the properties of medicines and their side effects. Therefore the opportunities for safe treatment during pregnancy are increasing. Use of certain medicines may be beneficial for the mother and safe for the baby, but there can sometimes be risks for the baby too. A woman expecting a baby should be openly informed about this. However, it is important for you to know that "the disease often poses a greater risk to the developing baby than taking pharmaceutical drugs" [1]. I myself suffer from diabetes and hypothyroidism; in my experience, I have a history of difficulty becoming pregnant, of miscarriages and a weakened immune system. During my pregnancy, I took a few drugs for chronic problems, but nevertheless I gave birth to a healthy daughter. There are many such women. You could even say that it's thanks to modern medicine that many of us actually became mums :-).

The most important rules for treatment during pregnancy. The iron rule is to only use substances with proven results. They must be tested compounds that have no teratogenic effect on the developing baby. Teratogenic means toxic effects on the unborn child, causing damage to the central nervous system, delayed fetal development, functional disorders, premature birth and even the death of the embryo. It seems reasonable to use drugs and supplements only when necessary. The treatment should be chosen so that the smallest possible doses are taken in the shortest possible time. It is best to avoid medication altogether in the first trimester.

Classification of drugs in terms of their use for pregnant women. Until 2015, a classification created by the *American Food and Drug Administration* (FDA) was in force. Medicines were divided into five categories: A, B, C, D and X, where A was the safest and X was absolutely prohibited. However, in 2014, the FDA announced the introduction of a new descriptive system which replaced this letter one. What does this mean for patients? As of 30 June 2015, you will no longer find information on which group the substance belongs to in the leaflets of new medicines. Instead, there will be more information under 3 subsections:

- Pregnancy – information on the dosage and risks to the baby with the use of the substance. In addition it's also required that a record of any side effects is included.
- Lactation – information on the possibility of use in breastfeeding mothers, the concentration of the drug and its effect on the baby.
- Reproductive abilities of women and men – information on, among other things, the influence of the drug on the pregnancy test result, effectiveness of contraception and fertility.

10 guidelines on the safe use of medicines during pregnancy
1. Only take medicines during pregnancy if you have to.
2. If at all possible, avoid taking any therapeutic substance in the first trimester.
3. Read the leaflet! Choose medicines that have been clinically tested, with proven efficacy, and which are safe for the fetus. Definitely avoid any substance that has any possible or suspected teratogenic effects on the fetus (in other words, the possibility of causing developmental defects).
4. In pregnancy, take medications at the lowest registered treatment dosages, and for as short a period as possible (but don't stop before full recovery).
5. Not all medicines can be taken in every trimester. For example: ibuprofen is only safe in the 2nd trimester, butamirate for dry coughs in the 2nd and 3rd, while paracetamol is safe in all three trimesters.
6. Our understanding of medicines used in pregnancy is still limited, so future mothers should be informed about the level of risk to the fetus. Don't be afraid to ask your doctor or pharmacist!
7. Folic acid, vitamin D, iodine, DHA are recommended for use during pregnancy, are taken for prevention, and are safe and effective for the fetus and future mother.
8. Before taking any kind of therapeutic substance, consult your doctor or pharmacist. Don't take any medication or supplements without the express recommendation of your doctor.
9. Natural medicines containing herbs have not usually been tested, and the vast majority of them are not recommended for use during pregnancy.
10. Remember! The illness itself is often a greater danger to the fetus than rational treatment, so don't avoid medication at all costs.

What should you do if you catch a cold, run a fever, have a sore throat or runny nose? A pregnancy does last nine months, after all, so there's a fair chance of some kind of infection happening. **Above all, don't ignore a cold!** You need to do all you can to stop it getting more serious. Don't count on it going away on it's own. Above all, slow down. If you're working – take a few days off, if you're looking after a child – ask the father, a grandmother or another trusted person for help. Get some rest, but also take action as soon as the first symptoms appear. Try home remedies at first (garlic, onion, honey, flaxseeds, ginger). If that doesn't work, go to the doctor's (your GP or gynaecologist), who will run some tests. Knowing how advanced your pregnancy is and what your health is like overall, a specialist will know what medicine to prescribe to avoid any harm to your unborn baby. You may be prescribed an antibiotic or some other strong medication. Doctors prescribe this if the illness, such as bronchitis, UTI or tonsilitis, could be more dangerous for the fetus than taking medication. At this point, you have to choose the lesser evil, and you should follow your doctor's advice.

Pain and fever. A fever is considered to be a temperature above 38 – 38.5°C. A raised temperature under this level is a low-grade fever. If you have a temperature just over 37 degrees, give your immune system the time and opportunity to fight the infection itself. But what should you take if your temperature goes up and you do run a fever?

The medicine of choice for pain and fever for pregnant women is paracetamol. You can safely take it in every trimester, as demonstrated in many clinical trials, but you shouldn't take it on a daily basis for a period of more than 4 weeks. Why? Because one clinical trial conducted in Spain indicated that pregnant women who took paracetamol regularly had a higher chance of delivering babies with autism spectrum disorders and attention-deficit hyperactivity disorder (ADHD). A lot more research is necessary to confirm this finding, which is why paracetamol is still regarded as safe, particularly in single doses, and not taken over a period of weeks. The usual dosage is 1g 3-4 times a day, at intervals of at least 4 hours.

Nonsteroidal anti-inflammatory drugs, or NSAIDs for short (e.g. ibuprofen, ketoprofen, diclofenac, naproxen) – were, until recently, considered fairly safe in the 1st and 2nd trimesters. However, according to recent guidelines, the use of NSAIDs in the 1st trimester is not recommended, due to disruptions in embryo implantation and increased risk of miscarriage. There was already agreement about the 3rd trimester – they are not recommended, mostly due to the risk of premature closing of the arterial duct (Bottala), which can lead to pulmonary hypertension in the newborn, as well as the risk of increased labour times and reduced amniotic fluid.

If you are in your 2nd trimester, have a fever or severe pain, and paracetamol is not helping, you can take a single 200 mg dose of ibuprofen (for example), and up to a maximum of 600 mg per day (200 mg up to 3 times a day, every 6-8 hours). Acetylsalicylic acid (Aspirin) at dosages above 150 mg and metamizole are contraindicated throughout pregnancy. Acetylsalicylic acid can be taken in cardiological doses (75-150 mg).

Dry throat, hoarseness. The main thing is to keep your throat moistened and lubricated:
- drink a lot of water throughout the day,
- give yourself inhalations with nebulized saline (0,9% NaCl) or hypertonic saline (2-5% NaCl),
- take a spoonful of flaxseed oil, rapeseed oil, olive oil or similar and swallow it slowly,
- soak some flaxseeds in water for about 8 hours or overnight and drink them with the water (if you are taking any medications or supplements, leave a few hours between taking them and the flaxseeds, as they coat the intestines and may decrease absorption),
- make some homemade onion syrup,
- take a teaspoon of honey, or some honey in water.

If the above methods don't help, get a spray, syrup or pastilles from the chemist's containing marshmallow, Iceland moss, glycerol, hyaluronic acid or oils such as olive oil.

It's important not to eat or drink anything straight after taking these treatments, in order not to cancel out their effectiveness by accidentally removing the protective and moisturising layer they provide. It's best to wait at least 30 minutes.

Sore throat. You can treat a sore throat by:
- gargling with sodium bicarbonate dissolved in water or a preparation from the chemist's,
- sucking or chewing on a piece of fresh ginger.

If rinsing doesn't help, you can use benzydamine hydrochloride in the form of a spray or pastilles. This will have an anti-inflammatory, analgesic, anaesthetic and antiseptic effect. Benzydamine is safe for the fetus and can be used during pregnancy, breastfeeding and in infants and children.

Runny or blocked nose. A runny or blocked nose can really ruin your day. What can you do to make things better? The first and most important thing to do is to clean out your nasal passages, starting as soon as symptoms appear. This will flush out the bacteria and viruses that want to "settle down" in your mucous membranes. It will also prevent the infection from spreading to your ears or lower respiratory tract. You can clean out your nasal passages using a sea water nasal spray or inhaling nebulized saline (0,9%) – using an adult mask, not a mouthpiece.

What if these methods are not working, and your nose is so blocked up that you can't breathe, or you can feel that there is some thick catarrh far down which it is hard to blow out? Use a hypertonic saline solution in an aerosol or give yourself an inhalation of nebulized hypertonic saline (3% NaCl). The higher concentration of salt cleans out, thins out and liquefies the secretions in your sinuses and nasal passages, and constricts and moistens the mucosa, making breathing easier. If you don't experience asthma or overreactive bronchial tubes when using hypertonic solutions, you can do so for up to 2 weeks. Using them for longer dries out the nasal membranes and may lead to further problems.

If nothing is helping, and your blocked up nose is stopping you sleeping at night, you can temporarily use a spray containing oxymetazoline or xylometazoline. Only use them for a few days, because both of them can be addictive and drying. Some doctors recommend using them at the lower dosages for children, as this introduces less of the active substance to the body and this half-strength dosage usually helps. If it doesn't, you can use the traditional adult dosage. The medicine of choice should be oxymetazoline, since it is a derivative of xylometazoline, with half the concentration but the same decongestant effect. If your nose is still stuffy and it is getting more problematic for you, definitely see your doctor.

A cough is one of the more annoying conditions during pregnancy. A cough can last a lot longer than other cold symptoms, and on top of that it can be so tiring that, in extreme cases, it can even bring on contractions. It can also be a symptom of a more serious disease such as bronchitis or pneumonia. So

don't wait for it to go away by itself, go to see your doctor, who will examine you and decide on further treatment.
- Dry coughs – take care to keep your throat moistened when you have a dry cough, using the same methods given above for dry throats and hoarseness. These are the only methods to use during the 1st trimester. Remember not to use expectorant medication for a dry cough. They can increase the coughing reflex and will do more harm than good. So what should you choose? The medicine of choice from a chemist's will be butamirate citrate – a non-opioid medication which reduces the coughing reflex. It is available as a syrup. If clearly necessary, it can be used temporarily in the 2nd and 3rd trimesters. Codeine and dextromethorphan are not recommended for use in pregnancy. They are thought to have teratogenic effects on the fetus (causing developmental defects). Treatments for dry cough can be used throughout the day and night, as needed.
- Wet coughs – if you've got a wet cough, you need to get rid of the thick secretions by diluting and liquifying the mucus. In this case, stopping the cough reflex can lead to a respiratory tract infection. Here, too, a nebulizer for inhalations will be useful. Used with a hypertonic saline solution (3% NaCl), it will help liquify and thin down the secretions. It is a very effective yet gentle method for getting rid of excess mucus. It is also completely safe for the developing fetus. If you have asthma or overreactive bronchial tubes, you can give yourself an inhalation with a lower concentration of saline, for example by combining normal saline with hypertonic saline in various proportions. Onion syrup can be helpful in treating a wet cough. You can add garlic, ginger and lemon to make it more effective. Persistent wet coughs in pregnancy can be treated with acetylcysteine, ambroxol, and bromhexine. However, it would be best for a doctor to examine you first. All the above-mentioned medicines are in category B, and should only be used when essential. It is best to take expectorant medication in the morning, and the final dose 4-5 hours before sleep. Inhalations of hypertonic saline are an exception – they can be used 2-3 hours before sleep.

Medication for use during pregnancy
- Antibiotics. If you have a serious bacterial infection like bronchitis, tonsillitis or cystitis, an antibiotic can become unavoidable. Your doctor will

then make a decision as to which substance to choose, for the safety of both of you. The safest ones include: amoxicillin, ampicillin, cefuroxime, cefaclor, cefadroxil, azithromycin, nystatin, natamycin. All these antibiotics belonged to formerly category B, so they are considered safe for pregnant women and their baby. The following antibacterial drugs should be avoided during pregnancy: doxycycline, triamycin, aminoglycosides (streptomycin and kanamycin), clarithromycin, gentamicin, ciprofloxacin.

- Drugs for heartburn and other stomach problems. It's better to prevent indigestion problems than have to treat them later. To minimise the risk of heartburn, eat less and give up fatty foods in favour of easily digestible foods. Do not lie down immediately after a meal. If this doesn't help, you can try calcium carbonate, magnesium carbonate, or sodium alginate in the form of milk or lozenges that neutralize excess acid in your stomach. As recommended during pregnancy, drugs for hyperacidity containing aluminium salts should be avoided as they may carry the risk of side effects in the baby.
- Anti-allergic drugs. Women who suffer from allergic rhinitis, seasonal allergies, skin allergies or other allergies, in the event of emergency certain antihistamines may be necessary even during pregnancy. In clinical trials, no significant risk to the baby was found when second-generation oral antiallergic drugs were used. However, they should certainly be used in the first trimester only in true crisis situations. Ask your doctor to choose a specific medication and the treatment should be as short as possible with the lowest possible doses. You'll probably be prescribed one of the 'formerly-B category drugs: either containing cetirizine, which is the safest in pregnancy, or loratadine, which is still safe but recommended only if cetirizine hasn't helped. Oral use of phenylephrine and pseudoephedrine carries the risk of many defects in the fetus, including the organs of sight, hearing, limbs and small intestine. As for preparations administered to the eye or nose directly, sodium cromoglicate is permitted in the second and third trimester, which is only slightly absorbed into the bloodstream and therefore its use is most probably safe during pregnancy.
- Vitamins. Most vitamins can be used during pregnancy. It is important to take them in the recommended doses. Before you start the supplementing, do a laboratory test beforehand to see if it is really needed. Folic acid

– necessary during pregnancy (formerly category A), vitamin D – recommended during pregnancy (formerly category A), vitamin B (B1, B2, B4, B6, B12), vitamin C and vitamin E are safe.
* Herbs. Our society is convinced that herbal preparations are completely safe and effective. For this reason, pregnant women and breastfeeding mothers very often reach for them with little thought. When I ask my pharmacy customers or blog readers about it, the answer is usually along the lines of: "because they're natural." Mums say that they prefer herbs to synthetic substances, because they do not have undesirable effects and will not harm the baby, and there are always so many negative effects written on medicine labels that it is better to avoid them. Nothing could be further from the truth! The truth is that the effect of vegetable raw materials on the body are not yet fully documented. This means that we don't know how the herbs will pass on to the baby, how they will affect its development and whether they might cause defects. Future mums should in particular avoid products with ginseng, coltsfoot, ginkgo biloba extract and juniper. Essential oils should also be removed as they have a potentially irritating effect.

It's natural to feel overwhelmed by the amount of information provided in this chapter. It is not about remembering everything, but about knowing what the possibilities are and what to ask the doctor or pharmacist. And remember that sometimes the disease itself is a greater threat to the baby than regular treatment. Sometimes it's necessary to choose the lesser of two evils and start the treatment. ◆

Anna – Pharmacy M.A., mother of Antonia and Misha, blogger on the proper use of medicines in children, pregnant women and breastfeeding mothers.

29. You mean folic acid isn't enough?! What supplements to take in pregnancy

Almost every woman who learns she is pregnant immediately starts to take better care of her own health and the baby developing inside her. She is aware that a balanced diet – the provision of essential building blocks such as vitamins and minerals – is very important. This is why many women make their way straight to a pharmacy for dietary supplements and multivitamins for pregnant women.

Do pregnant women really need multivitamins? The number of TV ads for them would suggest that, yes, they do, but are they truly needed for the health of a future mother or is it all just great marketing? Perhaps it's ok just to take only those vitamins and minerals that are necessary? Or simply take some tests and only go for specific supplements if there's a deficiency?

Undoubtedly, a balanced and varied diet containing natural vitamins and minerals will cover most needs. Unfortunately, so far there are no clear recommendations as to which ingredients should be supplemented during pregnancy. In reality different gynaecologists will recommend different ones. Yet there are several vitamins and minerals that have proven (in clinical trials) to have a positive effect on pregnancy and the growing baby. These include **folic acid, vitamin D, iodine and DHA fatty acids**. It is important to take them in specific doses and times of day.

Folic acid (vitamin B9)

- Is it a necessary supplement? YES
- Who should take it? All women aged 15-49 regardless of whether they plan to get pregnant or not, but especially women planning to get pregnant (at least three months before trying), during pregnancy and while breast-feeding.
- Dose for a healthy woman: 0.4-0.8 mg/day
- Form: folic acid and active folates
- How and when to take: at a fixed time, after a meal
- Is an overdose risky? YES

It seems that each of us knows that we have to take it, but there are still many uncertainties. First of all: what is it for? Will a balanced diet protect us from a shortage of folates? When to start taking it? What to choose: folic acid or active folates? And finally: what dosage? One thing is certain, **all women of**

childbearing age (15-49 years) should take folic acid. Statistics tell us that around 40% of pregnancies are unplanned. In such a situation, the prophylactic use of folic acid will significantly reduce the risk of nerve coil (NTD – neural tube defect) defects in the fetus. And what is this? It is a syndrome of congenital malformation of the central nervous system and spine formed in the first four weeks of pregnancy, so when the woman is not aware of her pregnancy. They can result in brain damage and spinal cord herniation of the embryo. To reduce the risk by up to 70%, use folic acid according to the latest guidelines, which are: a minimum of 12 weeks before pregnancy, and then during pregnancy, during the postpartum period and until the end of breastfeeding.

Folic acid plays many important roles in the human body, including:
- enabling the complete closure of the spinal cord, which ensures the healthy development of the baby's central nervous system,
- being a coenzyme (assistant) during the formation of DNA – that is in every cell of the human body,
- prevents heart, urinary tract and limb defects,
- prevents a cleft lip and cleft palate in the child,
- prevents pre-eclampsia,
- prevents anaemia that occurs in 40% of pregnant women and breastfeeding mothers.

Unfortunately, even a balanced diet cannot provide a daily dose of folic acid during pregnancy. Of course, a future mother should try to consume as much folate as possible, which is found in lettuce, spinach, cabbage, broccoli, brussels sprouts, red pepper, whole-grain cereals, liver, eggs, nuts and cheese. In order to meet your increased needs, however, you need to additionally supplement vitamin B9. It is also important to choose supplements with documented ingredients and effects.

MTHFR mutation. This rather unexplainable mutation, specifically the gene variety, is currently in the vocabulary of many women. This is thanks to a lot of nonsense and false information that can be found on the web. The truth is that "MTHFR mutation" occurs in about 50% of women. Nevertheless, according to reputable gynaecologist associations, there is no justification for performing tests for the presence of the MTHFR mutation. Why? Because regardless of the absence or the presence of a genetic variation of MTHFR (and there are dozens of types of MTHFR polymorphisms) a standard prophylactic folic acid dose of 0.4-0.8 mg/day is sufficient to prevent this mutation. There is no recommendation to use any treatment in this situation.

Recommendations. What dose of folic acid is currently recommended? The question is not a simple one, but according to the latest guidelines, women are divided into three groups: preconception, pregnancy, postpartum and breastfeeding.

A low risk group of fetal malformations and pregnancy complications, involving healthy women with no history of pregnancy concerns, should take 0.4-0.8 mg of folic acid per day. Those at increased risk of fetal defects and pregnancy complications are those who:
- gave birth to a child with a congenital malformation of the fetus, or a close family member,
- have fetal hypotrophy and/or pre-eclampsia in previous pregnancies,
- have prenatal diabetes mellitus type I or II,
- have gastrointestinal diseases (ulcerative colitis, Crohn's disease, coeliac disease),
- have liver or kidney failure (dialysis),
- have had a bariatric operation (operation to reduce the capacity of the stomach),
- are obese,
- are permanently using the following medications: metformin, methotrexate, cholestyramine, sulfa-lazine, antiepileptic drugs,
- smoke cigarettes and abuse alcohol,
- have reduced MTHFR activity.

In the high-risk group it is recommended to take folic acid at a dose of 0.4 mg per day plus another 0.4 mg preferably in the form of active folates. A vitamin B12 supplement is also recommended. The high risk group of fetal malformations and pregnancy complications, which includes women who themselves, or their partner or offspring, have birth defects to the nervous system. Supplementation is recommended:
- a minimum 12 weeks before the planned pregnancy and in the first trimester of pregnancy – 5 mg of folic acid daily, including active folates and vitamin B12.

- in the second and third trimester of pregnancy and during lactation – 0.8 mg per day, including active folates and vitamin B12.

You may ask why vitamin B12 is recommended at higher doses of folates? This is because an increased supply of folic acid during pregnancy can mask the deficiency of vitamin B12, which can lead to metabolic disorders and consequently complications in pregnancy.

At what time of day should you take folic acid? It is certainly recommended to take folate at a fixed time and around a mealtime, for example after breakfast.

Should men also take folic acid? In general, there is no recommendation that fathers should also take vitamin B9 every day. The exception is if the andrologist recommends it, for example due to poor sperm quality or reduced fertility.

Paradoxically, taking too high a dose of folic acid may lead to an increased risk of complications during early pregnancy.

Did you know that the demand for folic acid from breastfeeding mothers is higher than during pregnancy? This just shows how important it is to use folate regularly during this period as well.

Vitamin D

- Is a supplementation necessary: YES
- Who should take it: everyone who has a vitamin D deficiency, newborns, infants, small children (up to 1 year of age), women planning pregnancy, pregnant and breastfeeding women
- Dose for a healthy woman: 1,500–2,000 IU/day
- Form: any available (tablets, capsules, drops)
- How and when to eat: with a meal, preferably one where there is fat
- Is an overdose risky: YES (but it is very rare)

Intensive research on the influence of vitamin D on the human body has been conducted for many years. It's only recently, however that its role during pregnancy is beginning to be appreciated. Vitamin D has extremely valuable properties, and its action is multidirectional. Among other things, it prevents the occurrence of pre-eclampsia and thrombosis, reduces the likelihood of the development of diabetes during pregnancy, reduces the risk of *bacterial vaginosis* (bacterial infections of the vagina), and helps to maintain healthy bones and teeth.

Unfortunately, vitamin D deficiency in many populations is common, including among pregnant and breastfeeding women. The main reason for this is a lack of exposure to the sun (especially from September to April) and insufficient supply from diet. Because of this, supplementation during pregnancy is mandatory. Together with your doctor, you should determine the right dose of vitamin D for you. Even better is to take a 25(OH)D blood test. This will help you find out your vitamin D concentration and make it easier to adjust the right dose.

Recommendation. Vitamin D3 should be taken by women planning to become pregnant, who are pregnant and during lactation. The dose of 1500-2000 IU per day is the recommended dose, and this should be included in the diet no later than at the beginning of the second trimester. It is a prophylactic dose.

What is important is that a mother's vitamin D level that is too low translates into a deficiency in her offspring. The newborns of women with low vitamin D are at risk of a number of complications. Some occur immediately, including the risk of seizures due to hypocalcemia (too low a concentration of calcium in the blood), reduced bone mass or rickets. Others may occur later, such as defects in tooth enamel, asthma, diabetes, susceptibility to fractures, autoimmune problems, metabolic or cardiovascular diseases. Do not wait for deficiencies in you or your little one. Check the concentration of vitamin D in your body and supplement it regularly.

Iodine

- Is supplementation necessary: YES
- Who should take it: women planning pregnancy, pregnant and breastfeeding women
- Dose for a healthy woman: 150-200 mc/day
- Form: potassium iodate or potassium iodide
- How and when to eat: with a meal
- Is an overdose risky: YES

Before, or as soon as you become pregnant, you should check your thyroid. If there are any abnormalities, you should see an endocrinologist for further diagnosis and treatment. This is very important because thyroid diseases can cause difficulties in getting pregnant, but also miscarriages, pre-eclampsia, prematurebirth, increased risk of intellectual disability, hearing loss and deafness in the newborn. The most common cause of insufficient production of thyroid hormones is iodine deficiency, and a deficiency of iodine can already be apparent in the first trimester of pregnancy, so from the very beginning of pregnancy future mothers should take this supplement, in fact ideally 12 weeks before conception.

What dosage is currently recommended? Iodine content in food depends on diet and on the amount released in the thyroid. However, the latest WHO and ATA (*American Thyroid Association*) recommendations on the total daily intake of iodine in pregnant and breastfeeding women are 250 mcg per day. Constant consumption of too high dose (over 500-600 mcg of iodine per day) during pregnancy may cause thyroid dysfunction in the baby.

Should every future mum supplement iodine? In the case of a woman with thyroid disease, iodine supplementation should be done while thyroid hormones and anti-thyroid antibodies are monitored. This situation requires the treating physician to adjust dose to the individual patient.

Polyunsaturated fatty acids (DHA)

- Is supplementation necessary: YES
- Who should take it: women planning pregnancy, pregnant and breastfeeding women
- Dose for a healthy woman: 500-600 mg/day
- Form: DHA from algae, fatty marine fish, seafood
- How and when to eat: with a meal
- Is an overdose risky: NO

DHA (docosahexaenoic acid) is one of the most important – but underestimated – components of the diet of pregnant women and breastfeeding mothers, because polyunsaturated fatty acids taken during pregnancy have a documented positive effect for both mother and child. They affect, among other things, the proper development of the child's brain and eyesight, as well as its psychomotor development, and in the case of a woman, they reduce the risk of premature birth and postnatal depression. DHA acids should be taken by every woman who is planning to get pregnant, is pregnant and also by breastfeeding mothers. Their natural sources are fatty sea fish (salmon, herring, mackerel, cod), seafood and sea algae. However, an additional supply of them is necessary. Ideally supplementation should be introduced no later than week 20, as in the second half of pregnancy the baby's central nervous system undergoes intense development. This does not mean that DHA acids cannot be taken earlier. Unless you're eating a lot of fish, it is worth supplementing it from the very beginning of your pregnancy.

Recommendations. According to current recommendations, a future mother should take:
- minimum 200 mg DHA – with a weekly intake of at least 2 portions (about 130 g/portion) of fatty sea fish,
- 500-600 mg DHA – if small amounts of fish and other DHA sources are consumed,
- 1000 mg DHA – in case of significant deficiency or high risk of preterm birth.

No side effects on the pregnant woman and fetus have been reported so far, even with high doses (over 1,000 mg) of DHA.

What to choose – fish or seaweed supplements? Well, both are equally valuable and safe when you choose a preparation with DHA acids from safe sources. The risk of contamination with heavy metals, dioxins or polychlorinated biphenyls (PCBs), which can be harmful to the baby, are in this case minimized. They can be taken safely.

Iron

- Is supplementation necessary: NO
- Who should take it: the doctor decides (based on blood test results) whether iron supplementation is necessary

- Form: iron salts, iron diglycinate, iron (II) fumarate, iron sulphate, iron (III) diphosphate
- How and when to take it: at least one hour before you meal and two hours after your meal
- Is an overdose risky: YES

It's not true that all pregnant women should take iron supplements. Indeed, according to various statistics only (or as much as) 25-40% of pregnant women really need it. Anemia – or anaemia – is most often caused by too little iron in the body. This mineral is an important building block of haemoglobin, so when there's a lack of it, haemoglobin levels in the blood decrease at the same time. Anemia can be divided into two groups.
- Physiological – this happens to all pregnant women due to a quitesudden increase (about 40%) in the volume of peripheral blood, and is characterized by a decrease in hemoglobin to a level 11-12.5 g/dl. In this case, an iron-rich diet, or dietary supplements from a pharmacy, is recommended.
- Pathological – when haemoglobin falls below 11 g/dl. This needs treatment with medication prescribed by a doctor.

Anemia resulting from iron deficiency may cause, among other things, a feeling of malaise, a deepening of pregnancy complaints (nausea, dizziness), increased risk of premature birth, fetal malformation, anemia in the child or increased risk of low birth weight of the newborn. Before pregnancy, it is best to go for a blood test and additionally check the concentration of ferritin, which best reflects iron storage. If it turns out that haemoglobin is at the lower end of the range, you should start supplementation. However, if you find out that you are pregnant, put the iron away and wait until you have finished week 8 of your pregnancy. This should be done because too high a concentration of this element in the follicle liquid may increase the risk of adverse effects on the developing embryo, which can lead to developmental defects.

People on a vegan or vegetarian diet, who have absorption disorders, women with heavy menstruation, pregnant women and breastfeeding mothers are all at risk of anaemia.

Diet is very important for the prevention of anaemia. So what do you need to eat to protect against anaemia? The best source is products which originate in animals, because they contain heme iron, which is well absorbed. These include: meat (beef, veal, rabbit), fish (herrings, sardines, mackerel) and egg yolks. Liver is also a rich source of iron, but it is better not to go over the top during pregnancy, because excess iron can harm the developing child. Plant foods are a less absorbent source, as they contain non-heme iron, but it is still worth including them in your diet. These include: legumes (chickpeas, beans, lentils, peas), cocoa, wheat bran, beetroots, spinach, broccoli, nuts, almonds, pumpkin and sunflower seeds, buckwheat, dark bread (rye). You can improve your iron absorption with the addition of vitamin C. How? Take pills or eat a meal with fruit juice rich in vitamin C, such as orange, blackcurrant or raspberry. The absorption of iron then increases by even 2 or 3 times.

Recommendations. Given that both excess and deficiency of iron negatively affect pregnancy, supplementation should be decided by a doctor.

What not to do during iron supplementation? Do not take iron preparations 'randomly,' but always at least an hour before a meal and two hours after. You can take them on an empty stomach, but if you take other medicines in the morning, for hypothyroidism or hyperacidity, do not take iron before breakfast. This stops the absorption of the thyroid hormone and anaesthesia. Also, do not drink coffee, tea or fizzy drinks after a meal or after taking iron supplements – this significantly weakens the absorption of iron. Instead of these drinks, choose a juice containing vitamin C. Do not take iron supplements together with magnesium or calcium. If you have to use all these minerals, spread them out throughout the day so that the interval between them is as lengthy as possible (at least 2 hours).

Side effects of taking iron. You don't often hear about the undesirable side effects of taking iron, but they can be really annoying. They include constipation, diarrhea, nausea, vomiting or severe stomach problems. If you have a stomach ache, take the iron after a meal, even though it's less absorbable.

Are you a vegan or a vegetarian? Vegans and vegetarians who plan to get pregnant, are already pregnant or are breastfeeding should also make sure they have an adequate level of vitamin B12. This is very important, because its deficiency is one of the causes of anaemia. Since vitamin B12 is well absorbed only from animal-based foods, women on a vegan and vegetarian diet should additionally supplement this vitamin, even though they take plant-based forms of vitamin B12 such as spirulina, chlorella, alfalfa sprouts, miso or sauerkraut, as these are forms that are unabsorbable by the human body. The dose of vitamin B12 should be determined by your doctor.

According to official guidelines, **you should supplement folic acid, vitamin D, DHA acids and iodine during pregnancy and during lactation**. This is indisputable, because supplementing them through diet is difficult or insufficient. As far as iron and magnesium are concerned, they should be used by women who are deficient or at risk of deficiency in their diet. It is also worth considering the supplementation of choline and vitamins B6 and B12. It is known that, together with folates, they help to maintain proper homocysteine metabolism. Lowering the concentration of this compound in the mother's blood has a beneficial effect on the course of pregnancy and the health of the newborn.

Remember that despite the huge variety of multivitamin supplements available for pregnant and breastfeeding women, it is certainly not the case that all the ingredients they contain are recommended. What's more, some of the added substances may have an adverse effect, such as hindering the absorption of others. This is the case with magnesium, iron and calcium. Those described in this chapter are necessary, and the rest – for a woman who feels well, does not get chronically ill and has good test results, are really UNNECESSARY! ◆

Anna – Pharmacy M.A., mother of Antonia and Misha, blogger on the proper use of medicines in children, pregnant women and breastfeeding mothers.

30. Pregnancy is not like illness? Lifestyle choices during pregnancy

Joy, euphoria, disbelief – two inconspicuous lines on a pregnancy test can turn your whole world upside down. Hormones go crazy, happiness is mixed with uncertainty. What next? This seemingly banal question is asked by every pregnant woman. Do I have to give up my lifestyle? What about work? What about my interests? Should I be active, or from now on should I lie down, try to relax, and plan the baby's room?

Officially, pregnancy is not an illness, but try convincing a woman who has experienced a whole range of ailments associated with this 'blessed' state. Horrible nausea, back pains, drowsiness, emotionally-negative indecision and distraction are just some of the side effects [1]. One of our mothers, Anna, wrote: "Everybody around me says pregnancy is not an illness and ok, maybe it is not an illness, but I have never felt as wrung out as I have at the beginning and end of pregnancy. And trying to explain what it's like to someone who has never been pregnant is like trying to explain what it is like to be hungry." On the other hand, maybe there is a grain of truth in the fact that women "are too hard on themselves" and demonise pregnancy-related ailments? They are actually superpowers! What else would you call the following:

- falling asleep in any position,
- creating unique culinary combinations such as herrings in honey or pickled, cucumbers in chocolate,
- sensing a trillion smells on a crowded bus,
- running the gamut of emotions, from euphoria to despair, all in one day,
- a sluggishness and forgetfulness worthy of an elephant.

Mysteriously, pregnant women become specialists in fragrances and fusion cuisine, and all this happens with a growing belly and dramatically shrinking bladder and brain capacity! The good news is that you will not experience all these symptoms. Every woman goes through this period differently. Does giving up work at such a moment show a lack of professional ambition? Certainly not. Think about the fact that each of us has a different story behind us, and different internal sensitivity or vulnerability to stress. Pregnancy is a time of huge changes not only physically, but also mentally. Some women need more time to adapt to their new situation, others less. It is damaging to say that women who go on maternity leave do so out of laziness, just as it is to stigmatise anyone who decides to carry on working until the birth.

Listen into yourself. The most important thing during pregnancy, mums agree, is to listen to yourself and to your needs, and to see the limitations our body places on us. Even though Kate was a triathlete before pregnancy, taking part in half marathons, she had to limit her sporting pursuits during pregnancy. "I also thought that pregnancy was an illness until I survived it," she recalled. If you feel good, that's fantastic. Work, travel, have fun. But if you feel like even putting on a tracksuit is too much effort, take it easy and stay in your pyjamas."

So everything is an individual matter. If you are in good shape and your doctor sees no contraindications, you don't have to give up your current lifestyle. Mums who were in good health during pregnancy walked in the mountains, swam, biked, practiced yoga and jogged. Considering that childbirth is not an easy challenge, all the more reason to take care of your physical condition. The best moment for this is the second trimester. Then you can feel a significant surge of energy. However, don't get too attached to this, because in the next few weeks fatigue and heaviness will probably take its place. This will be the perfect time to slow down a bit and start preparing for the birth. If your pregnancy has complications and your doctor recommends that you take it easier, don't blame yourself. Are you in a melancholy mood? Anxious? It's natural. "Just don't spend all day worrying. Give yourself an hour and then enjoy life," [3] a wise person once said. Keep a sentiment like this in your heart and remind yourself of it when it gets tough.

What about socialising? Traveling? Self-fulfilment? Pregnancy is a wonderful moment to get back to being yourself, to rediscover your inner child and do what you have always lacked time for. Proof of this is the mothers who are writing this book. "Who said that pregnancy is a bad time to make your dream holiday come true? If not Peru, maybe Spain? Leaving in the 6th month of pregnancy? A campervan? Anything is possible!" – proclaims Mariola.

It is said that pregnancy and the way a child was born are permanently written in the human limbic system [4]. Consider what feelings and emotions you would like to convey to your unborn baby. Do you want to nurture fear, insecurity, a sense of threat, or would you prefer joy and fulfilment? Meeting friends, going to concerts, making handicrafts, writing books? Our contributing mothers are proof that there are no major limitations. "A happy mother is a happy baby. Do what makes you happy and satisfied and what you have the strength to do," adds Joanna.

What conclusions can we draw? There is no one universal truth about how to navigate these exceptional 9 months. Pregnancy is not an illness, but the first time we take responsibility not only for ourselves, but also for our unborn baby. So experience it as best you can. Listen to your intuition and don't let ambition, a sense of duty or false beliefs drown it out. ♦

Sylvia – mum to Peter and Hannah.

31. Nourishing both of you, without eating for two. A healthy diet during pregnancy

A pregnant woman's diet has an impact not only on the development of her unborn child, but also on her mood and, to some extent, on the course of childbirth and the postpartum period. Poor nutrition may affect the weight of the baby, which can result in a longer birth time or birth by caesarean section.

How many calories? We now know that the calorie requirement during pregnancy increases only slightly, by about 340 kcal in the second trimester and less than 450 kcal in the third trimester. So you can put the saying "eating for two" back with the fairy tales and focus on the quality of the food you eat.

Folic acid. A future mother should remember first and foremost (but not only!) about supplementing folic acid (vitamin B9), because the amount in your food is insufficient (▶ I – 33).

Water. An adequate supply of water is also extremely important, as the volume of blood circulating in a pregnant woman's body is about 40% more than normal. You need to drink more than two litres of non-carbonated water per day.

You already know that you should focus on the quality of the food you eat in order to provide your baby with the nutrients it needs to develop healthily and to enable you to prepare for the birth. A pregnant woman's diet should not be calorie or product-oriented. Only highly processed foods or fast foods are not recommended, but nothing will happen if you occasionally satisfy a strong desire to eat fries or crisps. It's only important that it doesn't become an everyday habit. Choose everyday products without flavour-enhancers or other unnecessary additives, just simple and natural ingredients. Use seasonal products, don't be afraid of fruit or legumes, just be moderate and ensure proper hygiene to avoid bloating, indigestion or food poisoning. Eat vegetables (especially greens) and whole-grain cereal products every day, which will provide many valuable minerals and vitamins. Nuts are a healthy snack. The water and fibre content of your diet will improve bowel movement, which may be prone to constipation during pregnancy. Regular and well-balanced meals seem to be effective against nausea as well. Unfortunately, there are cases of severe vomiting, which – due to their intensity – require special dietary attention and medical care to prevent significant weakening of the body. There are various ways of dealing with nausea through diet, including eating a small meal in the morning while still in bed, smaller but frequent meals, choosing dishes with a less intense smell, ginger tea, fresh ginger added to water, water with lemon, snacks rich in vitamin B and almonds (good for heartburn).

Food hazards. Many women, especially in their first pregnancy, have a lot of dietary concerns. After all, choosing the right foods to eat is not only about satisfying your hunger, but about nourishing your growing baby, and it can seem more important to watch what you eat during pregnancy than when you're breastfeeding. In addition to the guidelines for a rational, balanced diet discussed above, you should also keep in mind a few other things:
- Toxoplasmosis – make sure you do toxoplasmosis tests. If you haven't had any contact with toxoplasma, you'll have to take additional precautions so that you don't get infected during pregnancy, as this could endanger your baby. The main sources of infection are cat litter (avoid cleaning the cat litter tray), raw meat (use appropriate heat treatment) and unwashed fruit and vegetables.
- Listeria is a disease caused by animal bacteria that is found in unpasteurised dairy products, raw meat or unwashed fruits and vegetables. In order to avoid infection, observe due hygiene in the preparation of raw products (heat treatment of meat, fish and seafood), also give up products made from

unpasteurised milk (we include here many types of cheese, including brie, feta, gorgonzola, camembert).
- Fungi and moulds – like to lurk in fruits and vegetables or nuts. It's a good idea to look carefully at these products before eating them. Throw them away if you have any doubts. Cutting out the spoiled area does not guarantee getting rid of tiny, invisible threads of mould.
- Heavy metals – accumulated in seafood, especially large, long-life predatory fish. Avoid – or only eat occasionally – tuna, shark, royal mackerel, marlin and swordfish. Choose cod, salmon, trout flounder or catfish. Remember that frequent consumption of fish, with its DHA fats, contributes to the healthy development of the child's brain and eyesight, so it's extremely important especially in the third trimester of pregnancy. If you can't eat enough of these fish, consider DHA acid supplementation.
- Caffeine – the safe dose for a pregnant woman is 200 mg of caffeine per day. This means you can allow yourself three cups of espresso or two black teas, or two coffees – or ten decaffeinated ones ;). Remember, however, that caffeine can significantly exacerbate unpleasant pregnancy symptoms, such as insomnia and frequent urination.
- Green tea – green tea is not recommended for women who are trying to get pregnant and those who are in their first trimester. Compounds in the tea reduce the absorption of folic acid, which is responsible for the formation of the child's nervous system. Reducing green tea is also recommended in women with anemia resulting from folic acid deficiency.

What about herbs and supplements? Not everything during pregnancy can be consumed without fear, and certainly not herbs, medicines or supplements. Ask your gynaecologist or nutritionist to make sure you take something safe. Remember that there are no stupid questions, especially if your baby's welfare is at stake.

The golden rule of nutrition, not only for pregnant women, is moderation. A cup of herbs drunk once in a while won't do us any harm, while a few cups drunk every day can have a real impact on you or your baby's health. Nettle, ginger, peppermint, chamomile and lemon balm are generally considered safe during pregnancy, but you should avoid raspberry leaves, hibiscus, sage, ginseng, aloe vera, hops or mint until the birth. Raspberry leaf tea is often used just before the birth, as recommended by the midwife or medical practitioner, to help prepare the uterus. Cranberries are considered safe to use during pregnancy and are recommended for their protective effect on the urinary tract.

Just remember that dried cranberries available in stores can contain a significant amount of sugar. ◆

Monica – clinical nutritionist.

32. Pregnancy diet for vegetarians and vegans

Well-planned vegetarian diets, including vegan diets, are suitable for people at all stages of life, including pregnancy – so says one of the largest dietary organisations in the world, the American Academy of Nutrition and Dietetics. Evidence-based analysis has shown that vegetarian diets can meet the nutritional requirements of pregnancy and benefit both the mother and the newborn. If you are a vegetarian or vegan, you can quite happily continue with a vegetarian diet during pregnancy, paying attention to a well-balanced diet (which applies to any woman expecting a baby). Remember that if you are a vegetarian or vegan, you should supplement with vitamin B12, which only comes from animal based products. ◆

Joanna – Kazik's mother, Panda's partner, caretaker of two dogs and a cat. She likes to parent closely, in the here and now – and loves baby wraps.

33. Munching cucumber with chocolate. The science behind pregnancy cravings

Do pregnancy cravings really exist, or are they just a myth? The mothers working on this book had a range of opinions, from utter denial of pregnancy cravings or disappointment if they didn't experience them, to a long list of rather strange combinations of food. As Dominica writes: "I didn't know I was pregnant until one day I ate a whole jar of mustard in one sitting. This craving continued throughout my pregnancy – I was drawn to mustard and vinegar pickles." We've all seen comedies and cartoons showing night-time snacking or sending a partner out to get a particular product. "For me it was banana cream eclairs. My then-husband-to-be sent half his family to look for this eclair, and he must have gone halfway around the town. He found it! But it was a one-off thing," Agnes recalls.

What is a craving? According to the dictionary, a craving is "a sudden, passing and often fanciful idea" [1]. Many future mums, however, would argue with this definition. Sylvia writes: "During my first pregnancy, I ate ice cream and kiwi... I passionately consumed whole baskets full of this fruit and people joked that my baby would be green." Pregnancy cravings are rather better defined as an unstoppable desire for something that was not particularly enjoyed before pregnancy, or an unusual combination of flavours. As Anna says: "I couldn't understand why they wouldn't leave me in peace to eat pickled cucumber with yoghurt or kefir... they go well together."

Symptoms of pregnancy and the connection to gender. Pregnancy cravings are common among women around the world. Studies of different populations show that at least 50% of pregnant women experience at least one craving. In some countries (and some studies) this percentage is much higher, reaching 80-90%. They are even described as a 'symptom' of early pregnancy. This phenomenon was experienced by Kate, whose pregnancy delicacy was... fried herrings in vinegar: "Every day, I ate a litre of mayonnaise... After 2 weeks we realised that this wasn't really a normal diet and... bought a pregnancy test."

In some cultures there is a popular belief that it is possible to determine the sex of a child on the basis of food cravings – sweet foods heralding a girl and salty or sour ones a boy (or it can be vice versa). This can be firmly placed with the pregnancy fairy tales. It does seem, however, that what we eat during pregnancy might have a bearing on our children's tastes. Agnes writes: "I have three sons. In the first pregnancy I had a hankering for salty and fatty food, in the second, sweet food, and in the third one, crunchy foods and crispy vegetables. And these are the kinds of food that each son likes to eat."

Where do pregnancy cravings come from? Cravings usually appear in the first trimester of pregnancy and weaken around the fourth month. They are sometimes associated with a more intense sense of smell and taste, nausea, vomiting and aversion to certain products, hence the strong belief that they are associated with hormonal changes in the female body. This theory is supported by evidence that cravings occur during two other periods of hormonal fluctuation, PMS and menopause. Some people regard pregnancy cravings as "superpowers" that evolution has endowed us with to guide us towards better nutrients and avoid toxins harmful to the baby. According to other hypotheses, they are mechanisms to indicate deficiency in certain ingredients. For example, a desire for chocolate points to a deficiency in magnesium. However, if this were true, such a craving would be for spinach or kale. A current theory is that cravings are caused by cultural and psychological factors, a theory which is becoming increasingly popular, and is confirmed by research. Pregnant women all over the world experience food cravings, but *what* they crave is definitely culturally conditioned. In the United States, chocolate is No. 1, and another bizarre whim is sucking ice cubes. Women in other parts of the world – who generally eat less processed food – crave fruit, meat, dairy or rice.

A social game. Cravings can also be a mechanism to draw attention to the needs of a pregnant woman – a strategy to gather social support. In this way, a man can be proud that he is able to satisfy his partner's wishes and needs, and it allows him to demonstrate his readiness to share in caring for her and their child. He actively participates in the miracle of creating new life. In this sense, cravings as a kind of social game play a positive role.

On the flip side, however, researchers point to a dark side of pregnancy cravings. Their intensification, especially towards products that are dangerous (like cleaning products) or inedible, may be caused by too much social pressure related to the role of the woman or the expected sex of the child. In this way, it is a kind of mental safety valve or stress relief [4].

I have a craving, so what's next? General advice would be "don't ignore the craving" for that which is forbidden tempts the most. If you have a craving for:
- Something healthy – bon appetit!
- Something that is forbidden for pregnant women, such as raw meat or alcohol, look for a substitute (like non-alcoholic beer) or an activity that will take your mind off the craving (physical or artistic activity).

- Something you consider unsuitable for pregnant women (fast food, sweets, coffee). Allow yourself to satisfy your cravings in reasonable quantities or look for a healthy substitute; you can make ice cream yourself at home by mixing frozen fruit (berries, strawberries) with banana, prepare apple "chocolate", or bake fries in the oven.
- Something inedible (chalk, washing powder) – consult a doctor or a midwife, as it may indicate a lack of some vitamin or mineral. In this case it might be necessary to perform tests. Perhaps it is also your body telling you that you feel threatened or stressed. Talk about this with your family. If you cannot find support among your loved ones, look for it among women in a similar situation (support groups or Internet forums), or contact a psychologist.

The most popular cravings, according to the mothers we spoke to for this chapter:
- fruit (oranges, watermelons and strawberries),
- sweets (especially ice cream),
- fermented foods (pickled cucumbers and small cucumbers or the salty, sour water which comes with them, or sauerkraut),
- fast food.

Cravings or whims can completely bypass you throughout your pregnancy, and can also support you in your healthy eating habits. If you're worried about something, try taking care not only of your body but also your mental health. One thing you should definitely get rid of here are feelings of guilt. If you sometimes indulge in unhealthy cravings which are not the basis of your diet, you don't have to worry. Feelings of guilt don't do you any good. And of course, you can give the future dad a chance to show off, not necessarily by sending him off for pickled cucumbers at 4 in the morning, but perhaps by asking him to find fresh fruit for you in his spare time. ◆

Natalie – mother of two boys.

34. How much coffee can a mum-to-be drink? Stimulants during pregnancy

Pregnancy often turns the mother's world upside down. From the very beginning, you want to take care of your baby as well as possible. You go to the doctor or midwife for check-ups, do tests and try to eat healthily. So, will a delicious morning coffee, glass of wine at a friend's house or a cigarette after a stressful day at work be harmful to your baby?

Coffee (caffeine). Due to hormonal changes which come with pregnancy, caffeine stays in the body of the future mother 2 or 3 times longer (about 10-18 hours) than in women who are not pregnant (4-6 hours) [10]. Caffeine permeates the placenta and therefore goes directly to the child. The influence on the course of pregnancy and development of a child is dependent on the dose of caffeine, the stage of pregnancy and whether the mother is smoking or not.

<u>Influence of caffeine on pregnancy:</u> increased risk of miscarriage, increased risk of premature birth and increased risk of anemia (caffeine reduces iron absorption).

<u>Influence of caffeine on the child:</u> lowering of birth weight and caffeine abuse in the third trimester of pregnancy may increase the risk of sudden cot death of infants.

<u>Recommendations:</u> The most common recommendation is to consume no more than 200 mg per day [3]. That's a maximum of two not very strong coffees a day.

<u>Tips:</u> Caffeine is not just coffee. It is also found in tea, cocoa, chocolate, desserts, energy drinks and cola. Therefore, when you drink another coffee during the day, consider how much caffeine you have already taken in other products [8].

1 cup 240 ml of brewed coffee	135 mg
1 cup 240 ml of instant coffee	95 mg
latte or cappuccino 180 ml	90 mg
1 can 355 ml of coke	35 mg
1 cup of tea (green has less caffeine than black)	40–60 mg
30 g of bitter chocolate	80 mg
chocolate ice cream	20 mg

Alcohol. The womb is not sufficient a barrier to protect vulnerable babies in the womb from alcohol. Alcohol causes more damage to the fetus than drugs [4]. The strongest toxic effects are in the first 8 weeks of pregnancy.

<u>Influence of alcohol on a woman and on the course of pregnancy:</u> miscarriage, premature birth, premature separation of the placenta (which can lead to haemorrhaging), stillbirth, hypertension, liver function disorders.

<u>The influence of alcohol on the child.</u> Consumption of alcohol during pregnancy may lead to many defects in the child's development, it may also

cause syndromes of co-existing defects, such as FAS, FAE, ARND. These are incurable diseases that may disrupt the functions of the child's body, causing, among other things, intrauterine growth restriction, small head syndrome, heart defects, damage to the central nervous system, facial deformities, sight and hearing disorders, but also problems in establishing social contacts in adulthood and many others.

Recommendations: **No amount of alcohol, regardless of its type, is safe when you're pregnant**. Experts also recommend giving up alcohol when trying for a baby (preferably three months before the planned effort), because in the first weeks of pregnancy the mother does not yet know whether or not she is pregnant.

Tips:
- If you can't stop drinking alcohol, contact a doctor or therapist for help.
- If you see a pregnant woman drinking alcohol, try to find a nice way to share some of the dangers with her – she may not know the effects of alcohol consumption during pregnancy.
- Do not sell, offer or invite a pregnant woman to drink alcohol.
- Alcohol is not necessary for good fun. In good company, sober meetings bring even more fun.
- At parties, make delicious cocktails, smoothies or fruit juices, go to yoga for pregnant women or go to the pool to relax.

Cigarettes. Both active and passive smoking are harmful to the mother and her unborn child. It can cause a number of complications in a pregnant woman, as well as in the fetus.

Influence of nicotine on the course of pregnancy: premature separation of the placenta, ectopic pregnancy, frontal placenta, premature rupture of the membranes, asthma, COPD, cancers of the oral cavity, larynx, lungs, cervix.

The influence of nicotine on the child: Intrauterine growth restriction – reduced body weight, tachycardia – heart rate, intrauterine death, increased risk of allergies, asthma, POCHP and decreased immunity in adulthood, increased risk of sudden infant death syndrome (SIDS), mental development problems, learning difficulties and motor hyperactivity.

Recommendations: In terms of smoking during pregnancy, the recommendations are also clear – **even smoking a small number of cigarettes can**

negatively affect you and your child's health. In society and among doctors there is still a misconception that it is better to stop smoking gradually during pregnancy, or that you shouldn't quit suddenly because it will be too much of a shock to the body.

Tips:
- If you are trying to have a child with your partner, give up smoking at least six months before.
- If you smoke cigarettes and you find out you're pregnant, give it up immediately.
- Electronic cigarettes are equally dangerous in pregnancy.
- If you can't stop smoking yourself, don't be afraid to ask for help from relatives or specialists.
- Do not be surrounded by smokers – this is as harmful as active smoking.
- If you see a pregnant woman smoking, see if you can talk to her about some of the risks of smoking for the baby's development – she may not know that she is harming her baby.
- Do not offer, sell or encourage pregnant women to smoke.

Other stimulants (drugs, 'legal highs'). Drugs (including marijuana) and other psychoactive substances have a negative effect on health, whatever your age or state of health. During pregnancy they are as dangerous as alcohol and cigarettes. **Every time they are taken, there is a risk of irreversible change in mother or child**, depending on the type of substance, method of administration, dosage.

Influence of drugs and weed on the course of pregnancy: premature unsealing of the placenta, premature childbirth, pre-eclampsia, miscarriage, postpartum haemorrhages, hypertension, depression, anxiety disorders, viral diseases related to – among other things – lack of hygiene and sterility of needles.

Effects of drugs and weed on the child: reduced body weight, congenital defects, prematurity, perinatal death, heart disorders, emotional problems.

Recommendations:
- If you're trying to get pregnant, stop taking any drugs.
- If you're taking drugs or weed and you've found out that you are pregnant, quit immediately, preferably with the help of a therapist and an addiction treatment centre.

Tips:
- Look for help from relatives and specialists – it is very difficult to deal with addiction alone.
- Tell your doctor or midwife about your problem – they will know how to help you.

Pregnancy does not have to mean renouncing all pleasures. Remember, however, that you are now also responsible for the little person inside you. Give up alcohol, cigarettes and other drugs. Enjoy the taste of iced coffee with ice cream in summer and hot cappuccino with cinnamon in winter.

If you're using any drugs while you're pregnant, tell your doctor or midwife – with their help you can quit. ◆

Isabel – qualified midwife.

35. Staying active — physical exercise and movement during pregnancy

Many women who become pregnant wonder how to tackle exercise and physical activity. Can you continue training? Or maybe your pregnancy has actually motivated you to get moving? In a nutshell: how to approach exercise during pregnancy.

The benefits of exercise during pregnancy. You may have concerns about physical activity during pregnancy. However, if you do not have any medical reasons not to, physical activity has many benefits for both you and your baby. I certainly hope that my advice helps convince you that exercising sensibly during pregnancy is well worth it.

Exercise can bring you the following benefits:
- help to maintain or increase your fitness, strength and mobility,
- contribute to shortening the delivery time: by learning to loosen up the muscles and be able to withstand more difficult births positions, like squatting,

- help to reduce the ailments typical of pregnancy, such as back pain,
- reduce the risk of developing gestational diabetes,
- help you control your weight gain,
- make you feel better,
- speed up the return to normal of your reproductive organs and ease its course (the postpartum period),
- reduce the risk of postnatal depression,
- improve bowel motility and reduce the problem of constipation and the risk of hemorrhoids,
- minimise the problem of swelling and reduce the risk of varicose veins,
- improve your pelvic floor muscles(▸ II – 106), reducing the risk of urinary incontinence problems.

Your activity also has a positive effect on the child:
- stimulates the child's cardiovascular system,
- reduces the risk of hypoxia (lack of oxygen at the tissue level) or early expression of meconium (earliest stool or faeces) by the child,
- reduces the amount of fat tissue in childhood, which reduces the risk of obesity in adult life,
- positively affects the development of the nervous system, vision and motor coordination,
- accelerates the newborn's brain development.

Safety rules. Dear Mum, every mother can find activity that will bring her pleasure. But every mother should also know the safety rules for exercising during pregnancy. Always be sensitive to symptoms. If you feel abdominal pain, weakness or blotting, stop exercising and consult your doctor.
- Avoid sports with an increased risk of injury, such as skiing, roller skating and contact sports.
- Avoid exercises that cause an increase in so-called abdominal pressure which can cause tension in the abdominal muscles. First of all, this may be the cause of premature contractions (the straight abdominal muscles compress the vena cava – the vein which carries deoxygenated blood into the heart – and uterus), and secondly, it strains the pelvic floor muscles

and can contribute to the formation of stretch marks in the abdominal muscles (▶ II – 105).
- Avoid exercises that require balance, such as exercises on one leg or one foot exercises. The center of gravity shifts during pregnancy, and our brain has to get used to this change.
- Try not to overheat. In the first trimester this is especially important because the child's thermoregulation is strongly dependent on the mother's thermoregulation.

How and what to exercise? You already know how not to exercise. So, what can you do? You can choose from a wide range of activities: walking, swimming, aqua aerobics, fitness classes for pregnant women, gym with training tailored to pregnancy, yoga (▶ I – 36), pilates, elliptical workouts, dancing.

Ideally it's best to be physically active at least 3 times a week. If you were training before pregnancy, as long as there are no medical reasons not to and you feel well, you can continue as before. Adjust the intensity of your activity to your current situation. However, if you are just starting, stick to the recommendations above. If you are new to them, start with 15-minute sessions, extending them to about 45-60 minutes.

What to pay attention to during exercises? The following tips are divided into consecutive trimesters. Each stage of your pregnancy is different according to the changes in your body.

First trimester. Work on your whole body. You can pay special attention to the transverse abdominal muscles, buttocks and back muscles. A relaxation hormone (relaxin) is released during pregnancy which relaxes the joints. Strengthening these muscles will have a great impact on your ability to maintain a correct posture and avoid pain.

If you are feeling well, there are not many restrictions on exercise during this period. Lying on your stomach can be troublesome because of your sensitive breasts. If this isn't bothering you, you can still use this position. Even if you feel well, keep in mind that your cardiovascular system already produces more blood in the first trimester, which is a burden on your heart. This is why you'll get tired faster. So your workout shouldn't be too strenuous.

Exercise for the abdominal transverse muscle (this is a breathing exercise): Lie down on your back. Keep your head on the floor. Put your hands on your stomach so that the fingers of both hands touch each other. Take a deep breath with your nose, relaxing your belly and enlarging your stomach. Move the fingers of each hand away from each other. Then slowly let the air out of your mouth, tightening your stomach. Imagine that your navel is getting closer to your spine and a corset is tightening around your stomach. Then move the fingers of each hand closer to each other. Do 10 inhalations and exhalations. Try the exercise in different positions: sitting, kneeling and standing.

Second trimester. At this stage, your heart has enlarged by about 12%, so it beats about 10-20 times a minute faster than before pregnancy and you may experience breathlessness. To minimise pain in your lumbar region, strengthen the so-called *core*, in other words your postural muscles. When exercising at home, go on all fours. A pool can also bring relief. At this stage, give up lying on your stomach. When your tummy gets really big, avoid static standing exercises. This increases the pressure on the intervertebral joints in the lumbar region and may cause pain. Do the exercises while sitting on or using an exercise ball.

Third trimester. When your tummy is big, a sitting position, lying down sideways or 4 point kneeling are very beneficial. If you haven't done this yet, it's worth introducing birth preparation exercises and breathing/relaxation exercises during this period. It is very important to relax the body during childbirth. Don't forget about the simplicity of walking. Avoid lying on your back for a long time – in this position your baby may be compressing the vena cava, which can lead to fainting. This is particularly dangerous if you exercise alone at home.

Physical activity during pregnancy can help you prepare for the many challenges of childbirth. On the one hand, you need to strengthen your whole body and increase fitness and on the other hand, you need to relax and breathe properly. By exercising, you learn to control your body. Childbirth is a marathon and it is difficult to fully prepare for it, but it will certainly be easier if you get to know your body through exercise. Remember the benefits you can get from physical activity. Some changes in pregnancy can't be avoided, but exercise can give you much more than just a better look. ◆

Pauline – an active mum.

36. Pregnant yoga — exercise for health!

Whether you practiced before pregnancy or not, yoga will have a positive effect on you and your little one. You can practice alone at home, but it's also worth looking for classes for pregnant women taught by an experienced teacher.

Benefits of practicing yoga during pregnancy. By becoming aware of your breathing you can learn to relax your muscles, which will greatly help during childbirth. Yoga strengthens the muscles that underlie the skeleton and protect it from injury, reducing the negative effects of additional strain on the spine. And you learn how to be in the "here and now", which has a great effect on your consciousness and concentration, and in turn makes you feel relaxed and calm.

When can I start? You can practice yoga from the beginning of your pregnancy after consulting your doctor. In the first trimester, the risk of miscarriage is highest, so I advise newcomers to start their yoga adventure from the second trimester. Depending on your condition, you can practice until the end of your pregnancy, and use the familiar breathing methods or relaxation techniques during the birth.

Contraindications. The main medical reasons not to practice yoga during pregnancy are: high risk pregnancy, multifetal pregnancy, low-lying placenta, hypertension due to pregnancy, bleeding during the second and third trimesters; premature birth in previous pregnancies, risk of premature birth in the current pregnancy, gestational diabetes, cervical weakness, gestational gestosis, pelvic nephritis, pregnancy rhinitis, cervical sutures and circulatory diseases [1].

I asked other mums about their experiences of doing yoga during pregnancy. Pauline says: "I've been practicing since the 6th month. It was an alternative to the intensive exercise I was no longer able to do. I also needed the silence that yoga gives." Anna adds that she started practicing in the second trimester under the supervision of an experienced teacher, who always took into account her condition and told her what not to do or how to modify her posture. The activity helped her not only during pregnancy but also during childbirth.

I hope that you, dear Mum, will also be tempted to practice yoga during pregnancy, which I strongly encourage you to do. ◆

Anna – hatha yoga instructor, mum of 2-year-old Simon.

37. 50 shades... of a future mother — sex during pregnancy

You're pregnant. Maybe you wanted and planned this for a long time, or maybe it was a surprise. For the vast majority of women, pregnancy is the result of an intimate encounter between two people. If you're a woman who became pregnant after a long period of trying, you may feel tired of sex and it may not have been satisfying during this time.

Expectations. Now, you may have expectations about your sex life during pregnancy. Perhaps you hope that this will be a time of carefree enjoyment of intimate closeness, without the pressure of tracking your cycle and conception. If, until this time, it has always been your aim not to become pregnant, these 9 months will be the first time in your mature life where you can forget about contraception and the constant need for protection.

And indeed, for many women pregnancy is a special period when they are more likely to have sex, explore their desires and experience unusual orgasms. But what if this is not happening for you?

Pregnancy is the beginning of a new stage in a woman's sexual life: the motherhood stage. It may seem strange to you, because the traditional image of a mother can be seen as not particularly sexual. In turn, the female narrative and some pregnant celebrities try to convince us that nothing changes in a woman's sex life. But this is not always true.

What does pregnancy change? It's a huge storm for your nervous system and for your hormones. Your body changes, your sensitivity to touch develops. You can experience fluctuations in your libido, your emotions are different, birth is imminent and a baby will soon change your life. This all affects your sexuality.

The first trimester can often be a time of fluctuating moods, nausea and sleepiness. You may also have doubts about whether sex is safe for the child. So it's important to know that in a healthy, physiological pregnancy there are no risks in having sex. The bladder, a long cervix and thick mucous membrane provide sufficient protection for the baby. If you feel any ailments or discomfort, give yourself time to feel better again.

In the second trimester, women often recover their desire for intimate connection. I write "often" because as a mother of 3 children, I know that it is impossible to put one standard to every woman, and that in every pregnancy our mood and needs – including sexual ones – are very different. Changing sensitivity to touch and an increased blood supply to the intimate organs may cause some women to experience orgasms that they have not yet experienced. Don't worry if you're not one of these women.

The third trimester may see your appetite for sex weaken, mainly due to the size of your abdomen, as well as ailments typical of the last weeks of pregnancy such as heartburn, pressure on your bladder or fear of causing premature birth. It is true that the prostaglandins in sperm can soften the cervix and induce birth, but only when the body of the woman – and child are – ready for it. During sex, take care of your comfort and choose positions that are best for you, so that you can derive the greatest possible pleasure.

What if the doctor in charge of the pregnancy recommends avoiding sex – or even bans it? If this is the case, ask the doctor whether it is a ban on penetrative sex or a ban on having an orgasm, and when the ban applies: is it until the end of the pregnancy, or until a defined time? The most common reasons for such a ban are: intimate infections, a frontal placenta, a shortening of the cervix or the risk of premature contractions. But even they do not necessarily mean the end of sensual pleasure! If you can still experience an orgasm, there are other ways to do it than having intercourse. And if you are forced to remove orgasms from your list of experiences, you can still find many opportunities to be close. Baths together, gentle massages, stroking, hugging, discovering your body, and knowing each other's fantasies – you will surely find your own ways to be close to your partner and strengthen your erotic bond.

A new stage of sexual life, which is pregnancy – although it can sometimes cause anxiety – can also be a source of joy for a woman, rediscovering her bond with her partner, celebrating moments just the two of you. Knowing the diversity with which women experience their sexuality during pregnancy, it can be both liberating and inspiring for you. ♦

Eva – doula and sex coach.

38. A pampered mum-to-be. What cosmetic treatments can you have during pregnancy?

Part I

I'm pregnant. Can I go to a beautician? The answer is "it depends". If your pregnancy is going well – if you're not at risk of premature birth and it's not a high risk pregnancy- you can do many treatments. You just need to know what to look for when choosing a treatment. Remember that pregnancy is not the time for experimentation. If you have used the treatments before your pregnancy, you do not need to give them up, but if a treatment is to be performed for the first time (this does not apply to mild, moisturizing treatments), you should think about whether now is a good time, or whether to put it off until after the birth.

For hormonal reasons, your skin is sensitive during pregnancy, and this needs to be taken into account by the person performing the treatment. It is important that you tell the cosmetician that you are pregnant, in which week, whether you have done the particular treatment before, whether you are sensitive to smells and if you're allergic to anything. This will make it easier to choose the right treatment.

Which salon to choose? The place you choose should be well staffed, unless you have a permanent beautician you've been going to for years, who knows everything about you and your skin. Your trust in her is more important than looking for a new place with specialised staff.

If you're worried about you or your baby despite assurances that the treatment is safe, don't do it. There's not only a physical dimension, but a psychological one too.

Apart from your mental conviction and readiness to undergo the procedure, your physical condition is also important. The treatment should be a pleasure and not involve holding your breath in order not to throw up.

Beauty treatments allowed during pregnancy. Below is a list of what you can use during pregnancy unless you have medical reasons not to have the treatment verified by your doctor or cosmetologist. Medical bans for all treatments are assumed if you have a viral or bacterial disease, fungal disease, fever, infection or skin wound at the place of treatment. Other bans can be related to the treatment itself.

Care treatments – masks
YES:
- Cream, gel, rubber masks.
- Algae masks for face, bust, etc. – only so-called alginates, i.e. plastic rubber masks that do not contain a large amount of algae which can affect the thyroid.

NO:
- Herbal masks.
- Masks with lots of essential oils or citrus.
- Intense green, ground, sea-smelling algae masks containing a lot of iodine.

Moisturizing and relaxing treatments
- YES: Moisturising and relaxing treatments. You can enjoy a prenatal, back, hands or face massage with peace of mind.
- NO: Nothing warmed up, irritating or which could cause an allergy or irritation, such as a massage with coffee or essential oils, hot rocks or a sauna.

Scrubbing treatments and peels
YES:
- Mechanical peels, or so-called scrubs – may contain natural husks or kernels (plum kernels, apricots, nut shells), sugar, salt or plastic mini-balls, as well as corundum or water. Remember that if you are allergic to something in your food, you should avoid it in cosmetics too. Mechanical scrubs include body brushing. This is a cooling method because, besides exfoliating the epidermis, it also improves blood circulation and makes the skin more elastic. Only avoid doing it too intensively, keep it gentle and calming. Remember to avoid overheating the body.
- Oxybrasion and microdermabrasion – forms of mechanical peeling. Oxybrasion is recommended for sensitive skins, as it only uses air and saline. Microdermabrasion is a more intense peeling, so if you have never done it before, put it off or ask your beautician to do it gently.
- Enzymatic peels are one of the most delicate skin peeling options. They contain enzymes that gently dissolve the dead layer of the epidermis.
- AHA Fruit Acids – if you used them before pregnancy, you can now use their softer versions. If you've never used them, pregnancy is not a good time to try.

NO:
- Some scrubs – don't choose those that have caffeine, carnitine, strong anti-cellulite or slimming properties. These scrubs can significantly warm up and irritate the skin, which is not advisable during pregnancy.
- Cavitation peeling is not recommended because of the ultrasound waves used. It's not yet fully determined how deep these waves penetrate the skin.
- Salicylic acid (BHA) and trichloroacetic acid (TCA) – cannot be used during pregnancy because they can get into the bloodstream.
- Medical peels – treatments performed by a doctor, not a beautician or a cosmetologist. They must not be done during pregnancy because deep layers of skin are wiped off during the process, which is associated with large (controlled) inflammatory and cellular conditions. A strong skin reaction (exfoliation, irritation, swelling) is common. During pregnancy the skin may heal worse or there may be scars or discoloration. In addition, substances that are used in medical peelings may penetrate the bloodstream.

Here I have only covered standard cosmetic treatments, not treatments performed by a dermatologist. In such cases, the dermatologist is responsible for their execution and he or she decides whether or not they are safe.

Hair removal treatments
YES:
- Wax – if you used it before pregnancy and your skin is used to it.
- Sugar paste – a softer method than wax, which is less painful and not allergenic.
- Disposable razors – can be used, as long as they are not reused multiple times, in which case there can be an issue with bacteria.
- Threading and pulling hair out with tweezers.
- A depilator, if it is disinfected, is not a risk.

NO:
- Laser hair removal, IPL hair removal and epilation are not recommended during pregnancy.

Rejuvenating and anti-cellulite and stretch marks treatments
YES:
- Light massages, application of lotion, elixirs, oils and masks – chosen by the beautician according to your needs. However, they should not warm up the skin.

NO:
- Treatments using vitamin A and its derivatives (e.g. retinol, retinoids).
- Treatments using RF (Radio Frequency).
- Photo-rejuvenating treatments using laser (e.g. laser lipolysis) and IPL light.
- Wrapping in foil or bandages, treatments with chambers or slimming suits which can cause pressure or overheat the body, and may cause an increase in blood pressure, potentially posing a threat to pregnancy.
- Treatments using coffee, L-carnitine and other products. Substances that significantly increase blood circulation and warm up the body.
- Treatments which involve electrical currents, like iontophoresis, galvanization or electrostimulation). The reaction of your body to such treatments can be unpredictable.

Sunbathing
YES:
- Safe plant-based self-tanner without artificial dyes (read the labels on the packaging!) and spray tanning (if it is done with safe and certified cosmetics) are not dangerous, because the cosmetic settles on the epidermis and does not react with the skin.
- Sunbathing in the sun? Yes, but sensibly! Apply cream with SPF factor 50, protect your head, put on sunglasses and try to sit in the shade. Avoid the sun during the brightest parts of the day. Remember that staying in the sun too long can cause sunstroke, overheating and can even lead to premature birth.

NO:
- Solarium – due to the large quantities of carcinogenic UVA radiation, which can cause sunburn, discoloration and even miscarriage.

Beauty treatments
Makeup
- YES, as long as you know that the salon respects the hygienic principle of washing brushes after use.
- Permanent makeup – with such treatments, the risk of infection at the treatment site or the healing of wounds increases. There can also be problems with the choice of colours for make-up, as they may come out a different colour than intended thanks to the hormone estrogen. This type of treatment is NOT recommended during pregnancy for these reasons.

Henna
- YES: If you have had your eyebrows or eyelashes coloured with henna before pregnancy and there was no allergic reaction, and if you know the person who is performing the treatment and they know you, there is no reason why you shouldn't use henna during pregnancy.
- NO: If you have had an allergic reaction to henna before pregnancy, you will almost certainly have one during pregnancy. Then I recommend that you paint your eyebrows with suitable pencils, crayons and powders, and put the henna away for a different time.

Hair dyeing
- YES: If you did it before pregnancy and there was no allergic reaction. But check that the dye doesn't contain ingredients which irritate the mucous membranes of the eyes or nose, or ammonia and aromatic amine that may be allergenic.
- NO: Perms at this time are a bad idea as a lot of substances that may be allergenic are used. It's also not worth dyeing your hair if you had an allergic reaction before pregnancy.

Keratin hair straightening treatments
- Hair straightening treatments are not applied to the scalp and are therefore not harmful, but most contain formaldehyde, which can get into the body through the nasal mucous membranes. They are also irritating and unhealthy if inhaled for a long time. There have been no studies on harmfulness, but I would recommend that you stop any treatments during pregnancy and during the first 6 months of breastfeeding.

Manicure and pedicures
- Manicure/pedicure: classic, Japanese, hybrid, titanium. If you know the manicurist, he or she operates in a ventilated space and uses certified cosmetics, there's no reason why you have to make any changes during pregnancy. If your due date is approaching, you might like to consider washing and painting your nails in a light colour, because during birth or Caesarean section your health is also monitored via the nail plate.
- Acrylics and gels: Artificial nails, acrylics or gels are not recommended during pregnancy (but not forbidden!) due to their chemical content, which is not toxic, but can irritate. These substances penetrate the nail plate and can cause irritation, so I simply recommend caution. In large quantities there can also be harmful substances which the mother is exposed to during the treatment, and which can irritate the eyes and nose. If possible, I recommend switching to hybrid nails during pregnancy and breastfeeding.

Aesthetic medicine and plastic surgery
- During pregnancy, no cosmetic procedures, plastic surgery, fillers, botox, injections, medical scrubs or dermatological treatments should be performed.

You must also not use cosmetic medicinal products (ointments, creams, masks, blends) without the consent of a doctor. ◆

Ada – mum of Sophie, Helene and Jack; MSc in cosmetology.

Part II

The hairdresser. Pregnancy favours the young mother's hair because it becomes exceptionally beautiful and thick. Nevertheless, you should inform your hairdresser about your pregnancy as some treatments, such as colouring, brightening or perms, may not meet your expectations due to hormones. The penetration of chemicals through the scalp is negligible and does not threaten your child's health, and hairdressers usually use cosmetics and dyes that do not contain ammonia or aromatic amines, which can cause respiratory irritation or sensitisation – but it's worth checking.

Sunbeds. Based on WHO recommendations [4], it is not recommended during pregnancy. The skin is more sensitive to UV rays and pigmentation spots may occur, the so-called melasma, and stretch marks. There is also a risk of overheating, which can cause dizziness, fainting, skin burns, increased pressure, and even unsealing of the placenta and bleeding. Even an alternative, such as spray tanning, should be considered carefully. Always ask your doctor for an opinion.

Dentist. Every expectant mother should have at least one check-up, as teeth and gums are more likely to be inflamed during pregnancy. If necessary, plaque can be removed but teeth whitening is not recommended as the procedure weakens teeth, which are already exposed to calcium loss anyway. Whitening preparations contain strong substances: hydrogen peroxide and carbamide, which can damage the baby's DNA structure if swallowed.

Tattoos and piercings. When pregnant or breastfeeding, it is better not to tattoo or pierce your body as these treatments carry the risk of HIV and hepatitis B infection. Besides, you don't know how your skin will react to the pigment used for the tattoo, and it may not meet your expectations as

– during pregnancy – your skin stretches and partially loses its elasticity. An alternative is a henna tattoo with natural ingredients that will not irritate, as can happen with artificial black henna.

Massages. Recommended from the second trimester of pregnancy, as long as safety measures are taken. If your pregnancy is without complications, you can go to a specialist for a prenatal massage, which is a safe whole-body massage that relaxes and unwinds you. It is also advisable to have a gentle massage of the spine (performed seated or lying on your side) and reflexology (hands, feet or head). At home, you can perform a firming massage on areas particularly exposed to skin stretching, such as thighs, abdomen and breasts. Lymphatic drainage can be performed on an expectant mother only by a suitably-qualified specialist. In pregnancy, do not use a Chinese bubble massage or so-called "cupping" – which may cause bleeding [9].

Kinesio Taping®. This is a safe and increasingly common form of muscle and skin relief which works by wrapping the area in question with special tape. This should be carried out by a qualified physiotherapist.

Hydrotherapy. Water has a very positive effect on your wellbeing. If it's an option, you can go to the pool and take part in aqua aerobics for pregnant women. At home you can use either a shower or a bath, however towards the end of your pregnancy you should do this in moderation because of the risk of fainting, bleeding and even premature birth. Thermal pools, water baths, whirlpools and saunas are also banned because of their high temperature, which can cause fainting, bleeding or cramping.

Aromatherapy. Essential oils themselves have a well-deserved place in natural medicine, whereas during pregnancy they are a subject of discussion. This is because you are not really able to predict your body's reaction (for obvious reasons there are no studies on pregnant women). Oils can contain substances which – in higher concentrations – may irritate the respiratory tract and have photosensitizing effects [8]. Some may even cause uterine contractions and lead to miscarriage (for example parsley oil containing apitol and savine juniper oil) [5]. As always, think carefully before going ahead, and always ask your doctor if in doubt.

Pregnancy doesn't have to be a period of sacrifice, but you are preparing your body for a challenge. Anything that puts your mind at ease is good, so if in doubt, consult your concerns with your doctor. ◆

Agatha – physiotherapist and mum to Simon and Jacob.

39. Read the label! What kind of cosmetics can you use during pregnancy?

Pregnancy is a time when everything can change, or maybe nothing changes. Your skin condition may improve or it may get worse. You may become allergic to something that you weren't allergic to before, and suddenly the smell of your beloved cream is unbearable. The problem with clearly defining what's harmful in pregnancy is obvious – experiments aren't performed on pregnant women.

Substances banned during pregnancy. There are two groups. The first group includes retinol and retinoids (International Nomenclature of Cosmetic Ingredients (INCI): retinol, all-trans retinol, retinaldehyde) because of teratogenic effects of vitamin A (which can cause developmental defects). The second is salicylic acid (INCI: Salicylic Acid), which can cause malformations.

Substances not recommended. Listed here are three types of undesirable substances. Permeate filters (INCI: Ethylhexyl Methoxycinnamate, Methoxycinnamate Octyl, Benzophenone 3-4, Methylbenzylidene Camphor, Dimethyl PABA Octyl, Homosalate), all substances which penetrate into the bloodstream with a slight proven estrogenic effect. Polyacrylamide (INCI: Polyacrylamide), very often accompanied by small amounts of acrylamide, which increases the risk of cancer. Algae masks belong to the last group.

Substances that are better avoided. This is a larger group, and here are some of them:
- formaldehyde and formalin derivatives – popular preservatives, can cause allergies,
- parabens – preservatives that can cause allergies,
- 2-Phenoxyethanol – a preservative, increasingly popular, can cause allergies,
- acids, all kinds: better to avoid them during pregnancy,
- essential oils are very often allergenic and photosensitizing substances.

Now you know what to avoid in cosmetics, it's time to go shopping – unless you have cosmetics without the above-mentioned substances on your shelf already. But if you want to refresh, here are some suggestions:

Body lotion. A good moisturiser will help to keep your skin well moisturised and therefore resilient. There is no cosmetic composition that guarantees the absence of stretch marks. This is a very individual issue, often genetic, and you usually have no influence on it. So there is no point in spending money on "specialist" creams.

Breast cream. Another great idea from cosmetic companies! Massaging your breasts has salutary effects. There is no need to buy a special breast cream, just body lotion. A well-chosen bra will work best for your breasts.

Suncream with a filter. In summer it is best to have SPF 50+, in winter it can be SPF 30. Why? You don't want pregnancy discolouration, the so-called melasma, which does not always disappear by itself, so you may need laser treatment to improve it. I particularly recommend mineral filter creams, which are less allergenic than chemical filters, but unfortunately they also offer less protection.

Intimate hygiene fluid. If you use a mild full-body wash without SLS and SLES, it is enough for you. There is no need to buy a "list" of cosmetics for intimate hygiene. If you prefer to buy it in liquid form, look for the mildest one, without any of the previously-mentioned elements.

Seasonal cosmetics. Not every mum needs a cooling winter cream for her legs. On the other hand, "summer" mums-to-be can attain welcome relief with a cooling cream applied to sore and swollen legs on a hot day.

You can read about two things that new mums often ask about, namely hair colouring and nail painting, in chapter (▶ I – 38).

With potentially harmful substances there is – as with alcohol – nothing like a safe dose. Keep in mind that specialist cosmetic lines are a way for companies to take more money from us. It is often the case that cosmetics dedicated to pregnant women are no more suitable than products for "ordinary women", but the price is usually much higher. Therefore, always check the ingredients and don't spend money just because someone wrote "for pregnant women" on the package. ◆

Anita – mum of two and chemistry graduate. She scrutinizes cosmetics and thoroughly analyzes their ingredients.

40. Pregnancy cosmetics for vegans and vegetarians

If you're a vegan or vegetarian and you are pregnant or breastfeeding, you will likely pay great attention to the ethical side of cosmetica: whether the ingredients have been tested on animals or whether any of the products have animal, or animal-based ingredients. Despite the total ban on animal testing in cosmetics and their ingredients throughout the European Union, and the declaration of companies in the industry not to perform tests, it appears that this applies mainly to European companies selling their products only in the EU. Yet most well-known companies are also present outside the EU. So how can you make sure that a company is really *cruelty-free*? The best way is to check its status on logicalharmony.net.

In terms of animal products, the most common are lanolin, beeswax or carmine. There will be many more synthetic ingredients, so if you want to be sure, always check the composition of your cosmetics in this respect. The 'beauty without cruelty' community can be a big resource as well.

There are special lines of cosmetics that are not tested on animals and have vegan ingredients which are dedicated to pregnant women or breast-feeding mothers, but there is no need to overpay. And do check what you already have at home – these products may be absolutely fine in the context of animal cruelty. ◆

Joanna – Kazik's mother, Panda's partner, caretaker of two dogs and a cat. She likes to parent closely, in the here and now – and loves baby wraps.

41. It's not always rosy... Getting through a difficult pregnancy

When you are pregnant, it goes without saying that you will want everything to go well, right up until the birth. Unfortunately, pregnancy is not always a beautiful time which passes happily. It can happen that there are problems with the baby or the mother. In this chapter I hope to help you deal with a "complicated" pregnancy.

How to take care of yourself and your mental health:
- Someone close by. First of all, try to make sure that there is someone close to you who will be a real support for you. This person shouldn't tell you what to do or what you're doing wrong. You don't need any extra stress. If you don't have anyone in your family or amongst friends, your community midwife could be a great support.
- Don't suppress your emotions. Get them out, and if necessary, don't be afraid to talk to a psychologist. As Dominica says, "it's hard without the positive attitude and support of others. I didn't need advice, just the presence of others and their empathy. It's a pity it wasn't available at the hospital.
- Don't blame yourself. A mother with a high-risk pregnancy can blame herself, but in most cases she hasn't had any influence on this. That's why it's worth talking about your fears and problems with someone you trust, or with a psychologist, to help you deal with your emotions.
- Don't worry in advance. It's no surprise that instead of thinking positively, you may worry about how things will turn out. That's not surprising, as

the little miracle is often long-awaited by its parents. Again, speaking with a loved one or a specialist will help you to overcome negative thoughts.
- **Try to think positively.** Your child will soon be here and by focusing on the wonderful moments you will have with him or her, you will soon forget about the days spent in a hospital bed.

How to arrange your time in the hospital or at home (if you can't go out). Fortunately, not every difficult pregnancy involves lying in bed or staying in hospital all the time. However, if you're in this situation, here are some tips for getting through this difficult time:
- Try to make a plan for each day – this way you won't feel like you are "doing nothing".
- Talk to other mums in the ward. I had to lie in the ward for a week and I know you can go crazy in silence.
- Ask your family and friends to visit you regularly – contact with your loved ones is important. Don't wait until they get in contact – call them yourself!
- Enrol in an online foreign language course, learn how to crochet or master programming. What have you always wanted to do but never found the time for?
- Make your debut as a blogger or a children's story writer – it can be a lot of fun. Or you could simply keep a diary of your pregnancy.
- Create your own cookbook from proven recipes – maybe you'll pass it on to your children one day?
- Sort out the pile of photos which has built up over recent years – how many times have you promised yourself you'd do it? The memories will hopefully have a positive impact!
- Take the time to really talk with your partner. The choice of a name, getting things ready for when you return from the hospital and sharing parental responsibilities are just some of the issues that need to be discussed beforehand in order to avoid unnecessary tensions later on.
- If you're worried about your diagnosis, do not search for information on the internet, consult another doctor – you have the right to do so. Getting a second opinion about you or your child's condition will give you more peace of mind even if the diagnosis is difficult.

- Find yourself a comfortable pillow – lying on your back for long periods can cause your back and neck to ache.
- Make sure you have your music and headphones with you – there will be moments when you want to cut yourself off from your surroundings, and there's no better way to do that than with music.
- Make sure you have coins to pay for food and drinks from vending machines.
- Don't forget your laptop (and charger), books, newspapers, crossword puzzles or board games. Buy a subscription to a VOD platform.

How to organize your life. The following advice is primarily a guide to not underestimating the problems of a future mum.
- Tell your loved ones that you need some peace. They need to think about whether you should be burdened with problems or bad news.
- Ask for help if you need it.
- If you run your own business, appoint a deputy to take care of everything in the company, so that you don't have to do it. This is not the best time for making important, stressful decisions. If you need to do some shopping, do it online.
- Ask someone, a trusted relative or a friend to take your other child or children – or dog – for a walk, if you're not allowed to yourself.
- Ask your loved ones to bring you a home-cooked dinner from time to time. For long stays you may well have had enough of the hospital menu.
- Think of some activities you can do with older children that won't tire you out, but will be fun for them, e.g. searching for things in books, reading books, finger puppets, shadow puppets. It's important that older children don't feel left out at this time.
- If it's an option, ask your partner to do a massage that will stimulate lesser-used muscles and relax your body.
- If you need to spend a lot of the time lying down, make sure to have a diet rich in fibre in order to avoid constipation. Groats, brown rice and whole meal bread are good, but go easy on heavy and indigestible dishes – and try to drink around two litres of water a day.
- Take care of yourself – do your make-up, paint your nails or pick a nice outfit which can have a very positive impact on your wellbeing.
- Little pleasures – give yourself treats in whatever way you can!

Don't do it to others! If you don't have problems yourself, but there are women around you whose pregnancies may be complicated, it's better not to do the following things:
- Don't tell a woman with a complicated pregnancy that the hospital isn't a prison. As Violet says: "It's annoying when the whole family tells you that the most important thing is the child, that the pregnancy will finally pass, that the hospital is not a prison, or that others have it worse. This will make you want to murder your visitors. Of course they want the best, but that sort of comment doesn't help at all. Above all, remember that the mother is also important, not just the baby, and it will be her who sets the priorities, not third parties. Lying in a hospital for months on end can really make you feel like you're in prison."
- Don't declare that pregnancy is not an illness. In a perfectly healthy pregnancy would a woman have to lie down, would she have to be hospitalised? No. That's why it can feel like a pregnancy is also an "illness".
- Don't tell a woman who has been put on bed rest due to complications during pregnancy that she doesn't have it so bad because she can lie down and do nothing. You think she wouldn't want to go out shopping, prepare herself a normal meal or go out for a coffee with a friend? Of course she would, but she also wants to have a healthy baby and in due course. That is why she rests.
- Don't ask for details of her condition. Don't be too inquisitive. Respect the mother and don't go to the doctor on duty to ask about her condition.
- Don't say what you'd do in her place. Keep your good advice to yourself.
- A future mother with a high-risk pregnancy needs support, not extra nerves because someone said she did something wrong or didn't do something which she should have done. ◆

Susanna – a devoted mum who went through a difficult pregnancy.

My story

When I became pregnant for the first time, after trying for a long time, we then had a miscarriage. I felt that we mustn't break down. I tried to think that this was the way it was meant to be. There had been "fireworks" – surprising my husband, parents and family with the news. Unfortunately, a week later, it was already over. So the second time was without the fireworks. I was both fearful and happy at the same time. The first trimester passed full of worry that it would happen again. Then a moment of respite as the second trimester started. I was in great shape, went to work and felt no need to slow down. The whole time I was under the care of a great doctor, who is also my friend.

After some tests, everything seemed to indicate that it would be ok. Then it was time to test glucose levels. Unfortunately it came back that I had gestational diabetes, but it was rather mild. Nothing else aroused my concern until the unlucky 12th September 2017. I went with my husband for an ultrasound. We were relaxed, because if the test results were good, why should we be stressed? The only thing that was bothering me was that the little one wasn't moving very much, and it was week 30.

I will never forget the visit. We were talking about nothing, it was a standard ultrasound, my husband was watching his baby on the monitor – and suddenly I saw my doctor's face. The ultrasound lasted a good half an hour, which felt like an eternity. I remember the focus on her face and the grimace of her expression, the silence in my ears alternating with the sound of the machine. It turned out that there was a weak flow in the umbilical cord and in the uterine artery. As I found out later, this was not a standard test that every pregnant woman has, even privately. My friend performed it with the diabetes in mind. And so it started: a referral to another doctor to confirm the diagnosis, continuous KTG check-ups, twice to hospital, a million thoughts in my head. It was all a bad dream. Pregnancy became a nightmare for me. The little person in my stomach was hardly moving at all, and then he had hypertrophy. I went to KTG several times a week, including once for a Doppler ultrasound, sitting like a time bomb and waiting for the decision – would my pregnancy be terminated? All those moments give me goosebumps, and tears appear in my eyes. This period, which was supposed to be beautiful, had become unbearable. Fresh in my mind were still the feelings from a year before, when – after the euphoria – I was left with nothing, with an emptiness in my heart. And now? Now I felt cheated. It was supposed to be plain sailing. After the first trimester it was supposed to be okay. No complications. A nice time to complete the baby list, and now it was to be taken away.

When I was in the hospital for the first time, I was released after a few days, with recommendations for frequent KTG and Doppler checks. Being in the ward had been mentally draining. Sharing a room with people who cried into their pillows could not help but have an impact on the emotions and feelings of a pregnant woman. Returning home didn't bring peace either. Just appointments, checks and the continuous sound of the KTG and flow tests. The sad thing for me was that at the end of the pregnancy we didn't watch our miracle at all anymore, we just listened to the sound of the Doppler and looked at the KTG chart, trying – with my husband – to interpret the results and decide whether it was time to go to the hospital or not.

Then another check-up at the doctor's and the advice that it's time to induce the baby. It wasn't supposed to be like this… But an earlier doctor had told me that it's better that it happens sooner rather than be a minute too late…

When I write it all, I wonder what my message to pregnant mothers with complications is. How can you share the pain and suffering with your loved ones, and not be afraid to speak up about what you are afraid of and ask for help when things seem unbearable? The bad time will pass, although I am aware that not every story ends successfully. Unfortunately.

I still remember talking at night to one mum who had a high-risk pregnancy, and a child with autism at home. At such moments, we are able to say we'll survive because we're not alone. It helped me a lot to share my emotions. It's a time when you don't have the strength to read or watch TV because of the thoughts that are buzzing in your head. But one thing is certain – everything paled into insignificance on October 23rd at 7.20 a.m. The moment when I heard: 10 points, healthy boy, weight 2240 kg. They bring you a little "chicken" who has spent the last eight months sleeping inside you, and now he is with you. And you don't think about that constant sound of the KTG, about all the complications. You take in the very moment. ◆

With thanks to A., Martina.

Emotions and the mental health of the future mum

42. Give me some space! Hormones and their effect on a pregnant woman's emotions

During pregnancy, changes occur both in the body and the mind. It is said that pregnancy is not an illness, but the amount of these changes and their nature trigger a lot of reactions in your body which can be unpleasant. They cover almost all systems and organs: from the gastrointestinal tract that causes you to be nauseous and vomit, through to the hormonal system, when progesterone and oxytocin levels rise, to an increase in saliva, blood volume and cavities. But most of all, there is a small person growing in you – and this is the biggest change you are facing!

The first trimester... is difficult. Your pregnancy is still invisible, and you're actually feeling your worst of the entire 40 weeks. "Pregnancy is a wonderful time in a woman's life," say some, and it is a beautiful time for many women. But during this period your emotions run a gamut: joy, anger, fear, loneliness. On the famous list of forty-four of the most stressful life events, created by two psychiatrists – Thomas Holmes and Richard Rahe – pregnancy is in twelfth place (40 stress units out of 100) and the appearance of a new family member is in fourteenth place (39 stress units out of 100). So what are new mothers most afraid of? Usually one thing: the CHANGE itself. Change of habits, life, yourself, your relationship with your partner. Raging hormones further intensify this fear and cause variable, unwelcome and discomforting reactions in the body. For example, nausea and vomiting are caused by human chorionic gonadotropin (hCG). It is this hCG that is detected in urine by pharmacy pregnancy tests. An increase in the production of further hormones can also be seen: an increase in progesterone can lead to constipation, flatulence and heartburn; an increase in estrogen can increase blood volume, and can cause bleeding in the nose and gums; an increase in prolactin causes sleepiness. Your body tries to adapt to all these changes, but it is not easy either physically or mentally.

How to deal with it? Listen to your body – don't ignore your needs. If you need to take the day off work, ask your attending doctor for a note. It is also good to look for a support group, to talk to other pregnant women in a similar situation. You may find yourself in various social situations without the support of a loved one, so it is important to look for such a soul mate. Try to find someone who will accept your fears, which are, after all, completely natural during this period. And someone who will not tell you in an all-knowing tone: "You should feel this and that, behave like this or that," but who instead can tell you: "I understand what you're feeling, I've felt the same!"

The second trimester is generally more enjoyable. Your energy is coming back, your body is 'coming to terms' with the changes that are taking place in it, and you feel more optimistic. Now you can feel that pregnancy is a beautiful time. Hopefully you won't have nausea or other ailments anymore. Women are beautiful and often slimmer after the first months of 'stomach problems' and their breasts are getting larger. They feel more feminine. They do not have a large belly yet, so they are physically strong. During this period the biggest changes are taking place in the body of the little one in the womb. What is happening in the mother, though, are big changes in hormones. High levels of progesterone, oxytocin and estrogen make you feel more like having sex. It's a great time to have a closer relationship with your partner!

How to make best use of this time? Make the most of it! Now can be a good time to agree with your employer on your work conditions or take advantage of parental leave. At home, think about the equipment you and your baby will need. If you plan to renovate your child's room, you will now have the energy to do it.

The third trimester. Your expanding uterus begins to compress the internal organs. You go to the toilet more often and it's harder for you to go to sleep. But regular visits to the toilet are important as urine retention can lead to kidney problems.

During this period, your legs can swell up, which is a result of hormones, water retention and a higher temperature in the body. You have less and less strength, and various thoughts start to go round your head. Basically, you feel the pressure of the impending birth. "It's coming soon – I should be ready and packed for the hospital by now!" And something else, something we don't really talk about: women just start feeling fat. They worry that the kilos they've put on will be hard to lose after pregnancy, that their breasts will not be firm, that their intimate relationship with their partner will suffer.

The third trimester is a time of waiting. You're already packed. On the one hand you can't wait, on the other hand you're trembling at the very thought of giving birth. You are getting heavier and heavier and having trouble sleeping. Walking and breathing are more difficult, now that the expanding uterus is compressing most of your internal organs. Towards the end of pregnancy, the level of progesterone in the body drops, and it is this drop that signals to your body that it's time to start the birth. It is also responsible for a potentially reduced postpartum mood and even depression. Just before the birth, various thoughts may also appear, for example thoughts related to death. For many women, childbirth is indeed such a moment of transition – something ends and at the same time something beautiful begins.

How to deal with this time? Talk to your mother, sister or friend who has already given birth and can share their experiences with you. Choose a hospital and a midwife if you haven't already. Talk about the actual birth – don't treat it as a taboo subject. After the birth it can take some time to get back in shape, but it is not impossible. Sometimes it just requires a little more commitment and exercise. And it is not only about extra weight, but also about uterine contractions and possible incontinence problems.

Be good to yourself. Accept your choices and decisions about the type of birth you want. If possible, it is a good idea to give birth naturally, not least because then the postpartum period is much less painful. This is not always possible, however. Don't expect a perfect birth like in a movie. Turn for support from your loved ones, talk about your feelings. Take care of yourself in those last weeks, strengthen yourself and your sense of value.

Pregnancy itself may not be an illness, but it is worth listening to your body and reacting to its needs. Above all, ask questions – don't keep your doubts to yourself. ◆

Annette – Bart and Tim's mother. Psychologist and managing director of a medical centre. Consultation: Dr Dominica Wojsz – family doctor, Stanley and Frank's mother, blogger.

43. It's not just physical — taking care of your mental health during pregnancy

There are many reasons why taking care of your mental health during pregnancy is not so much advisable, as necessary. Feeling good when you're pregnant contributes to the physical outcome, to the subjective feeling of a 'good' birth – one that takes place as naturally as possible and reduces the number of medical interventions. It also makes the transition to your new life after the birth easier and reduces the likelihood of postnatal depression [1]. In this way the mother establishes a stronger bond with her child and positively influences its emotions once it's in the world. How can this be achieved?

Express any emotion. It is perfectly natural that when you are pregnant, a roller coaster of emotions are part and parcel of the experience – joy, pride, sadness, fear and anger towards yourself, your partner, your child and the new situation. Each new experience brings with it a whole range of emotions, from positive to negative. Changes can be difficult because they require you to react in new ways, and pregnancy hormones also have an impact. I know that it can be frightening, and feelings of guilt can arise. However, each of these emotions indicates your concerns and needs. Expressing them can bring you relief and sometimes a solution. Think about them consciously, write them down, take some steps back, then talk about them with someone you trust, maybe your partner, your mother or a friend.

Accept your concerns and give yourself time to change. One of the greatest changes in your life is ahead of you. As with any breakthrough event, it takes time to adapt to the new situation. In a private conversation Annette, the mother of 3 children, shared what helps her: "Accept situations. Every phase passes. Enjoy them, because they'll never happen the same way again."

Imagine your child. The internal representation of a child by its mother is understood as a set of conscious and unconscious judgements, feelings or fantasies defining who the child is for the mother [2]. Imagining what it will be like, fantasising about holding or feeding it, talking to it, evokes positive emotions and makes the child more familiar and expected. This can have a significant impact on the sense of bonding.

Talk to the father of the child about your fears, desires and joys. This is your child together. You have it with you all the time but the father doesn't. By telling him what you are experiencing, you bring him and the child closer together, and it's an opportunity to be heard and understood. And shared joy is more strongly felt. Caroline, the mother of 2 girls, recalls a funny situation: "It was late at night and I was crying because there was no mayonnaise in the fridge. My husband was ready to go to the shops. He was laughing, but I felt his love and acceptance." (▶ II – 123)

Contact other women and experienced mums. Who, if not another woman – especially an experienced mother – will understand and support a future mum? This is Kate: "I was afraid of giving birth and a woman said to me: 'Women have given birth, are giving birth and will give birth. This is the order of things in this world. Nature.' It reminded me that I am not the only woman in this world who will give birth. If you don't have such a woman in your circle, you can go to support groups for pregnant women, birth story circles or workshops. If you have to stay at home or be in hospital, look for support groups on social networking sites. Surround yourself with women who remember their birth as a beautiful, enriching experience. Avoid stories of traumatic births – this can only cause worry.

Learn about pregnancy and childbirth, monitor your baby's development. What you don't know can be a source of anxiety. Your imagination creates different scenarios, often scary and usually wrong. Therefore, give yourself knowledge. You can dispel doubts, make what awaits you feel real, and gain a sense of control over the situation. Look for literature on the course of pregnancy and childbirth, check how your baby is developing, which also allows you to start building a bond with him or her during the prenatal period. Take a birthing course – either in a class or online – and meet with a midwife or doula.

Choose medical care consciously. It is important to feel that you and your baby are safe during pregnancy. Contact with a trusted gynaecologist and/or midwife contributes to this (▶ I – 23).

In the case of a pregnancy with complications, look for additional psychological and information support. Ask for help. If the pregnancy is not developing as you'd expected, it causes great concern for your health and that of your baby. It can cause depression, despair, mood swings and irritability. Make sure you get the support of loved ones and the care of specialist doctors.

If your emotions are very intense, stop you from going about your daily routine or last more than 2 weeks, ask for help from a gynaecologist, midwife, psychologist or psychiatrist. This is not a failure, it is taking care of your child and yourself.

Take care of your changing body. Your body's needs are different from those before pregnancy, which can cause you confusion and frustration. Try to look at your body with empathy: you are carrying your baby, there are two of you, so the effort is greater. Your body has to change in order to accommodate your growing baby. Rest, relax with a bath, music, or a walk. Think about your health and eating habits. Take care of your appearance – maybe change your hairstyle or try out new makeup.

Be active – the way you like it. Some women work until the end of their pregnancy, which gives them a sense of belonging, continuity and fulfilment. Others give up work straight away and pursue passions they have never tried before or had time for, such as crocheting, sewing or restoring furniture (▶ I – 30).

Be physically active in a form that fits your condition. Body and mind are connected. Physical effort causes the secretion of endorphins which give you feelings of happiness, relaxation and satisfaction. These hormones can relieve stress and even reduce pain. Through well-chosen, safe physical activity like pilates, swimming or gymnastics, you also prepare your body for childbirth and the postpartum period (▶ I – 35).

Let go, delegate tasks and find time only for yourself and your pregnancy. Perhaps you like to take everything into your own hands and have everything in place and in order around you. At the same time you feel tired and overwhelmed. Try to accept that if you take time for yourself and the baby you are carrying, there won't be a disaster. Divide up household chores – it will pay off. You will be more rested, and your loved ones will be able to show you support and care.

Pregnancy is a time of hormonal and emotional transformation. Taking care of your own mental health is an investment which pays off in the future: It helps childbirth, the postpartum period and supports your bond with your new baby. You have many ways to improve your well-being, but it's up to you to make it happen. ◆

Alexandra – mother, psychologist, psychotherapist.

44. Meditation and the well-being of the future mother

One of the methods that mums can use to calm down and relax is meditation. Over the last few decades, a number of scientific studies have shown the positive influence of meditation on wellbeing. Jon Kabat-Zinn, the creator of *Mindfulness-Based Stress Reduction* (MBSR) training, conducted a study on mindfulness meditation together with neurologist Richard Davidson in 2003. The study showed that participants were more active in the left prefrontal cerebral cortex than those in the control group. This part of the brain is stimulated when we are satisfied, as opposed to the right prefrontal part, which is active in people with depression or who are feeling depressed [1].

Meditation benefits:
- improves the functioning of the respiratory, circulatory, nervous and muscular systems,
- stabilizes hormonal balance,
- helps to alleviate the symptoms and effects of depression and reduce insomnia.

How to meditate? Meditation, in simple terms, will guide you to being in the here and now. If you've never encountered meditation before, all you have to do is start with one minute a day, gradually extending the time. You can sit, lie or walk while listening to relaxing music.

Make sure you're comfortable and that there is nothing around to distract you. Wrap yourself in a warm blanket, and if you're lying down, put a pillow under your head.

One form of meditation is to focus on your breath. Close your eyes. Don't try to lengthen or slow your breath down, just be aware of it. Feel the air flowing in and out through your nostrils into your body with every breath and exhalation. Notice how your lungs and stomach fill up, rising and falling. Concentrate on your breathing all the time. If at some point you notice that your thoughts are wandering – and this is sure to happen – don't worry about it. It's perfectly normal for your mind to wander – that's what it does. Be aware of your thoughts. You can give them a name, for example

– planning, worrying, recalling, and then, gently, focus your attention back on your breath. At the end of the meditation, take a deep breath, exhale and slowly open your eyes.

You can use this method at any time. Let it be an "anchor" for you, to help you calm down and relax in difficult moments. ♦

Anna – hatha yoga instructor, mum of 2-year-old Simon.

My story

There is a lot (although still not enough) talk about postnatal depression. People list the symptoms, raise awareness and offer help. However, little is heard of depression during pregnancy. Pregnancy is a beautiful and joyful time of waiting, after all! It's a time to complete a nursery, attend birth school and have mythical culinary appetites. As it turns out, this is not always how it works... Let me tell you my story.

I was never a fan of children. I didn't even know if I really wanted them. Maybe you felt the same? My partner and I had been together for years, before we decided to have a family. Perhaps that's saying things too strongly. We just left things to fate. And here's the first surprise: I thought we were going to try, try and try – but after a month, I was already pregnant. Surprise, fear, horror but also curiosity and... joy. Yes. I was even happy at first. I chose a wonderful doctor (it would later be confirmed how well I chose), I started to read parenting literature, I signed up to an online forum. Everything was going along its peaceful path, until around November – I got pregnant in September – I received poor cytology results. A procession of doctors, diagnoses and examinations started. Then it was Christmas time and I had no time to think about what was happening. In the meantime, a strange thing happened. Since the beginning of my pregnancy I had suffered from vomiting and abdominal pain. One day, however, I woke up and felt... Nothing. Absolutely nothing. It was about the 4th month, so I hadn't felt any movements yet. I had no way to verify this strange feeling. I ended up in the hospital for an ultrasound. Fortunately it turned out that everything was fine and in the evening I got a wonderful reward in the form of some first movements :). I didn't know yet that the fear that I felt that day would stay with me till the end...

It started to get serious in late January. I went to see my doctor... who didn't recognise me. I had been lying at home crying for some time, out of powerlessness and fear of the unknown. I came to the visit pale and swollen. I didn't even know what my doctor was saying to me. He examined me quickly and asked my partner to come to his office. He told him that my behaviour was not normal for a pregnant woman. That I needed help. A doctor like that is a treasure. Within a week, I was given psychotherapy by a wonderful specialist. For the first few meetings, I just cried. I wasn't even able to name most of my feelings. And she listened. Patiently, without interrupting, handing out tissues. It was very important that – with only the few months that we had – she focused mainly on preparing me for the birth, on calming my crazy emotions. I felt calmer with each meeting. Although the fear had not entirely disappeared, she managed to "tame" it so that it stopped paralyzing me. I even started to feel a kind of excitement about meeting my child. Before this, negative emotions had obscured everything.

I think that – thanks to the great support of my gynaecologist, partner and therapist – I managed to make it to the end of the pregnancy calmly and did not end up with postpartum depression, which, frankly, most people around me anticipated. I'd like to stop for a moment and draw attention to a few things that were crucial in my case. I think the first and most important choice is the choice of the attending doctor, who should make us feel safe and who will clarify any doubts and – if necessary – will refer you to the appropriate specialist. If you are not comfortable with your doctor after the first or second visit, find a new one. The second thing I encountered was the "nightmares of childbirth" that women have when they are pregnant. And here's my appeal: Dear Mum, let's not do this. Let's refrain from telling terrible details, tragedies and nightmares about pregnancy, births, whether they're yours or things you've heard. It's not the time or place for this. Let's be carers, not enemies. The third thing is the ability to ask for help. I didn't have it. My doctor did it for me. Please don't hesitate to ask for help. Talk about your fears and emotions with your partner, husband, parents, friends. Talk to other women. Maybe someone else is going through the same thing? Maybe you just need to talk and know that you're not alone in this? Look for support, if not on the Internet, then in support groups. Choose a midwife in advance, with whom you can talk from the heart about your fears. The most important thing is not to suffocate these emotions within yourself – to find an outlet for them.

I don't want what I write to alienate anyone. It is worth remembering that the threat is real and knowing about it beforehand can help. ◆

Caroline – Philip's mother, infant & child nutrition advisor.

---

45. Lions and tigers and bears, oh my! The fear of giving birth and other pregnancy worries

Pregnancy can bring a lot of joy, but can also bring fear. On the one hand, you are happy to see your baby's heart beating on the ultrasound, but on the other hand, you are worried about whether the little one is really ok. Some mums are afraid of pain during natural birth, while others are worried that medical intervention or a caesarean section will be necessary. On top of that, you may be doubtful whether you can handle not only the birth itself, but also the baby's care: "During my first pregnancy I was concerned about the baby's health and whether I could handle my newborn," writes Justina. "Now, in the second one, what I fear most is childbirth – this pain, pain, pain and pain again." And Betty adds: "I wasn't afraid of giving birth myself, but of the possible C-section."

Fear or anxiety? In this chapter we deal with fear and anxiety, which are natural for each of us. These terms are often used interchangeably, but it turns out that they mean two different things. This distinction is important because often the mere analysis of the concepts leads to a deeper understanding (and familiarisation) of them [3]. Fear is a reaction to a specific thing. For example, during pregnancy it could be the fear of your baby not developing healthily or the fear of a difficult birth. Fear appears in response to a real danger, but for it to appear, there must also be an awareness of the danger [2]. Anxiety, on the other hand, is vague and unfocused, meaning that you cannot put your finger on the cause. In pregnancy, it could be a fear of change; a fear of the future, and even of death [1, 3]. This fear of death can be understood literally or metaphorically -metaphorically, in that the childless woman dies and a mother is born. Who will she be? It is not possible to say that before she is born, and after she is born it is not that easy either. In this way of looking at it, the fear that you feel is actually a fear of yourself, and the other side of the fear of death is the fear of life – of yours and your child's.

Fear and anxiety, of course, accompany us throughout our lives and are common to almost everyone, not just pregnant women [2]. But pregnancy is a time when they can often intensify. After all, it is not only your body that is adapting to the needs of the baby, but also the head and heart that are preparing to take on new roles. Sometimes fear and anxiety can paralyze everyday functioning and take control over the person. In such cases, it is necessary to go to a specialist for help, as you may have a phobia or anxiety disorder.

Fear management strategies. The cure for fear is to eliminate its cause. You may smile and think, "Sure, but how am I supposed to eliminate the pain of childbirth?" The fact is, pain is unavoidable in the case of a natural birth, but you can change your attitude towards pain. How can you do that? First of all, find out what the pain is for and how you can alleviate it, in terms of appropriate positions, exercises and forms of relaxation. As with all other fears, the first step is always to try to understand more deeply what it's really all about and then work towards finding the best possible strategy for you to deal with it. A concrete strategy, in the case of childbirth, would be to choose a good birthing school or birthing preparation course. This will make sure that your experience of birth is as natural as possible and that you have the strength to do it.

What you shouldn't do is open yourself up to stories that will compound your worries and send you into a spiral of fear. This is not to say that you don't have a right to be worried – you do, especially if you've previously experienced loss or have had a difficult time getting pregnant. But just because your friend had a difficult birth or has a sick baby, this does not mean that you will too. Every woman is different, both in terms of physical predisposition such as pain threshold or ways of dealing with pain, and in the mental or spiritual dimension. An awareness of this helps distance oneself from worrying stories. You can also choose to listen only to positive stories. Listening to such stories, especially in a circle of women, has a very good influence on the pregnant woman's mental health.

Remember that a pregnancy is not isolated from other life experiences, and therefore many different factors influence the way in which it is experienced. These include family relationships, one's material or financial situation, or your previous experiences. How you deal with these can help with working through your pregnancy fears. Seeking support from others is invaluable, particularly women who have had similar experiences. If there is no one within your circle of family or friends, then do look for professional support, such as individual therapy, group therapy or support groups.

Should you fight anxiety? Anxiety has no specific cause, so a different strategy has to be applied. The first step is to realize that it is an inevitable aspect of our experience in this world. Often people simply do not realise that they have anxiety, or develop mechanisms to protect themselves from feeling it – they run away or hide from it. Escaping from anxiety can consolidate a pattern of avoidance, and as a consequence the anxiety persists and can even lead to phobia. Yet anxiety is important, as it can draw attention to a problem [2]. The fear of giving birth, and the fear of a huge change, is often drowned out by throwing yourself into the preparation. Preparation is of course important and necessary. The problem arises when it serves to avoid thinking about what lies ahead. You are dealing with the bustle instead of trying to think deeply about what you are experiencing and what is happening to you. However, if you try to talk – either to yourself or to a person you trust – you can turn it around to be an experience that will strengthen you and develop your personality. In this way, fear allows you to prepare for change and for the completely new role that awaits you, contributing to your daily comfort and security. This is a great opportunity to face up to the different worries that you experience in everyday life. It is often the case that such a confrontation with yourself has never taken place before, and becomes an opportunity to undergo psychotherapy. Pregnancy can make a woman start to reflect on her own history, and in this sense the process of psychotherapy itself is a continuation of this thinking; it often involves a person's history and her relationship with others, including her own parents.

Often the very understanding that fear is something that is a permanent part of your existence is enough to stop it paralyzing you. The next step is to try to find the answer to the question: "Why am I afraid?". As it has already been said, in the case of pregnancy we are broadly dealing with a fear of change, which requires you to build a new image of yourself and the world around you. Before you build this new image, there can be an empty period where your old self no longer exists and your new self is not yet born. This is your "little death". Nietzsche stated that the first time we are born is from our mother's womb and the second time we are born is when we give birth ourselves to a conscious and responsible life [4]. Pregnancy is a time of preparation for this second birth.

The best cure for fear is to reflect on it and understand its inherency, and to give yourself time. Give yourself time to go through these incredible changes that are yours. Let yourself experience all the emotions that come to you. Being fixated by fear is counterproductive. If you accept it, you take away its power over you. It also involves abandoning any excessive desire you may have to control things, in favour of allowing things to happen. The desire to control everything is a consequence of experiencing fear, but it is an ineffective strategy for dealing with it because – simply put – you cannot control the whole world. You don't have an influence on everything that happens to you, but you do have an influence on your attitude towards what happens, including difficult situations. You may think that what happens in life is "punishment for sins", and you may say that life is trying to teach you a lesson, or giving you a chance to grow, and that overcoming the crisis will strengthen you and make your life more complete. But try to replace these negative, unhelpful thoughts[8] with an attitude of trust. Who should you trust? Trust yourself that you can handle what life will bring you, and that it will give you what you need. You can trust in God or a higher power or in fate, or in family, friends and loved ones. That's why a support network is so important. Once you trust, it becomes easier to ask for and receive help, which is extremely important.

---

[8] I am talking here about a medium severity of anxiety, which comes with a changing situation, as pregnancy is. Since anxiety is one of the most frequent psychopathological symptoms there is, if it is very intense and is connected with a number of somatic symptom disorders such as insomnia, appetite disorders, clear and long-term low moods, you should seek specialist help. If the anxiety is severe, it may be a symptom of prenatal depression. It is difficult to judge on one's own when anxiety goes beyond the basic level and becomes destructive, especially since everyone's limits and thresholds are different. The tendency towards severe anxiety is strongly related to your nervous disposition.

Fear and anxiety are inseparable companions in our lives. It is impossible to completely eliminate them, but it is in your power to develop an attitude that will help you deal with them well. In the case of fear, it can be a kind of inquisitiveness ('what am I really afraid of and why?') and a desire to work toward finding the best answers. In the case of anxiety, it will be a way to live through it and an ability to accept it with confidence in what life brings. Starting a family, although a natural part of life, requires a lot of effort from you and involves overcoming difficulties. Fortunately, it's an undertaking which you are equal to. ◆

Monica – philosopher, artist, novelist and mum to Mary.
Mary – Tom's wife, Sofia, Margaret and Matthew's mum; psychologist.

What else should you know?

46. Shopping with your bump... and not necessarily replacing your entire wardrobe

In this chapter, we will focus on picking your essential items! I will tell you what I think is worth buying during pregnancy and motherhood, but remember that each of us is different – what is absolutely necessary for one mother may not be useful at all for another. Nowadays there is a huge selection of products available, so you just need to think about what you really need and what your budget is.

Accessories useful during pregnancy
- Sleeping pillow (croissant) – designed to relieve strain on the spine and support the pregnant tummy while sleeping. Later on, it can be useful to support your baby while breastfeeding.
- Fitness ball – for exercise during pregnancy (unless you are not allowed to). After the birth it can also be used to rock the baby or calm it down.
- Car seat belt adapter – lowers the seat belt to the height of the hips below your belly, providing both comfort and safety for the travelling mother and child.
- A woven baby wrap – you may have already heard about baby slinging (▶ II – 36). If you buy a baby sling, you can also use it when you are pregnant to support your tummy, thereby relieving strain on your spine, pelvis and hips. Additionally, the sling will warm up your tummy if you are pregnant in winter, and you can practice tying it before the baby is born.
- Cosmetics – it is crucial to choose the right products, as substances contained in your cosmetics can harm your baby (▶ I – 39).

Pregnancy clothes. A woman's body can change dramatically during pregnancy. It is a special time and every future mother wants to feel not only comfortable but also beautiful. Whether you need special maternity clothes will depend on many factors including the size of your baby bump or the season. When choosing maternity clothes, pay attention to the natural composition of the materials.

Again, every woman is different. Some future mums will fit into their existing clothes, and they may just button their pants with a rubber band or special inserts, while others feel better in maternity pants, leggings or dresses. "In both pregnancies I didn't have any maternity pants (although my stomach was big)," writes Kate. "At the very end I was wearing jeans that didn't fasten, but a rubber band helped. However, if it turns out that you can't fit into your regular pants, you can find maternity pairs which will make you feel comfortable and beautiful." For comfort, you'll need leggings and pants with an elastic waistband, especially after the birth.

You don't have to buy special maternity blouses or dresses, you can choose looser cuts. As Betty advises: "I had a few pairs of maternity pants. I sincerely recommend them, but I know I can do without them. And I bought second hand blouses, a few sizes bigger."

The clothes you buy may depend on the season – in winter you might need a jacket that warms your tummy and in summer loose, airy dresses. Pregnancy clothes are now readily available, so there's no need to stock up. When shopping, try to pay attention to the natural composition of materials. These clothes can also be useful for the first months after the birth, before your figure returns to how it was before pregnancy. Amelie attests to this: "During my second pregnancy, I appreciated that the clothes can be worn both during pregnancy and during breastfeeding."

You may need a bigger bra already during pregnancy. You can buy an extension, or a new, regular one, or one for breastfeeding mothers, ideally with detachable shoulder straps that can be used both during pregnancy and after birth. In addition, it's worth buying a sleeping bra – soft, but one that will support your breasts.

Pregnant women sometimes need bigger shoes due to the effect of a hormone called relaxin. The joints and ligaments relax, which can make your feet bigger (and stay that way). In winter you need to think about shoes which will be safe on slippery pavements. Comfortable shoes will also be useful for pushing a pram.

As far as other necessary items for your wardrobe are concerned, you may need new panties (choose models that either end under your tummy or pregnancy ones that cover your entire abdomen) and compression tights (which will help to reduce swelling in your legs) or ones specifically made for pregnant women (with a belt that covers your abdomen, so you don't have to keep pulling your tights up).

Accessories useful for childbirth – (▶ I – 62).

Accessories useful after childbirth:
- Thermal mug – a hit for mums putting together this book! Prepare coffee or tea in a thermal mug, because you never know when you will find a moment to sip your favourite drink.
- Bag for a stroller – choose one that will still be your favourite thing even when the children have grown out of the stroller. A practical bag with compartments will serve you well on walks, for shopping or for travelling for many years.
- Breastpump (manual or electric) – may come in handy if you are breastfeeding and plan to leave your baby in the care of others from time to time. Some mums advise buying one 'just in case', others only when it is needed. If you decide to express your milk, you need to make sure you store it properly (▶ II – 45).
- Breast pads – appreciated by every breastfeeding mother. Before your milk is established, it can leak from your breasts and give you a surprise that will be visible on your clothing. Breast pads can be disposable or reusable – find out which one works best for you.
- The childbirth cushion is an invention which was supposed to make sitting down after childbirth less painful. Nowadays it is not recommended by gynaecologists or physiotherapists.
- Feeding area – a feeding corner should be prepared accordingly. You'll need water, snacks and a book. Keep an extra pillow and blanket on hand, as well as a thermal mug and a telephone. You will spend a lot of time here in the first few months after the birth, so making it comfortable is a must. Justina recommends stocking up on snacks "like nuts, dried fruit, something easy to eat quickly and with one hand – when you're breastfeeding, you get terribly hungry," as well as "some VOD subscriptions for good TV shows."
- Cosmetics – read chapter (▶ II – 115).

Clothing for breastfeeding or pumping
- Nursing bra – one should be enough in the beginning until your milk is settled, as well as the size of your bust. Once this happens, it's worth

getting 2 or 3 nursing bras, which you will wear during the day and which will allow you to give your baby easy access to your breasts.
- A nursing shirt or pyjamas – blouses or t-shirts which you already have may be sufficient. The main thing is easy access to your breasts, because the last thing you want to do at night is to fight with buttons on intricate blouses. If you decide to buy a nightshirt or pyjamas, consider choosing a style that has poppers, giving easy access to your breasts for feeding.
- Nursing tops and vests – these make a great bottom layer for any chosen outfit. You can put a sweater, top or shirt on top, which can be taken off or unbuttoned, leaving the vest which makes breastfeeding easier and more discreet. They are not an essential, however, if you feel comfortable lifting up or unbuttoning ordinary tops.

Every woman and every pregnancy is different. As a result, there are different needs. The market for mums and kids is huge, so before you spend your money, think about what you really need. Although I know it can be difficult, try not to stock up – buy what you need when you need it. I hope that the list above, combined with my advice, will help you make good purchasing decisions. The most important thing to keep in mind, though, is that your satisfaction and comfort are the most important things. After all, a happy mum is a happy baby! ◆

Anna – Iga's mother.

47. Mum's essentials — must-haves in the home medicine cabinet

Future mums often don't know what they should pack for the birth (▶ I – 62). In this case, it's best to go to the hospital website or call them and ask what you need to bring.

Maternity underwear. They certainly come in handy for mothers after the birth, both natural and caesarean. The main task of maternity underwear is to keep maternity pads in place and to ensure that air can get to the seams – especially

to the crotch or to the area of the caesarean section. There are two types of underwear on the market:
- disposable interlining underwear – made of artificial material and airtight, they're stiff and allergenic; not recommended,
- washable mesh underwear – in this case it does not matter what they are made of, the most important thing is the structure of the mesh, and that they are airy; they are soft, flexible and not tight; highly recommended.

Underwear are divided into those with low and high waist. If you are going to give birth by a caesarean section, you will need to choose the latter so that the elastic band does not compress the wound. Once the bleeding has subsided and you've given up maternity pads in favour of absorbent underwear, you can go back to wearing your regular underwear. It is important that they are made of cotton (for ventilation), a little too big rather than too tight, and without lace or other elements that may irritate sensitive skin.

Postpartum pads. These are large, absorbent, delicate and skin-friendly cotton diapers for women ;). Although they don't look very flattering, it is worth using them in the first days after childbirth. Postpartum pads, as opposed to ordinary sanitary towels, provide ventilation. Depending on the intensity of postpartum bleeding, some mums use them for a few days, others even for a few weeks. Postpartum pads maintain hygiene, helping to prevent infections and inflammation.

Cleansing of postpartum wounds. The hygiene of postpartum wounds is very important. Whether you gave birth naturally (and had a perineal tear) or through a caesarean section, the care is similar. I recommend:
- sachets with benzydamine hydrochloride to prepare a solution – this works as a disinfectant, anti-inflammatory, anti-oedema and local anaesthetic,
- octenidine spray – thanks to its broad spectrum of effects (antibacterial, antifungal and antiviral), it effectively prevents infections in intimate areas and accelerates the healing of the wound. It doesn't sting and can be applied to skin and mucous membranes.

Intimate areas can be washed with mild body wash. Do not introduce water (or any washing agents) into your vagina. It is not recommended to use intimate hygiene products in the early postpartum period as it can disturb the bacterial flora, which may lead to an increased incidence of intimate infections.

Disposable sanitary pads. If the hospital does not provide them, you will need a few 60 cm × 90 cm pads after the birth. Bleeding is greatest during the first 3-7 days, while the uterus shrinks and is cleansed, so it is good to protect the bed from possible leakage.

Breast pads. They will certainly come in handy for every new breastfeeding mother. The breast pads you put in your bra are designed to absorb the milk that excretes from your breast between feeds. They differ in thickness, absorbency, size and material. We distinguish between them as follows: disposable inserts (with cotton or moisture-absorbing polymer), reusable inserts (usually cotton or bamboo), lactation shells (made of soft, thin silicone; they protect cracked, irritated nipples, giving them time to heal). Which ones to choose? Whichever suits you best.

Ointment for irritated nipples. Pain, swelling, breast irritation and even a rupture in the epidermis of the nipple which can lead to bleeding – these are the most common problems that breastfeeding mothers initially struggle with. What to do in such a situation? First of all, it's advisable to seek help from a Certified Breastfeeding Advisor. You may not be properly adjusting the baby to the breast or the newborn baby is not sucking well. Act as soon as the first symptoms appear. To start with, rub and moisturise your breasts with your own breast milk. If this does not help, try cream from the pharmacy, whose main task is to moisturise and regenerate the epidermis, prevent excessive water loss, protect from the outside world (minimising the risk of infection), start the healing process and relieve inflammation.

In the pharmacy you will find several products that will help in the regeneration of irritated nipples. The best choice is almost certainly 100% lanolin, which fulfils all the above-mentioned tasks. It has a therapeutic effect, but you can also use it as a preventive measure as well. You don't have to wash it off before feeding again. There are no side effects. An alternative is ointment with dexpanthenol, allantoin or vitamin F (the same as is used for babies) which moisturise and relieve well, but they need to be washed off before feeding again.

Prenatal vitamins. Remember to use vitamins during breastfeeding. According to official guidelines, during lactation mothers should supplement with:
- folic acid at a minimum dose of 400-800 mcg/day,
- vitamin D at least 2,000 IU/day,
- iodine at 150-200 mc/day,
- DHA acids at a dose of 500-600 mg/day.

As for iron and magnesium, they should be taken by mums who are not getting enough from their regular diet.

Lactation aids. For the health of mother and child, it is important that you choose a product that does not contain fennel. Fennel contains an essential oil which – in excess:
- has a neurotic effect, leading to intoxication and seizures (anethole),
- has an estrogenic effect, which inhibits lactation (anethole, estragole),
- is a genotoxic carcinogen (estragole).

These should be avoided too:
- aniseed & dill (which can have an allergenic effect),
- goat's rue (contains galegine, which has no documented efficacy, but has proven toxicity),
- fenugreek (when used during pregnancy it can contribute to preterm birth or miscarriage; during breastfeeding it negatively affects the baby, causing nervousness and digestive tract problems),
- herbs which can prevent breastfeeding – sage, mint, parsley and walnut leaves.

Although many mums claim that breastfeeding teas stimulate the production of milk, this hasn't been confirmed in clinical trials. If you like herbal-fruit drinks, you can drink them in moderation, 2-3 cups a day maximum. Also remember that they change the taste and smell of your breast milk. In a practical sense, the only advantage of drinking breastfeeding teas is that the mother hydrates her body, an effect which can be achieved by drinking water.

Barley malt is the only substance with a positive, scientifically-proven effect on milk production. Not all malt is the same, however. It is important that it contains large amounts of beta-glucan and is standardised – only then will it work effectively. Bavarian, cereal coffee, lactose-free beer and other concoctions are simply myths passed down from generation to generation

Pain medication. Whether you give birth naturally or by caesarean section, you may experience pain after the birth. If the pain is strong enough to make it hard for you to function and look after your baby, take a pill or suppository. First choice should be paracetamol or ibuprofen, but if they are too weak, try diclofenac or ketoprofen. All substances can be bought in a pharmacy without a prescription. If you are going to breastfeed, pay close attention to the dosages and intervals to be observed when using this group of medicines.

Constipation. This is quite common for mums after birth, and to deal with it, movement and exercise are definitely the most important thing. If possible, get out of bed and walk. Sitting or lying down for long periods generally worsens the problem. Drinking a lot of water is also important, as is eating fibre-rich food. If necessary, you can also use a glycerine suppository or lactulose syrup from a pharmacy.

Hemorrhoids. Varicose veins around the anus can be very troublesome. Most often they cause inflammation, pain, burning, irritation and even bleeding from the rectum. If you're breastfeeding, you should see a doctor, who will assess the severity of the case and choose the right treatment. During lactation you can apply:
- white oat bark – can have an astringent effect, although it should not be used in the early postpartum period,
- ointments, gels and rectal suppositories with anti-oedematous, anti-sclerosis, analgesic, anaesthetic and disinfectant effects.

Likewise with diarrhea or gastrointestinal problems, it's worth going to the doctor and not trying to deal with it by yourself.

As you can see, there are far fewer products needed for a mother than for a newborn. Don't forget about yourself, though. Remember that the health and inner peace of the mother makes the baby calmer. Good luck! ◆

Anna – Pharmacy M.A., mother of Antonia and Misha, blogger on the proper use of medicines in children, pregnant women and breastfeeding mothers.

48. There are two of you now. Staying safe during pregnancy

For as many women as there are, there are just as many reactions to the news of pregnancy. Joy, happiness, shock, horror. From now on, you are responsible not only for yourself, but also for the little one growing in your belly. By taking care of yourself, you take care of both of you. The health and safety of your child depends on your health, well-being and care.

Mum with a tummy at home. Safety starts at home, so you should pay special attention to your immediate surroundings at the beginning of the pregnancy. A lot of mums emphasise that hygiene is extremely important. "For me, safety during pregnancy means washing vegetables and fruits thoroughly, washing and cutting meat – washing my hands," Paula writes. That's why you need to look at your diet and eliminate alcohol, mouldy cheeses, raw meat, fish, seafood and eggs due to the risk of toxoplasmosis or listeria infection (▸ I – 31).

Focusing on daily care, make sure that the cosmetics you use are safe for you and your baby (▸ I – 39).

Household chores that are better done by others:
- Hanging curtains. Your body has been doing a lot of work since the beginning of your pregnancy. Your heart needs to pump more blood and standing with your hands raised can result in dizziness, fainting or falling. Keeping your arms raised for long periods can also lead to straining of the ligaments which support the uterus [2].
- Cleaning with strong chemicals. Unfortunately, most have toxic and irritating substances in their composition, with intense smells (▸ II – 20).

Avoid contact with such agents. Inhalation of fumes is not good for your health, and during pregnancy you don't need any help getting nauseous or dizzy. It is worth taking a look at reliable pages online and learning the secrets of a naturally clean house.

- Shopping. Of course, you can go shopping, but heavy groceries are better left to others. A pregnant woman should not lift more than 4-5 kg. If you have to lift something, squat first and lift with your legs.
- Remember to get out of bed properly – first lay on your side, support yourself with your hand and slowly lower your legs, ending up seated on the bed. Do not make any sudden moves. Let's give ourselves and the little one a moment to adjust.

Car safety. According to the law in some countries, a pregnant woman is not obliged to wear a seat belt [1]. Unfortunately, this is not a sensible idea, and fortunately most mums know this. "Whether I drive 100 m or 100 km, my first instinct is to fasten my seat belt. ..."After all, they protect you from going through your windshield in an accident," stresses Violet. So how can you travel by car in a safe and comfortable way? Just remember a few simple rules.

- Firstly, the belt should always be fastened. The hip belt should be placed under the belly, as this is the most important part of your body to protect in the event of an accident. The shoulder belt should run over the belly, between the breasts and over the shoulder, but should not touch your neck.
- If the regular car seat belt doesn't fit, then the best option is a belt adapter for pregnant women – this will provide safety and comfort.
- If you drive often, remember to keep a safe distance between your belly and the steering wheel on account of the airbag. It should be about 20-25 cm, which is enough for the airbag.

Mum with a tummy in town. To make journeys on public transport safe, always hold on to handles and protect your belly from accidental nudges from other passengers. In buses and trams, comfort is not always ideal. Do take a seat to avoid falling over if there's a sudden stop. If possible, find a seat near the window. If there isn't one available, don't hesitate to ask someone to give up theirs.

In the city, it's best to avoid large gatherings, for example at concerts. In crowded places it's not only easy to get pushed around or bumped into by accident, but also to catch the flu or a nasty cold.

Don't smoke and try not to be in the company of smokers. Passive smoking is very harmful to you and your little one. Especially during the winter months, monitor air quality before going for a walk. If there is pollution, think about buying a smog mask with a suitable filter.

The safety of an active mum. If you do exercise and you feel ok, you don't have to give up your favourite activities such as cycling(▶ I – 35), but first consult your doctor. Remember to drink plenty of water and keep your clothes airy to prevent dehydration and overheating. Rest whenever you feel the need. Don't forget your helmet, reflectors and other protectors.

Safety gadgets. When you leave the house, take the following with you:
- an "I'm pregnant" sign – from the first months of pregnancy, it is worth having something on you in case you faint or have an accident; anyone who helps you will then know immediately that you are pregnant,
- a pregnancy card with information about your blood group, diseases (e.g. diabetes), the pregnancy medication you're taking,
- a bottle of water,
- a charged phone or an additional portable charger.

Each woman experiences her pregnancy differently. This is an exceptional state, but the same rules apply to all future mums. It's only 9 months, and the decisions you make, to a great extent, can have an effect on the safety of your child . ◆

Anna – Tim's mum fascinated by attachement parenting and Self-Reg.

49. On the plane with a baby bump?! Travel during pregnancy

Your child will soon be born and you already know it will be a big change in your life. For this reason many people think about going on holiday and recharging their batteries ahead of this. "I love travelling, and going away during my pregnancy was a symbolic farewell to my current lifestyle (only for a while, of course!)," writes Lena. What should you keep in mind when you plan such a trip?

Are you sure you should travel? Pregnancy in itself is no reason not to travel, as long as you are well and you feel good. There are, however, situations in which travelling is not advised or prohibited: with chronic diseases (e.g. hypertension, asthma, heart disease, diabetes, kidney failure, severe anaemia), problems in previous pregnancies (e.g. miscarriage, premature birth, fetal membrane rupture), multiple pregnancies, or a woman's age (younger than 15 or older than 35). In these cases you need to discuss further with your doctor. **Rule No. 1 – ALWAYS consult your doctor before you plan your trip and shortly before you leave.**

When is the best time to set off? There is no clear answer to that, as usual. Most doctors advise against travelling in the first trimester as it's the time of the highest risk of miscarriage. Furthermore, many women experience unpleasant pregnancy problems during this period, so they do not want to go anyway. In the third trimester, your bump can be quite large, affecting the comfort of travelling. The closer to the end of the pregnancy, the higher the natural risk of premature birth, so travel after week 36 is discouraged (after week 34 in the case of twins – or more!). The second trimester is considered the best time to travel, preferably the period between about week 20 and week 27 – the pregnancy has stabilised and most women feel their best then.

Which direction? There are a few things to consider when choosing your destination.
- Security – exclude countries in conflict or where there is a threat of terrorism. Rule out places with an epidemic risk or where there is a risk of

picking up infectious or tropical diseases (check which vaccinations are mandatory or recommended – many cannot be done during pregnancy). Information about current threats can be found on the website of your country's foreign ministry. Areas located high above sea level are also not recommended due to the risk of hypoxia (low oxygen in the blood). Also take into account the level of medical care in the country, and how easy it is to access – whether you will receive professional medical assistance in the event of any complications, a caesarean section or the birth of a premature baby.
- Distance – spending a long time travelling (whether on a plane or by car) is not advisable, so it is best to choose a destination which is no further than 3-4 hours away, or split the trip into sections, with overnight stays.
- The climate and the current weather in the destination – pregnant women are more sensitive to low or high temperatures, so even if you're usually good with the heat, it can be much harder when you're pregnant.
- Hygiene and food – choose places where there is no problem with cleanliness and access to good quality water (not only to drink, but to brush your teeth as well – it's best to use bottled water) and food. However, there are no reasons why you can't eat local cuisine.
- Local regulations – in some countries there are restrictions enforced – and even bans – against pregnant women who are not citizens of the country. Airlines don't take responsibility for this, so you can end up flying to the country but not being allowed to leave the airport.

Which type of transport to choose? It is very much up to you – your safety and comfort is the most important thing. Whatever means of transport you take, remember to move around – stand up, stretch your muscles, move your arms and legs – to ensure good blood circulation (against the risk of thrombosis) and not overload your spine (by staying in one position for too long). It is also important to drink plenty of fluids, eat regular food and have easy access to a toilet.
- The car. Traffic experts advise pregnant women to sit in the back, but if this isn't possible, move the front seat back, allowing for the safe opening of the airbag in case of an accident. Remember the rules of safe driving (fasten seatbelts below your belly or think about buying an adapter, do

not turn off the airbag, do not keep loose objects like water bottles in the car, and take breaks). If you're the driver, remember that pregnant women get tired faster, their eyesight often deteriorates and their concentration is lower [2]. In the later stages a large bump will also make it difficult to drive, and the child's intense movements may distract you.

- The train. This seems to be the most comfortable choice – you can stretch your legs, and sometimes even lie down. Take into account possible crowding on the train and reserve a seat if necessary. The disadvantage of travelling by train is the difficulty of getting quick medical help if you feel unwell.
- Bus or coach. This may be the least ideal method of transport: small leg room, no chance to stretch your legs while it's moving and the toilet is often difficult to access. If for any reason you have to take a bus, buy a seat in the middle of the vehicle to avoid the bumps over the wheels.
- Plane. Flying while pregnant is controversial in some countries and many myths have grown up around it. If your pregnancy is healthy and safe, you can choose this means of transport without worrying. The risk of a deep vein thrombosis applies to all air passengers, although there is a slightly higher risk in pregnant women [2]. Consult your doctor, who may recommend antithrombotic injections. You shouldn't fly if you have sickle cell anaemia or thrombotic vein inflammation, but other things such as 'cosmic radiation', hypoxia related to altitude or X-rays at customs have all been scientifically proven not to be harmful [3].

Air travel – what to remember? Be sure to read the airline regulations as regulations for pregnant women vary from carrier to carrier. Most airlines take women up to week 36 (or week 32 in the case of multiple pregnancies). You may be asked to show a recently-issued certificate or a pregnancy card to confirm which week you are in. It may be best to prepare the certificate in the language of the carrier, and it may be useful to have an online copy which you can download from the website. Additionally, some airlines do not take women and newborn babies on board for the first few days after birth, so take this into consideration when planning your flights.

Insurance. When going abroad, it's important to buy proper travel insurance dedicated to pregnant women. Standard insurance usually covers only the costs of the hospital stay, but rarely includes the costs of treatment for the baby, transport to a medical facility or return with a newborn baby to your country. Check the costs of childbirth in the country you are going to and any countries you will be passing through, choosing the appropriate amount of insurance. Most insurance companies will provide cover only up to week 32 (up to 18 weeks in a multiple pregnancy), and some even earlier.

Also consider buying travel cancellation insurance, which will allow you to cancel your trip without losing money if things change.

What to take with you:
- A birth plan, preferably translated into the language of the country you are going to travel to or through.
- Your most important medical documents: pregnancy card, current pregnancy tests, result of the last ultrasound examination, document stating your blood group, your doctor's contact number.

- ID card.
- A list of maternity hospitals along the way (also in countries you pass through).
- A list of important emergency numbers and your country's embassy contact details in the country that you will be staying in and any country you pass through.
- Hospital bags – it's worth taking them with you if your pregnancy is advanced. You will want your things with you.
- Phrasebook in a given foreign language with medical, pregnancy and childbirth terminology. Pictorial dictionaries can be helpful.
- First-aid kit, which additionally contains medicines and supplements taken during pregnancy and cosmetics appropriate to the destination, such as insect repellent or sunscreen. Hydrating salts are always a good idea.
- A child seat – worth taking if you are in the advanced stages of pregnancy, especially if you are travelling by car.

If you are travelling by plane, pack your most important things, such as your medical documents and identity papers, in your hand luggage, in case your luggage is lost or delayed.

Pregnant women invariably encounter a warm and friendly reaction from people they meet during their travels, so don't be afraid to ask for extra water or help with carrying a suitcase. People will be glad to lend a hand.

A trip during your pregnancy can be a fantastic adventure and the last moment to relax before the baby arrives. However, it really is worth preparing for it so that it doesn't turn out to be a source of stress instead of pleasure. Remember, the most important thing is to consult your doctor – tell him or her when and where you are travelling. ◆

Barbara – mum of two young men, passionate about distant travels.

50. The baby shower — your child's first party

Imagine your favourite cafe, where one of the rooms is decorated with balloons, and there are decorative baby bottles or dummies hanging on ribbons or bunting. In the middle of the table you see a cake, next to it there are gifts piled up, and on top are tiny shoes. Around the table laden with your favourite treats, friends and relatives are waiting. You enter this room surprised and happy — you and your baby are being thrown a baby shower!

What's a baby shower? The name comes from the most important part of this event, which is a deluge — or shower — of gifts related to the baby and your pregnancy. The theme of such an event is therefore closely related to the birth of the child and the role of the future mother. The custom itself comes from the United States, although Anglo-Saxon culture already had a tradition of women meeting on the occasion of an upcoming birth back in the 18th century. During these gatherings, more experienced mums would share their advice with the pregnant woman and give her handmade gifts. Such get-togethers were intended to tighten female bonds and relax the future mother.

Who hosts the baby shower? Usually, the organisers are friends or relatives who know the mother best. Unless it's a surprise, it is worth asking her to make a list of gifts she would like to receive. In this way the mother's baby list can be shortened or even completed.

If you feel that the organisation of a baby shower is too overwhelming, there are professional companies that prepare and organise such events.

Where and when is it best to organise a baby shower? Such a party is best done when the future mother's tummy is visible but she's not too far advanced that the due date is just around the corner. Baby showers usually take place around the seventh or eighth month of pregnancy. Depending on your preferences and budget, the party can take place in the organiser's house or apartment, in a favourite pub, in a cafe or in the open air. If mothers with children are invited to the party, you also need to think about a place where the little ones can play.

What attractions await during the baby shower? Apart from female chit chat around a tasty table and showering the pregnant mother with gifts, various competitions, quizzes and fortune-telling games can also be organised.
- Who knows mum best? The winner is the person who knows the most answers to questions about the future mother (e.g. name of first boyfriend, favourite colour etc.).
- Who's that baby? Each participant should bring a childhood photo. All photos should be attached with clips to a string. The winner is the person who correctly identifies as many photos as possible within 10 minutes.
- Who's first? For this you need a doll and a set of clothes. The winner is the person who dresses the doll the fastest.
- What's the song? Prepare a playlist of well-known children's songs. The person who recognises the most titles wins.

Why not organise a mini photoshoot during the baby shower. It will be a fantastic souvenir!

Is it worth having a baby shower? It all depends on the temperament of the future mother. But surely spending time with good friends – which, after the birth, not every young mum will find time for – is a very big advantage of this event. Another advantage is the gifts, especially those chosen by the future mum, saving her a lot of expense. Don't forget – even Fiona in "Shrek 3" had a baby shower!

Baby stag or Dad's baby shower. The equivalent of mum's baby shower is usually organized after the birth of the baby, even before the mother and baby come home from hospital. The place to party can either be the home of the freshly-baked parents or the favourite bar or restaurant of a proud dad. A meeting of the guys can be an opportunity to share experiences and to relieve the stress of the birth and new responsibility. And again, it's another opportunity to give an appropriate gift to an enlarged family, perhaps with a humorous touch, such as a supply of nappies or coffee after sleepless nights.

A baby shower can be a very good idea for mums who need to relax before the birth, or to exchange opinions and listen to advice from experienced mothers and relatives. ◆

Caroline – wife, mother and solicitor.

51. Crazy for animals. Preparing pets for a baby's appearance

You, your partner, Fifi and Felix, are living a peaceful life when suddenly – with two lines on a pregnancy test – the world is turned upside down. And not just for you, but for your pets too. How can you prepare animals for a new family member?

A natural and calm approach. For both animals and children, you should be like a refuge. With you they should feel safe and calm – always close by and comforting. Despite all the stressful situations with pregnancy, take a positive approach and don't be afraid of getting things wrong. After all, until now it was only you guys, and all attention was focused on Fifi and Felix. Therefore, it is best to start at the beginning of pregnancy, when you still have a lot of time to practice and get the animals used to the new reality. Carers can also play a very important role here. Yes, you can help your pet understand what is happening and let them know there is no cause for stress.

Before the baby shows up. If your animals have any behavioural 'problems' that you have not been able to deal with so far, they will become more difficult after the arrival of your baby. This is the perfect time to start working with your dog or cat. Perhaps the animal is hyperactive, jumps on you, pulls you along on walks, playfully bites you, and perhaps it hasn't bothered you before? This will now change, however, especially if your dog is big and heavy. Jumping on your tummy won't be so cute any more.

Preferably, get the advice of an experienced behaviourist to analyse your pet's behaviour and choose the appropriate exercises and games. Then all you have to do is practice, practice and practice again! Relax, you still have a few months. If you start early enough, it will probably not be difficult for you or your dog or cat. You'll have the time needed to shape their new behaviour.

New in the apartment. You're preparing your home for a baby. You buy or get a lot of new, sometimes big things and even furniture. It's best if these larger items come into the house a little earlier than your child. If the new items come into the house a few weeks earlier, the animals will be able to get used to them. It is also a good idea to walk with an empty stroller so that the dog gets used to it and learns to walk with it.

Special attention should be paid to cats when changing the decor of the apartment, as they can be extremely sensitive to changes. It is very important that the cat has time to get used to any new furniture or equipment in the home.

Preparing for new sounds. You can, while still pregnant, play recordings of a baby crying or laughing and watch the animals' behaviour. Playing sounds also familiarises dogs and cats with the new noises which will soon be part of their daily routine. Some animals do not react at all to the crying of a child, others may be curious, anxious or even frightened – in which case the help of an experienced behaviourist will be useful.

Contact with children. If animals have never had contact with babies and you have the opportunity to invite friends with their baby to see their reaction, take the opportunity. Be cautious and respectful of both the child and the dog or cat. If your cat is scared, let her go to a safe place.

New places to sleep. If your pets are sleeping with you in bed or in the same room, and you'd like to change this before the baby is born, it's worth taking your dog or cat out of the bedroom now and setting up a new place for it to sleep. Especially if you're planning on sleeping with your baby – a little one, you, your partner and a dog or cat in the same bed may be too much of a good thing.

A visit to the vet. Take your animals to the vet as soon as possible for a thorough check-up. Does your dog or cat have up to date vaccinations? Are they protected against ticks? Do they have healthy teeth? Are they dewormed? It is a good idea, especially for older animals, to have an abdominal ultrasound or chest X-ray. These are things that every animal carer should take care of, but animals in a family with a pregnancy should have their health status under control. If there is something wrong with your animal, now is the time to start treatment.

WHEN THE BABY SHOWS UP...

We are family. The appearance of a child transforms your life, and you need to take care of every member of the family, including the dog or cat. You know your pets best. You know that Felix likes long walks and Fifi adores evenings on your lap. However, things have changed a bit. But try to make time for your pet's little pleasures too, if possible. Many baby experts recommend that you gradually move your pets away and pay less attention to them. No! That's a straightforward route to an unhappy dog or cat and may result in behaviour like wetting its bed or destroying things. And that's not what you want at all.

You can already assume that you will have less time for your pets (especially if you have more than one), so you should consider introducing them to a pet sitter or carer at the beginning of your pregnancy. Such a person will not only help you after the birth by taking your dog for a long walk or playing with your cat, but before or during the birth too. He or she can take care of the animals while you are in hospital.

The smell of a baby. After the birth, while you are still in the hospital, it's a good idea to prepare your pets for a completely new smell in their environment – the scent of a newborn baby. Your partner, friend or family member can bring home the clothes or nappies the baby was wrapped in, for example. You can put them in different places around the home, not necessarily in their beds – that's their safe place, which is better to keep baby-free for now (until the baby starts crawling!).

First contact with a newborn. This first meeting will be a big experience for the animal. It is important for everyone to feel as comfortable as possible. You can introduce the animals to a new family member outside the apartment – in the corridor or the garden, for example – and enter the home together. Dogs can go out for a long walk and when they come back, you can wait in the foyer with your child – it all depends on the situation, as well as your child's health, the season, the weather, your pet's personality. Allow your dog or cat to sniff out the new member of the family so as to satisfy their curiosity. Observe the situation to see if the animals are comfortable. Behave as naturally as possible – the animals need to feel that everything is under control.

Let Fifi and Felix participate in the daily care of your child. Don't chase them away, don't scream, don't isolate them. The more you inhibit contact with your child, the more your animals may want to get to know them. After all, a newborn baby is the object of your greatest interest, so it must be very important, valuable and interesting – worth knowing at all costs. Animals can be very vulnerable to isolation and rejection, which can even affect their health.

The arrival of a newborn baby at home will surely be a small revolution for everyone. But don't push the animals to the side. Living with dogs and cats is good for the baby on many levels – contact with animals helps emotional development and teaches respect, responsiveness, sensitivity, empathy to all living beings – and that animals are our friends. Walking and playing with your dog or cat is a great way to get a good dose of exercise during the day. When difficulties arise, having a chat with a behaviourist will be helpful. Such a person will explain what is causing the situation and how to resolve it. ◆

Joanna – Kazik's mother, Panda's partner, carer for two dogs and a cat.
Consultation: Olympia – animal behaviourist, feline therapist, dog trainer.

THE BIRTH

52. Attitude matters — preparing mentally for childbirth

From the moment you get the pregnancy test results, you know deep down that, all being well, this journey can only end in one way. As time goes by, the feeling of impending birth becomes more and more alive and tangible. If you have listened to scary stories about birth, fear may start to build up. How can you prepare mentally for the birth so that you can await the arrival of your baby in peace and enjoy your pregnancy?

First of all: prepare for YOUR birth. "I was afraid of childbirth and its complications. Listening to the stories of other mums made me panic and I was constantly thinking about how I could avoid being damaged," remembers Maggie. You need to keep in mind that every birth is different, even for the same woman, and her experiences can be influenced by many factors, such as her mental state, support – or lack of it, physical activity during pregnancy or the choice of people present at the birth (for example, a midwife or doula). Do not take to heart all the stories you hear – especially the negative ones.

Meet the unknown. There are many sources from which you can draw information. First of all, ignorance can cause fear. To minimise fear, find out what birth looks like: what the signals are that the birth has started, what the courses of the first, second and third phases are, what pharmaceutical and non-pharmaceutical methods of pain relief there are, and so on. Active birthing classes, good books or websites, talking to your midwife – these are just some of the most popular sources of knowledge. Remember, however, that childbirth is not only about physiology and dilatation of centimetres. Childbirth is also about emotions and the mental side of experiencing it.

Make an informed decision. The more knowledge you have, the more informed the decisions you can make for yourself and your child, and this will help you distinguish between routine and non-routine medical procedures and decisions.

In the last trimester, write a birth plan. Going through its successive points will allow you to envisage what awaits you.

Think positively and surround yourself with positive people. Positive thinking is very important during pregnancy and birth. During pregnancy, it reduces the level of stress hormones, and during childbirth, it can lead you to a happier natural birth. "When I was afraid of giving birth, a woman told me that women have given birth, are giving birth now, and will continue to give birth," remembers Kate. "This gave me encouragement. If other pregnant women were able to do it, I could too. And I did :)." Accept the support of other women. Hearing about their experiences and reading positive stories can significantly ease your fear of giving birth. If you do not have women in your immediate environment who can support you, look for a support group in your area. In most areas there are usually several local initiatives promoting mindful and positive preparation for birth.

Know your options. Who, where and how? To answer these questions, you should take time to consider your options. The choices you make during pregnancy can enhance the quality and the memories of your birth.
- Who? The doctor who supervised your pregnancy or the one you'll meet on duty? Will you take on a private midwife (▶ I – 59), or is this unnecessary? Will you have a partner, sister, doula (▶ I – 60), mum or friend at the birth?
- Where? The hospital or at home (▶ I – 56)? Choose a place where you will feel safe and a place which will meet your needs.
- How? Naturally or by caesarean section (▶ I – 54), drugs or no drugs (▶ 64), or maybe hypnobirthing, standing up, in water or lying down? There are plenty of possibilities, and a free choice is your right!

Know your rights. Many women recall memories of friends or family talking about 'forcing' things or being forced to take certain actions during childbirth. Unfortunately, there is still a conviction in many people's minds that when we cross the threshold of the hospital we become completely dependent on the medical personnel and that we ourselves have very little or nothing to say in the matter. This couldn't be further from the truth! Most countries have national standards of perinatal care. Exercise your rights!

Ask for support. Proper support during the perinatal period is invaluable (▶ I – 58). "I was very scared," says Marta. "My husband's support and the conversations we had in the last days before the birth really helped me. At that time my mood swings were at their greatest and tears alternated with smiles. It is important that a decision to give birth together is a conscious decision by both sides. 'Pulling' men into the delivery room by force or emotional blackmail ("You caused it, so you have to be there") is not a good idea. Whichever person meets your needs, whoever they are, will be a valuable support. It could be someone who is actively supporting in the form of massages, in choosing positions, etc., or just 'being' there. A partner, doula, mum, sister, friend can go with you to the birth. Remember your rights! No one can tell you who you should give birth with. One accompanying person is standard but many hospitals accept the presence of two, such as a partner or a doula.

Accept and verbalise your concerns. Every birth is unique and special. If it's your first birth there is also the element of novelty and surprise. And that's OK! You can be scared, it's completely normal and natural. The question is how you deal with it, whether your fears will drive you to prepare and find out as much as possible, or whether they will paralyse you.

The birth cannot be planned. It is impossible to predict how it will turn out. It is worth preparing for this event consciously by thinking it through.
And being surrounded by people who will make you feel positive about giving birth can completely change your attitude and the last weeks or months of waiting for delivery. ◆

Beatrice – mother of three children and a hypno-doula.

53. Yes, yes, you can (and should) prepare your body for delivery!

Is it possible to prepare yourself for the birth? Can we learn something to help us give birth better? Is it worth practicing natural, instinctive breathing?

Instinct or preparation? In fact, in obstetrics there are two trends for the preparation of birth. The first one is the view that birth comes to us instinctively and the body knows what to do. The second assumes that it is worthwhile teaching a woman how to consciously use the wisdom and skills of the body during childbirth. Dear Mum, believe me, your body can give birth (▶ I – 52). Get over any fear of giving birth that you might have, fear which often results from an ignorance of what really happens in a woman's body during childbirth. Try to discover and embrace your femininity and strength. This is a time when you can meet with doulas and support groups of other future mothers, speak to your midwife or have private sessions with a psychologist, do relaxation exercises or birthing meditations. From a preparation point of view, childbirth resembles a date that ends with a good night. Only taking care of your body by making sure it is well groomed and visually pretty, is no guarantee of fulfilling sex unless we feel full of femininity and some level of maturity. Sometimes preparing for childbirth on a psycho-emotional level may seem much more challenging than preparing the body itself. On the basis of my own experience, I believe that both forms of preparation should take place at the same time, and that the exploration of oneself should begin long before pregnancy...

What to look out for during pregnancy? Certainly, physical activity during pregnancy (▶ I – 35) is a big plus in your preparation. However, there are women who are unable to exercise during pregnancy, so preparation for the birth itself should take place around week 36, when we approach so-called full term (exactly week 37). This is the time when you have every chance of giving birth on time, without any medical treatment or intervention. Around week 36 is the optimal time to learn about 'birth behaviour'.

Important elements in body preparation are:
- learn the right breathing path:
    - take long, deep breaths (avoid short, sharp breaths),
    - abdominal breathing,
    - chest breathing,
    - breathe and release the sound "aaaa" when you exhale;
- learn conscious pelvic movements, as often pelvic circulation involves the whole body instead of just relaxing parts of the pelvis,

- learn to engage the abdominal muscles for both spontaneous and classic pushing, while relaxing the perineum,
- prepare the pelvic floor muscles and the perineum area,
- normalise the position of the sacrum and hip bones (a visit to the physiotherapist is recommended),
- find exercises that have a positive effect on the position of the baby in regards to its head position, for example its head should be down and its bottom up from week 32, only the midwife or physiotherapist/osteopath may perform such exercises,
- conscious relaxation and the ability to feel when the body is feeling extremely tense, and know what methods and techniques can help bring relaxation,
- work with the simulation of the contractions in the early part of labour – how to breathe and move in rhythm with the contractions,
- improve respiratory and exercise capacity, if the course of your pregnancy allows it (moderate performance exercises with breath control).

If you were physically active before pregnancy, think about the kind of exercises that you did and if it's possible to modify them to include more relaxation elements, focusing on conscious and natural movement.

Where can you learn all this? All these elements should be included in specially-designed exercise classes for pregnant women, whether you choose yoga or fitness classes. It is important to work with your body to match the stage of pregnancy and find awareness of what natural childbirth requires (i.e. the importance of your body's competence and its ability to 'manage' the act of giving birth).

As a future 'parturient' (woman in labour), look for and choose really good quality classes or individual training sessions with specialists who, in addition to safe exercises, will create a programme suitable for birth preparation. Birthing schools don't generally offer courses for working with the body, or if they do, they don't go into a lot of detail. ◆

Isabel – Nadia and Leon's mother, qualified midwife, pregnant conscious-training coach, author of books on childbirth.

54. Natural childbirth, caesarean section, vbac – different forms of childbirth

Childbirth is a natural consequence of pregnancy – a physiological function of a woman's body, and at the same time an incomparable event, shrouded in a mysterious aura. Each birth is a unique, often surprising journey and there are no two exact same birth stories. Nevertheless, looking at births in general, there are certain patterns that form a logical sequence of regularities, the knowledge of which allows us to approach this life-giving process with respect and humility, but also with calm and without fear.

Types of childbirth:
- Natural childbirth – birth by means of nature's force, which takes place without medical intervention and without anaesthetic drugs or pain relief.
- Natural childbirth with medical interventions, such as the use of synthetic oxytocin and other drugs, planned rupture of the fetal membranes, episiotomy (perineal incision) and anesthesia.
- Assisted delivery – with the help of a vacuum or forceps.
- Surgical childbirth – C-section.

The best and healthiest ending to a pregnancy, for both mother and baby, is a natural birth. We are, of course, talking here about a situation in which there are no medical concerns or needs on the part of the mother or child for medical intervention or completion of the pregnancy by surgery.

CHILDBIRTH
Childbirth is a process that runs in parallel on many levels and includes all aspects of human functioning, which intersect and influence each other:
- the physical sphere, due to the body's delivery mechanism and the hormones involved in childbirth,
- the mental sphere, due to the strong emotional experience of the woman becoming a mother,
- the sexual sphere as a continuum of feminine sexuality. In childbirth there are many features common to intercourse; both acts require a certain

rhythm, supported by the same hormones, and if they run in a healthy way, they have a similar ending – a feeling of fulfilment, joy and release,
- the spiritual sphere – for many women, childbirth is a mystery or a kind of rite of passage,
- the social sphere – it's not only a medical event, but also a family and societal one.

Birth itself is divided into four stages:.
- First stage – the time when the cervix (which is a solid 'closed door' during pregnancy, allowing the baby to develop safely in the uterine cavity) opens up, enabling the baby's passage into the world. The hormones that condition the proper course of this stage of childbirth are oxytocin and endorphins, while the hormone that slows its course down is adrenaline. **The necessary condition for the undisturbed course of the first stage of childbirth is a sense of security, intimacy and relaxation** (low stress level). In the first stage of childbirth there are two phases: the latent (or slow-development) phase and the active (accelerated dilation) phase.
- Second stage – from the moment the neck of the uterus is fully opened (approx. 10 cm) until the birth of the baby. During this period there are two phases: the 'passive phase', which includes the baby's head moving down into the mother's birth canal and the stretching of the woman's pelvic floor muscles (important for effective perineal protection!), and the 'active phase' – the time of the active displacement of the baby. The hormones which maintain the correct course of the second stage of childbirth are mainly oxytocin and adrenaline (in the active phase).
- Third stage – the time from the birth of the child to the delivery of the placenta.
- Fourth stage – the first two hours after natural birth.

The childbirth. The birth can start with strong and regular contractions of the uterus or with the spontaneous rupture of the fetal membranes (waters breaking). If the birth starts with contractions, its beginning can be difficult to determine because often the contractions become gradually predictable, but they are not necessarily linear (i.e. periods of heightened tension followed by calm). Initially, contractions can easily fit into normal everyday life. As they become stronger and longer, they will require you to interrupt your activities and focus on your body while practicing deep breathing and rhythmic movement. In the active phase of delivery, due to the hormones surging in your body, you will start to switch off from the world around you. The powerful and extremely intense process taking place in your body will absorb all your attention. There may be moments of crisis – for example at 7-9 cm dilatation (the so-called 7 centimetre crisis), accompanied by a feeling of resignation and lack of strength. You can do it, Mum! When the time comes to push your baby out into the world, the adrenaline rush will give you the energy you need to complete the job!

Remember, the ability to give birth is within you – your body knows how to do it. So listen to the signals it emits and follow them. Find your own birthing rhythm. Change positions – this will help your baby to move down into the birth canal. Breathe calmly and deeply – for yourself and the baby. If you feel lost, listen to the midwife's guidance – she is your birth guide.

Push (second birth stage). Once the cervix is fully dilated and your baby is low enough in the birth canal, the birth contractions will change in character – you will start to feel the unstoppable need to push. By following this need, you'll help your little one to overcome the last centimetres of the birth canal. If you take a vertical position during the push, your effort will be supported by gravity. In addition, a position other than lying on your back and spontaneous pushing (reflex-like, in accordance with the body's needs, in the way and for as long as the mother feels the urge) will help to better oxygenate the baby as well as protect the perineum.

Sometimes, for example because of fear or pain, spontaneous pushing can be ineffective (the mother refrains from pushing). The midwife can then help the mother concentrate on the effective use and strength of the contractions of the uterus, giving her the right guidance.

There is also a kind of Valsalva maneuver where the midwife or doctor instructs the mother how, where and when to push. Often the woman gives birth in a less active position, lying on her back. Apart from exceptional situations (for example when the mother has received an epidural, in which case it is necessary to complete the birth quickly or perform a surgical delivery), this type of push is not recommended because of its adverse effects on the mother (higher risk of pelvic floor damage, exhaustion and burst blood vessels on the face) and for the baby (reduced oxygenation and higher probability of heart rate disorders). The scientific evidence supports spontaneous or 'mother-led' pushing wherever possible [5].

Protection of the perineum. In regular labour and by working closely with the midwife, most women can give birth without significant injury to the birth canal or perineum (easily healed abrasions and minor, first-degree tears on parts of the perineum). Protection of the perineum is helped by, among other actions, birth in a vertical position, birth in water and spontaneous pushing. It is extremely important to respect the physiology of the second stage of labour (the latent phase) and not to speed up the birth before the pelvic floor muscles have had time to relax and stretch out.

When the head emerges, it is important that you work with the midwife so that the baby is born slowly and your muscle tissues have a chance to move the baby down and out. Warm compresses during the second stage of labour and the use of moisturising and lubricating agents (obstetric gels) are also helpful. Work done on the perineum and pelvic floor muscles during pregnancy also has a beneficial effect on the elasticity of the perineum during childbirth – a gentle massage of the perineum with vegetable oils and breathing exercises are all helpful. The importance of the atmosphere in the birth environment cannot be overlooked during childbirth – a sense of security, intimacy and calm is important [3].

In a few cases, an incision of the perineum (episiotomy) is needed. Reasons for an incision include:
- the need to complete the birth quickly (due to complications or concern over the fetal heart rate),
- obstetric procedures (use of forceps, vacuums, internal adjustment of the shoulders),
- a breech baby or if the baby is not engaged.

A properly-made incision is not painful – sometimes you can't feel it at all, or it's equal to the discomfort of a pinch.

Skin-to-skin contact. Immediately after birth, your baby should be placed on your belly or chest. This is where your skin-to-skin contact begins. The newborn baby is dried and covered, and the pediatrician or midwife assesses its condition on the Apgar scale. If the baby is born in a good condition (7-10 Apgar) and does not require attention, your continuous skin-to-skin contact should last at least two hours. This is an extremely important and unique moment to bond, and a chance for the new baby to adapt to the new environment in the safe arms of their loving mother. It is also the best time to start breastfeeding. Remember, weighing and measuring can wait, and the pediatrician can perform the first examination of the baby on your belly!

Cutting the cord. Usually, except in the case of a lotus birth, the umbilical cord is cut at birth. In many hospitals it is already standard practice to wait until the umbilical cord stops pulsing before clamping and cutting. Late clamping has many advantages:
- allows the newborn to start breathing on its own in a calm and gentle way while he or she is still getting oxygen from the umbilical cord blood,
- umbilical cord blood supplies him or her with important components such as iron (reducing the risk of anaemia) and plasma clotting elements (reducing the risk of bleeding in the neonatal period).

In most cases, a late clamping is possible and beneficial. Exceptions are if the baby has hemolytic disease, or the mother has certain conditions such as HIV infection, or if there is a threat to the life of the newborn.

Placenta and the "golden two hours." After the birth of your baby you will enter the third stage of childbirth when you will have to deliver the placenta together with the amniotic sac or fetal membranes (the so-called afterbirth). This period can last up to an hour, but it is not as intense as giving birth. The hormone that determines the correct course of this period is oxytocin. In many hospitals a dose of synthetic oxytocin is given intravenously to speed up the birth of the baby and minimise bleeding. However, an artificial hormone will not be needed if you are in constant contact with your baby and it starts sucking your breast, causing the release of natural oxytocin in your body.

When the placenta peels off and the midwife sees that the umbilical cord is lengthening, she will encourage you to push a little. While waiting for the birth of the placenta, the midwife will make an initial assessment of the perineum.

At the end of the third stage of childbirth, there is time for the treatment of genital tract injuries, if there are any. Generally you will spend the next 2 hours after birth in the delivery room under the supervision of a midwife who observes the bleeding from the genital tract area and the contraction of the uterine muscles. This is also the time to start feeding your baby if it has not started sucking on your breasts yet. If, for some reason, the baby has had adaptation problems or the mother has had complications (for example, if there is heavy bleeding or a need to evaluate the uterine cavity) and it has not been possible to do proper skin-to-skin, it is worth repeating it as soon as possible.

After 2 so-called 'golden hours' following the birth, you and your baby will be taken to the maternity ward. If it was an uncomplicated natural birth you will generally stay in the hospital for two days. However, in some places you may be able to be discharged only a few hours after the birth.

The 4 P's. The course of natural childbirth is conditioned by 4 groups of interacting components, often referred to as 'the 4 P's'.
1. PELVIS – the physical side (especially the pelvis structure) of a woman giving birth.
2. POWERS – birth forces (the strength and efficiency of uterine contractions).
3. PASSENGER – the baby being born, in particular its position in the uterus and the way it is positioned in the birth canal. Ideally, the baby should have its head down and its body facing towards the mother's back. This is called the occiput posterior position (OP). During labour the baby should be encouraged to reach a left or right occiput anterior position (LOA or ROA) where its head is slightly off centre in the pelvis with the back of the head towards the mother's left or right thigh. This allows the baby to tuck its chin under and is considered the easiest and safest position for the baby to be born. If your baby is still in a position other than head down after week 32, it is worth doing some appropriate exercise (consulting with your doctor first) or asking about the Bowen technique. If the unfavourable position is still seen in week 36-37, an external cephalic version (a rotation procedure performed by an obstetrician) may be the solution.
4. PSYCHE – the mental state of the woman giving birth affects the hormones secreted by her body, and these affect both the birth itself and the child

being born. The broad sense of security of the woman giving birth is of fundamental importance.

Childbirth pain. An important part of labour, although not necessarily the primary part, is labour pain. It is felt by most women giving birth and is the result of the contraction of the uterine muscle, the opening of the cervix, and the the lowering of the baby in the birth canal (pressure on the sacro-lumbar nerve plexuses), as well as the stretching and compression of the perineal tissue. Although labour pain is not a pleasant experience, it has its purpose and a role in the birth. In physical terms, it motivates the woman to move, which helps the birth progress and protects against damage to the birth canal – the woman instinctively chooses positions where she feels the least pain associated with the compression of the baby's head. It also regulates the secretion of birth hormones, influencing the secretion of endorphins responsible for introducing the woman into the state of natural anaesthesia and adrenaline necessary in the second period of labour. Childbirth pain also has important psychological and emotional aspects: it helps to make the birth of a baby feel real, reveals incredible inner strength in a woman, positively influencing her self-esteem after the birth, and helps to build a bond with the baby.

Childbirth pain is necessary. Try to see it as a huge portion of life-giving energy at work in your body. However, this does not mean that a woman has to suffer during childbirth [5]. You can alleviate labour pain and find ways to deal with it (▶ I – 64).

Benefits and risks of natural birth. Natural childbirth has many benefits for the child. Its body is "massaged" during the contractions, which facilitates the emptying of the airways of amniotic fluid, activates deep and superficial sensations and stimulates internal organs. During childbirth, the bacterial flora of the digestive tract is also colonised, and the secretion of stress hormones helps facilitate adaptation outside the uterus.

When the subject of childbirth comes up, there are almost always questions about its safety. Childbirth is undoubtedly a seminal life event which arouses the strongest of emotions. Fortunately the percentage of complications associated with childbirth is really small.

The risk of any particular complication arising in childbirth depends on many factors, including the state of the mother's health, whether or not pregnancy pathology occurs, the health of the baby and the degree of medical assistance during birth. Here are the three basic principles of safe childbirth:
- The greatest virtue in obstetrics is patience and careful observation.
- A good birth is not necessarily a quick birth.
- Interventions should be employed as an exception and not routinely, starting with the least invasive.

Note: interventions during birth are sometimes necessary and can be life-saving. However, in some countries or cultures interventions are performed far too readily. They should be treated as a last resort.

CAESAREAN SECTION

Over the past few decades we have witnessed a global trend in the increase of birth by caesarean section. The development of surgical and anesthesiological techniques have made caesarean section an increasingly safe operation. Nevertheless, it is still not without risk for the mother and child, both short- and long-term, so should be treated as a way to save health and life, and not as an alternative to natural birth. Short-term maternal complications include bladder injury, uterus or intestinal damage, thromboembolic or anaesthetic complications (including postpartum depression). Long-term maternal complications include intraperitoneal growth (which may cause pelvic pain syndromes or intestinal obstruction), a caesarean scar, endometriosis in a caesarean scar or an abnormal placenta. Possible negative effects of a C-section on the child may include: breathing disorders after the birth,(so-called wet lung syndrome), disorders of the bacterial flora in the newborn's digestive tract, increased risk of autoimmune diseases in later life, as well as asthma and allergies.

In what situations should a C-section be performed? Each case is individual and the physician decides whether to perform a C-section after analysing many factors. If it is necessary to have a scheduled C-section, the doctor conducting the pregnancy will present you with the benefits and risks of performing the operation, so that you can give your conscious and informed consent. If the need for the C-section appears during the birth, the doctor (unless the situation requires immediate action) should also briefly present you once again with the pros and cons. In this case, you must also give your consent (in writing) for the caesarean section. Only in a situation where the woman is unable to give informed consent (when she is unconscious) and there is a life-threatening condition, the doctor can perform a C-section without the consent of the mother.

The duration of a C-section is about 30-40 minutes, but it can be longer especially if surgery or previous caesarean sections have already been performed in the abdomen.

What does a step-by-step caesarean section look like from the moment you consent to the operation?

1. The midwife prepares you for surgery by inserting a cannula, a bladder catheter and administering irrigation fluids through a drip. You are also given an intravenous prophylactic dose of antibiotic.
2. In the operating room, the anaesthesiologist inserts subarachnoid anaesthesia by means of a puncture at the lumbar spine (the majority of current caesarean sections are performed under this anaesthetic; only in exceptional cases, general anaesthesia is performed). During this anaesthesia you will lose sensation from about half of your abdomen to your feet. What is important is that during this anaesthesia you will not feel any pain in the targeted area, but you will not lose the feeling of touch and movement. There's no reason to worry or panic.
3. When the feeling of warmth and tingling begins, the medical staff will help you lie down on the operating table. From this point on, the anesthesia starts working.
4. The obstetrician starts the C-section. At this point you may feel pulling in different directions, but you should not feel any pain. The moment your baby is emerging you can experience an unpleasant pulling feeling and pressure. Remember to breathe and relax. In a few moments you will see your baby.
5. The child is transferred to the care of the neonatal team. The neonatologist assesses the condition of the child (▸ I – 66) and its ability to adapt to the outside world. If everything is OK, the baby will be presented to you and pressed against your cheek. In some maternity centres, the baby is placed on

your chest in full contact with your skin (▸ 67) and attached to your breast. If the baby is born in a good condition, this is the best possible scenario for both of you. If skin-to-skin contact with mum is not possible, you can ask for the baby to be handed to dad, who can also provide skin-to-skin.
6. Obstetricians continue the surgery. They have to extract the placenta and suture the wound.
7. From the operating room, a woman can be taken to the post-operation or residence room, where she usually stays with her child (although this depends on the institution). In hospitals, the length of stay in the recovery room varies depending on the centre. In most hospitals, a woman can have skin-to-skin contact and breastfeed her baby during this time. In some hospitals the so-called *vaginal seeding* is performed, which is the rubbing of the baby with gauze that has been soaked in the mother's vaginal discharge. The procedure aims at covering the baby with bacterial flora, as would have happened during natural birth [13].
8. The young mother stays in the post-operation room until she is on her feet. This takes place 6 to 12 hours after the operation (depending on the hospital). The catheter is then removed from the bladder and the woman takes a shower. Getting upright is usually not an easy moment, but it is important to get mobile, as being active after the operation helps with recovery and prevents complications.

If you need to have a caesarean section during your pregnancy, you may want to ask the following questions:
- Can an accompanying person be present in the operating room? It depends on the hospital. You can try and request this, as well as ensure full skin-on-skin contact and early placing of the newborn to the breast after the C-section.
- What does skin-to-skin contact look like in the hospital of your choice after a caesarean section? Is full skin-to-skin contact practiced while sewing the uterus and abdomen, or just a short pressing of the cheek?
- Can an accompanying person do skin-to-skin with the child immediately after birth? If so, where and how can this be done?
- Are you going to have your baby placed to your breast immediately after the surgery is over?

◆ Can an accompanying person be present in the post-operation room?

VBAC (*vaginal birth after cesarean*): natural birth after caesarean section.
If you have had a caesarean section, your next baby is likely to be born naturally. Current research and based on the recommendations of expert teams, such as the RCOG (*Royal College of Obstetricians and Gynaecologists*) or ACOG (*American College of Obstetricians and Gynecologists*), consider such a birth to be a sensible and safe solution for most women after one – and some women after more than one – caesarean section. The chances for a successful VBAC (i.e. natural delivery of a baby after earlier caesarean sections) are high and amount to around 72-75% in women after one CC and around 71% in women after two CCs [12]. If, apart from caesarean sections, you have also undergone natural births in the past, your chances for successful VBAC increase to even over 90%.

If you decide to have another pregnancy after a C-section, you need to know that each way of giving birth – the trial of labour after caesarean (TOLAC) or the pre-planned caesarean section, involves some risk. In the case of multiple caesarean sections, this risk is particularly related to abnormalities in the structure of the placenta (the frontal, anterior or oversized placenta, which is the result of the caesarean section), which may cause massive bleeding and even the need to remove the uterus. In the case of attempting to give birth naturally after a caesarean section, the complication which doctors fear most is a uterine rupture from the scar of a previous caesarean. The good news is that the risk is low at – 0.5% [11]. ◆

Kate – qualified midwife and mother to Antonia, Iga and Frankie.
Magdalene – qualified midwife, doula and mother to Nicholas and Mary.

55. Back to school — choosing an antenatal class

Most future parents have feelings of both joy and apprehension. Antenatal classes allow you and your partner to prepare for a new role, to calm your fears and to equip you with the knowledge of what to expect.

The benefits of participating in antenatal class (birth school). The topics discussed during the classes will mainly concern childbirth, including learning to breathe during birth, methods of pain relief and the role of a companion at the birth. A very important aspect of the postnatal period will also be discussed, which involves the body's return to physical and mental form. For example, if you're going to have a caesarean section, the birth can still begin naturally. This is the sort of information you can expect to find out, and you'll also meet people in the same exciting boat as you. Your fellow attendees will often be a source of support.

Antenatal classes are an important part of preparation for the birth, something which is backed up by research. For example, a conscious attitude while giving birth is very beneficial for both mother and baby, and is something learnt at the classes. If a contraction appears, the woman focuses her attention on the contraction and relaxes, resulting in an optimal flow of blood through the vessels. The woman interprets her body's experience in a natural way, the contraction is natural and the birth is benign for the baby. This is a very valuable observation, and many studies confirm the benefits of participating in antenatal classes.

When to attend classes? Antenatal classes usually last about five weeks. The number of hours and the duration of the sessions vary from school to school, but most often there is a 1- or 2-hour session per week. There are also short, intensive courses, for example at the weekend. You should ideally finish the classes 4-6 weeks before the due date. Taking these factors into account, you should start the classes at the latest around week 30, although you can attend them much earlier, from around week 20, when a woman usually feels best. Make sure to sign up a few weeks in advance.

If your pregnancy is at risk or you have irregular working hours, you may need individual classes. There are also online antenatal schools that allow you to go through all the material at any time. The disadvantage of such a school is lack of contact with other couples expecting a child. And when you do the exercises, nobody is there to check if you are doing them correctly.

What to consider when choosing an antenatal class. Pay attention to who is leading the sessions: whether it is a midwife, doctor, obstetrician or other specialist. There are places where all subjects are discussed by one person, while in others there are different specialists for different topics. Some training programmes are more focused on natural childbirth, minimizing medical interventions. Prenatal classes at hospitals prepare mothers for childbirth in that particular institution – you will learn about the practices and approach of the hospital, such as its methods for relieving labour pain and its approach to medical interventions such as perineal incision. This also gives you the opportunity to get to know some of the staff who work in the hospital. There are also antenatal classes in clinics and at birth homes and it's worth getting to know their programmes.

When choosing a birthing school, take into account practical considerations such as location and travel time, class hours, your work schedules (so that your partner or companion can take part in the classes too), location (whether at the hospital, at the birthplace or independent) and price (not all classes are free).

Advantages and disadvantages of group versus individual antenatal classes. The advantages of group antenatal classes are undoubtedly the exchange of experience, support and the opportunity to make friends. Of course, a lot depends on a random factor – which group you will be assigned to. The more active the participants are, the more valuable the classes will be. The disadvantages of group antenatal classes may be: too many people, too small a group, late hours or difficult location. If you are considering an individual antenatal class, the attraction is of course the possibility to choose topics and talk about your feelings one-to-one, the flexible class times and often the possibility to do them at home. The downside is that you can't exchange experiences with people who are in a similar situation.

Partner's participation in classes. If you participate in a group class, your partner has a chance to meet other future dads, see their commitment and feel more in touch with the situation. They can find out what their role is during childbirth and how to take care of you and your baby after the birth. Participating in classes can help the father build a relationship with his unborn child. Sometimes not all classes can be attended by a partner, and most topics discussed in the antenatal classes are important. Therefore, when choosing a school, take into account whether the dates of classes fit both of your schedules. If you know in advance that for some reason the father of your child will not be able to attend the class, invite another loved one, such as a parent, sister or friend, to attend.

Online antenatal classes? Yes, it is possible, and it can be an ideal solution for those who do not have access to a course near their home. It can also be a wonderful addition to a regular birth school.

Costs of participation in antenatal classes: free and fee-paying schools. Some birthing schools are funded by the local authority, foundations or associations, which means that they are free for participants. Where the antenatal classes are a business, prices can vary greatly.

What if for some reason you can't attend antenatal classes? Then, as I said, you should take an online course. There may be a chance to have sessions with a midwife near you. You can also have individual consultations with your midwife on a specific topic of your choice. I encourage you not to wait until the last moment – I sometimes hear mothers saying that the due date is imminent and there are still so many topics to talk about. ◆

Kate – qualifed midwife, Certified Lactation Consultant, mother of a daughter.

56. Choosing where to give birth

In most countries, a woman can choose where she wants to give birth. For several decades most women have given birth in hospitals, but this is not the only possibility. In this chapter we will look at the available options, their advantages and disadvantages.

Here are, generally speaking, the options:
- At home – where healthy pregnant women give birth when no medical intervention is needed. Home births are supervised by midwives (▶ I – 59).

- **A birthing centre (or midwifery unit)** – for women who wish to give birth naturally, without medical intervention, in an environment similar to home.
- **Hospital** – for healthy women as well as women at risk or with complications during pregnancy. The hospital is also able to care for babies born prematurely or who are ill. This is the only place that allows birth by caesarean section.

Selection criteria. When preparing for childbirth and choosing where to give birth, take into account both physical and mental safety (sense of security, and technical and logistical issues such as distance from the house to the hospital). In our discussions while putting this book together, the most common sentiment was that a woman should choose a place where she feels comfortable and safe. This is to some extent subjective, but also related to safety in general. Complications may occur during childbirth, but the risk of their occurrence varies. If your pregnancy is progressing normally and without any complications, you have the widest choice. Unless limited by finances or lack of a suitable bed, you can give birth in your home without any problem. But if you know that you have a baby that requires specialist care after birth, that you might want to have a C-section or you just feel safest in hospital, you should rule out the idea of a home birth.

Home. For centuries women gave birth at home. It's only in the last few decades that the hospital care system has developed. Nowadays, an increasing number of women are deciding to give birth at home and the number of midwives to assist in such a birth is growing. Studies show that home births in low-risk pregnancies are as safe as those at hospital [1].

Advantages:
- Your baby is delivered in a place you know very well.
- You don't have to go anywhere – there are no worries about getting to the hospital on time.
- The medical staff are guests in your home so they are no longer strangers.
- There is less risk of unnecessary medical interventions. Equipment and means that are not in place cannot be used.

- The medical staff assisting you in childbirth are only focused on you, so potential complications are spotted faster.
- There is no limit to the number of people who can be around you.
- The child has contact primarily with your bacteria. There is no risk of contact with hospital microorganisms or bacteria.
- It's much easier to hold off with the clamping and cutting of the umbilical cord for as long as you want. It's also possible to have a lotus birth.

Disadvantages:
- The cost – midwife or doctor's assistance is not always covered and can be expensive.
- There is a risk of having to move to the hospital if complications arise.
- The possible difficulty in finding a midwife or a doctor to assist, particularly in rural areas.
- The need to make an appointment with a paediatrician or neonatologist after the birth, which you will most likely have to pay for.
- You can quickly slip back into your daily routine, hindering your ability to properly rest after the birth.
- You will need to provide your own equipment, such as a birthing pool, if there is no bath, and you want to have a water birth (apart from this, a home birth does not require extensive technical preparations).

After a home birth, it is up to the parents to ensure that the baby is vaccinated, screened and given a hearing test.[9] The baby will also not receive an injection with vitamin K straight away, nor will the Credé procedure be carried out (eye drops with silver nitrate solution to protect against gonorrhea conjunctivitis). According to Kaya: "The most important thing is to choose a place where you feel safe. In my opinion, it is crucial to know as much as you can about birth, and on this basis you can decide where you feel best. For me it was at home."

Birthing centre / midwifery unit. These are special facilities which create friendly, home-like conditions for women, while providing medical and

---

[9] A hearing test can be performed in a specialist clinic after a referral by the paediatrician. The blood for the screening can be taken by a community midwife, something which must be arranged in advance.

technical support. In a birthing centre, the procedures and the working style of the staff are aimed at supporting natural childbirth. Studies have shown that labour in a birthing centre is safe and has lower instances of medical intervention [3]. In fact, delivery rooms in hospital wards are increasingly being set up in a similar way to birthing centres. Often in birthing centres, it is also possible to book the individual care of a specific midwife during labour, although you have to pay for such a service. Such care provided by a person you know, with a similar attitude towards your birth, increases the chance of a good birth experience [4]. As Sylvia writes: "I would like to see home births become more normal – after all, it was once completely natural. The first time I gave birth in a hospital, which I knew well and where I knew the personnel. For my second I would like to give birth at home, but my husband doesn't support this option, so I will think about a birthing centre as a happy medium."

Advantages:
- Less risk of unnecessary medical intervention than in a hospital.
- The largest choice of midwives to accompany the birth.
- Access to a variety of equipment to assist in childbirth, such as birthing balls, birthing stools and water baths.
- Immediate transfer to hospital in case of complications.

Disadvantages:
- The small number of such establishments in most countries.
- The need to pay for the care of the midwife.
- No pain relief drugs are administered to relieve labour pain.
- You have to qualify medically to be accepted by a birthing centre – it is not an option available to all women.

The hospital. Most women in western countries give birth in hospitals, which is – again for most – the obvious choice as healthcare systems have been operating for several decades.

Advantages:
- Relatively good accessibility, even in smaller towns. In larger cities you can choose from several hospitals.

- Access to pain relief drugs during labour.
- Availability of equipment (birthing balls, stools, baths).
- Possibility of quick medical intervention, including caesarean section.
- Access to the neonatal department.
- The possibility to perform vaccinations, administer vitamin K intramuscularly and to perform screening and hearing tests.
- Post-birth care, including lactation counsellors.
- Once you have received help and care during childbirth, you can leave the hospital at any time, assuming that neither you nor your baby need further hospitalisation.

Disadvantages:
- Higher chance of unnecessary medical treatment during the birth.
- You have to get there, decide when to go to the hospital and maybe wait in a queue on arrival.
- There is a risk of lack of space in the chosen hospital and you may be asked to go to another hospital or be transferred to it (depending on the stage of delivery).
- Most of the people around you are strangers. There is a risk that the staff's working style will not meet your expectations.
- You're giving birth – and your baby is entering the world – in a strange place.
- You have to go through hospital admission procedures, often during childbirth.
- Risk of insufficient support from medical personnel due to the number of people giving birth. Possible lack of continuity-of-care during childbirth.
- Depending on the conditions in the hospital, it may not be possible to have an accompanying person, or be limited to only one accompanying person.[10]

---

[10] Unfortunately, there are still facilities which, due to the conditions of the premises, are not able to provide separate rooms for mothers giving birth. In these cases, out of respect for the privacy of other women, the mother cannot have a companion with them. Sometimes, despite the presence of other mothers behind the screens, the medical staff allow a companion to be present if there is no objection from others. This is an issue that should be raised in advance.

If you decide to give birth in a hospital, it is a good idea to do a thorough checkup of the environment in advance, as well as doing a visit to find out what they offer in terms of:
- availability of single rooms,
- forms of pain relief during birth,
- a policy of allowing free choice of birthing position in the first phase of labour,
- giving birth in water,
- the percentage of perineal incisions and caesarean sections – the higher the percentage of such interventions, the less chance of avoiding them, even if your pregnancy is healthy; data on such things can usually be found on national or local pregnancy or birth websites,
- standard procedure when you pass your due date, including induction methods,
- the possibilities and conditions for choosing an individual midwife to care for you during the birth,
- the possibility of giving birth with more than one companion, e.g. a partner and doula,
- the standard of handling your newborn baby after birth (both natural and after caesarean section), in particular the skin-on-skin contact,
- breastfeeding support,
- access to milk from a Human Milk Bank – this is especially important for premature babies.

In addition:
- Check feedback on the facility. Find out which hospital will provide the right level of care if you or your child's health requires it. Although a specialist neonatal unit can help you feel safe, think about whether a large hospital, with lots of births, will be the best place for you. It is possible that the medical staff will be more restrictive in observing certain time frames imposed on the course of the birth, and these may not necessarily be consistent with your birthing speed.
- Determine what your expectations of care are and – based on the current standards for maternity care – prepare a birth plan. Check which facility

gives you the best chance of meeting your needs, taking into account the facilities and style of personnel.
- Remember that the care of the mother in the hospital is primarily the responsibility of the midwife, so if you want a natural childbirth, choose a hospital which allows you to have a dedicated midwife care (for a fee).
- If you are preparing for a caesarean section, it would be best to choose the hospital where the operation can be performed by the doctor who is supervising your pregnancy. Also think about your expectations in terms of care in the event of a caesarean section – maybe it's important for you to have a partner in the operating room or the opportunity for you or your partner to have skin-to-skin with the baby. If there is a risk that there will be a lot of births in the hospital, consider a backup hospital. And consider where you would like to give birth if the birth starts prematurely.
- Think about when you will set off for the hospital, bearing in mind the distance and how you feel in places like this. Maybe you can find a midwife who will help you make the decision, or who you can call when labour starts? As Monica writes, it is worth "finding out what the policies are like in hospitals in your area, and deciding which one suits you best... collect birth stories from people who have similar expectations to you. Attending antenatal classes in the hospital I was planning to give birth in was very helpful for me. After the classes, I no longer had any doubts that this was the right place for me :)."

Just like all aspects of childbirth, it is worthwhile taking the time to choose where you will give birth, and to start the search in advance. The environment in which you give birth is one of the most important factors influencing the course of childbirth and your whole birth experience, so choose carefully and consciously. ◆

Anna – mother of two children, enthusiastic about the benefits of natural and home births.

57. Preparing for childbirth at home

The choice of where to give birth is primarily determined by safety. If you feel safe surrounded by a team of specialists and connected to monitors, hospital is the best choice. If familiar surroundings are important to you, a home birth may be a better choice.

How to decide. The decision on where to give birth should ideally be made together with the father. Even if he does not want to participate, it is important that he agrees on where it should happen.

The decision to give birth at home is not made only on the basis of what the mother wants. Strict criteria have to be met. During the entire pregnancy any risk factors that could complicate the birth will exclude this option. Midwives only agree to attend to home births if the pregnancy is low-risk. Here are some of the reasons why a woman may not qualify for a home birth:
- pregnancy complications (hypertension, diabetes, cholestasis), or chronic or genetic diseases,
- the baby is misaligned or there are twins (or more),
- the previous birth had a life-threatening issue or was a C-section,
- there is infection of the reproductive tract or other active infections,
- a past gynaecological operation,
- the mother is very young.

HOW TO PREPARE FOR A BIRTH AT HOME?

Physical and mental preparation. Getting ready for home birth is primarily a mental preparation. A woman should know her body well, have confidence in it and learn to interpret the signals coming from it throughout the pregnancy. This trust makes her feel calm and confident that the birth will go well.

I strongly encourage women who are expecting a child to talk a lot about it with their families. Find safe, friendly places where you will be able to share your emotions and doubts. These can be good antenatal classes, women's clubs or birth groups.

The choice of midwife. A woman planning to give birth at home should undergo regular health tests, as well as on the baby. A very important element of preparing for birth at home is getting to know the midwife and being able to discuss all important issues with her and those who will be present at the birth. It is worth taking the time and energy to choose the right midwife, one who will treat the birth as a natural process and intervene as little as possible. Her job is to support the mother, tell her what is happening and let her know what may happen next.

If you decide on a home birth, start looking for a midwife to support you through the birth as early as possible. You can settle and organize many issues with her help. If you decide ahead of time, she can bring a large ball, bean bag or birthing chair with her for the birth. She will also tell you what hygiene products and medical equipment she will have with her (e.g. a Doppler monitor, IV drips for rehydration, anaesthetic supplies, sutures).

Other supporting people. It's important you and your partner take the time to talk frankly about each other's expectations of the birth. Partners need clear information about how they can help – what they can do and at what stage of the birth. A partner who prepares for the birth because he wants to, is an invaluable support for the mother.

You may also consider inviting other women or people close to you to attend the birth, especially if the father is absent. You can also use the services of a doula, whose task it is to provide non-medical but emotional and physical assistance to the mother.

A birth at home is an amazing experience for the family. The intimate atmosphere makes it easier for the mother to bear the pains of childbirth and enjoy the first moments of a child's life. She is cared for and all her needs are met.

What to prepare for a home birth? A birth at home does not require much preparation. You will need a covering or sheet to cover and protect the surface on which you are going to give birth (floor, carpet, bed), a hospital sleeper chair ideally, large sanitary towels, towels, maternity pants or so-called 'adult nappies', paper towels, waste paper bag, massage oil and sterile gauze. You should also have a bag packed in advance in case you need to go to the hospital. Have a car ready and a charged phone on hand to call an ambulance if necessary. Before the birth, contact a neonatologist or paediatrician who will come to examine your baby after the birth (within 48 hours). Prepare your favourite snacks and meals to make the time more pleasant and give you the strength that you will need for the birth. Before the birth you can also arrange to rent a birthing pool if you want to give birth in water, but a typical bath is enough. You need a bathroom with hot water at all times. Bathing in the bathtub has a very soothing effect and can help relieve the pain of giving birth.

When the birth begins, call the midwife. She will be able to tell you over the phone at what stage the birth is and whether she should come over immediately. Of course, if you want her to come, she will come right away.

After the birth. Once the baby is born, the family has special time for themselves. During this time, the midwife checks the newborn baby and assesses its condition using the Apgar scale. A dozen or so minutes after the birth, the umbilical cord clenches on its own and can be cut, although it is not necessary (in the case of a lotus birth, the umbilical cord is not cut – the placenta is delivered naturally and remains attached to the baby until it is discarded). The uterus shrinks intensively and the placenta comes out together with the fetal membranes, which are checked carefully by the midwife. When the mother takes her baby, the midwife also assesses whether she has suffered any injuries during the birth which require attention. She writes out an information sheet about the birth and any procedures which have been carried out, and leaves a certificate of birth. Parents receive a health booklet and a newborn child immunisation card. Further care for the mother and child is taken by the community midwife who helps to arrange for the baby to be vaccinated. It is up to the parents to decide when the first vaccinations are given. With the help of a midwife or health visitor they can order the vaccinations at the Sanitary and Epidemiological Station, at the outpatient clinic or at the vaccination clinic. Screening tests can be carried out by the midwife during the postnatal visit. It is good to establish these details before birth.

Home births have been part of our cultures from the beginning of humankind. The decisions about how and where to give birth should be a conscious decision of both parents but it is often the woman who is the main driver of the birth because she trusts her body and wants to be in control. ◆

Agatha – pedagogue, speech therapist, traveller, mother of four children born at home.

My story

When we found out that we were expecting our first child, the thought of giving birth at home slowly began to grow in us. I was thinking about how I would like to welcome my child into the world and I shared it with my husband. He saw that I was convinced of this idea and he supported me.

We are a family living close to nature and in harmony with its rhythms. We treat pregnancy and childbirth as one of the elements of this life. The choice of a home birth was therefore a result of our lifestyle. We are very connected with each other, we trust each other, and the house provides us with an atmosphere of peace and security. Believing in active and intuitive childbirth, in the strength and wisdom of a woman, I had no doubts or fears about making the decision, especially because the pregnancy was fine and the baby was healthy. Together we started to plan the birth of our daughter like a family holiday and a very intimate event, something we wanted to experience at home. We felt that it would be the safest and most comfortable place for our little one and for me. I read a lot about home births, talked to other women, and prepared physically and mentally for active childbirth. We met with a midwife who specialises in home births and got to know a home birth association.

It started in week 40. I had waited a long time for Marta, but I was sure she'd pick the best moment. I woke up at 11:30 p.m., and I felt like I was leaking warm water. I was so excited! I had no idea what was going to happen to me or how long it would take. I called Chrissie, our midwife, and she calmly advised me to go to sleep. What do you mean, "sleep"?! I'm not going to fall asleep with these emotions! I turned on some music, turned on some lights and watched my husband sleep. About two hours passed and the pain started to become stronger and more regular. I could no longer think about sleeping or lying in bed. I was walking all the time. Around four o'clock I woke up my husband. I wanted him to be with me, although there was not much he could do. He was asleep, and I was swaying, imagining meeting our daughter.

About seven o'clock in the morning, I was very tired and sore. I wanted Chrissie to be with us. She came, examined me and said: "You have about 5-6 hours (4 cm dilated) ahead of you." I cried out of tiredness and resignation. I didn't think I could stand it any more. I started to experience weakness and pain. My husband was still close to me, and I closed my eyes. I was falling somewhere inside myself. He helped me sit a little in the bathtub with warm water, rocked and massaged me.

Then our second midwife arrived with fresh rolls for breakfast. She and Chrissie happily chatted about how beautifully I was giving birth, while I was sailing away. I don't know how much time passed, but I was on the verge of physical and mental exhaustion. Waves of pain flooded me one by one. This moment was the most difficult for me as a woman, as it required complete forgiveness – for myself and others. I wanted to get away from it, and yet I had to be there. I had to confront the pain and participate in it. I kept saying it was beyond my strength, and yet I was able to do it. I surrendered to the wisdom of nature. It was the time when I was born again as a woman – as a mother.

The girls saw that I needed a rest. They persuaded me to go to bed. The examination showed an 8 cm dilatation. I went to sleep. I was woken up by another wave of intense pressure and contractions. I saw that my husband was anxious. He asked the girls what was happening to me and heard that the contractions were causing high levels of oxytocin hormone in my body. It was time to give birth. They helped me slip from my bed to the birthing chair right on the ground. I was in a completely different world. Someone was stroking my head, someone was holding my hand, I was making some sounds... Everything happened so far away. I felt my body. I felt the body of a child. I felt that my husband was close. I felt like I had given in to some energy beyond me. The strength and character of the contractions had changed. I heard my scream. Right afterwards, I felt another life emerging from me. Then I experienced the power of love, the miracle of life, strength, and agility. My daughter's head was already outside. With another contraction, a warm, soft body came out.

After fourteen hours of an extraordinary journey, I could hug my little Marta. She was so calm. She looked at me and my husband with curiosity. The world stopped for us. It was the most beautiful thing it could have been. With my husband, under the affectionate care of Chrissie and Bozena, without haste, magically... Bearing a child changes you forever. Nothing has ever given me such power as the birth of our daughter. Home is a place where a person should be born, where the birth is most beautiful. And now our third miracle has been born here. ◆

Agatha – pedagogue, speech therapist, traveller, mother of four children born at home.

58. Who to give birth with? A companion in the delivery room

Who do you choose to accompany you to the birth? What can he or she do during childbirth? What qualities will be useful? Here's how to make a good choice.

Your choice of a companion says a lot about the approach to childbirth you are taking. Will it automatically be your husband / partner? Or someone else? Assuming that childbirth is a unique event of the utmost importance, it is worth making an informed choice.

What should you be guided by? Ask yourself the following questions:
- Do you feel safe and comfortable with this person, do you trust them?
- Is it a person who knows your personality, character and knows how you react in difficult situations?
- Does this person know your ways of dealing with stress and pain, do they know what helps you?
- Is it a person who will be able to go beyond his or her vision of giving birth and be able to control his or her emotions to follow your needs?

You can discuss the second and third points before the birth so that the accompanying person can prepare. It is important that they know your birth plan and what you care about. It could be that the criteria above will be met by a person not necessarily from your immediate surroundings or family, but perhaps a friend who has had a positive birth experience. Sometimes we instinctively trust a person who we don't meet often.

I think one of the most important points is the last one. Remember that this is your birth. Your needs and emotions are the most important during the birth. If you are worried that you will have to take care of your companion – if you are not sure of his or her behaviour – consider another candidate. Most mums seem to choose their partner, if our group is anything to go by. At the same time, many of them point out a very important point, which is the mutual consent to his or her participation in the birth. As one mum wrote: "Dad has the right to vote too." It is also worth noting that the presence of an accompanying person does not exclude the participation of a midwife or doula.

What is the role of an accompanying person? They should be present 'at your fingertips', keep an eye on your mental and physical condition, and follow your needs. If they see that you are tired or drained, they can offer you rest, a gentle massage, a change of position or activity, a snack or a drink. They should constantly support you: telling you that you are doing great, that they are ready to help. They should accept your emotions and behaviour unconditionally, taking care that your birth plan is followed as you – due to pain and emotion – may not be able to follow it. The role of an accompanying person is also to ensure that the midwife or doctor keeps you informed about the tests being carried out.

What can surprise a companion in childbirth? Above all, it may be surprising to see the untypical behaviour of the mum – it may be the first time a husband, sister or mother hears you screaming so loudly or using fruity language. Sometimes the strength of the mum, squeezing her companion's hand with all her might, can be surprising. A companion may also be surprised that their presence alone is enough, that the mother does not actually need physical or verbal support. Also the duration of the birth may turn out to be a surprise. The companion may feel that nothing is happening or that the process is far from the end. Then he or she needs to be patient, because the birth can take anywhere from a few to several – or even several dozen – hours.

Is it a difficult role to be a childbirth companion? It requires a little physical and mental endurance, but above all empathy, open-mindedness, and the willingness to support the future mother on her own unique path to motherhood. And the satisfaction of helping a mother give birth to a new life – priceless! ◆

Alexandra – psychologist, doula, Shantal Massage Instructor, Babywearing Consultant; mum to Remy, Casimir, Flora and Frederic.

My story

Probably most of us, when we get used to the idea that we are carrying a little miracle, wonder what the birth will be like. Especially with the first pregnancy, there are many fears and question marks. One of these questions usually comes up right at the beginning: will the dad want to participate in the birth? In our case, everyone was interested in whether Matthew would be at the birth and tried to influence our decision. Around week 12, I was on the phone with my husband's aunt (!) who was asking about my well-being, cravings and other pregnancy issues. She then added in a very serious tone: "I would like you to listen to an appeal from our family. Don't drag Matthew into the delivery room. There's nothing to see there, and for him it will just be unnecessary stress. I preferred giving birth alone, that's the most comfortable way." This conversation surprised me so much that I didn't know what to say – and I don't usually have a problem with a good comeback! I only said that it would be my husband's own decision whether or not he would like to participate in the birth. From the beginning I assumed that I would give him a free hand in making this decision – after all, he is an adult. He told me that he honestly didn't know and he had to think about it. I was surprised that anyone would think it's ok to meddle in such a private aspect of our lives as childbirth. When I told him about the conversation with his aunt, my husband just smiled and advised me not to worry. I knew, however, that during the upcoming family get-together this sensitive topic would be raised again... In the meantime, my husband's grandparents and uncle – who had been at the birth of his daughter not long before – talked about the birth (which wasn't easy) and kept saying that Matthew was "not to be persuaded to do all this". These comments and the stories they told over and over again irritated me, but there was no point in wasting time on discussions. I just let them talk, letting the "advice" slide.

About two months later, during another family event, the same aunt asked my husband directly: "Matthew, have you decided?" He didn't even have time to answer as the uncle interjected. "What does he have to say? She'll decide for him whether he'll be with her or not." I couldn't stand it any longer:"As far as I know, Matthew is not incapacitated and has the right to decide for himself. No one, including me, has the right to impose anything on him. And it's rude to stick your nose in such private matters."

The uncle shyly said that he liked this suggestion and the subject was closed.

It was not until the end of the pregnancy that my husband's grandmother (who had advised him strongly against taking part in the birth) said that a companion was needed in the delivery room, because "then the staff take better care of the mother than when she is alone." My family also said something similar. It struck me that all these comments were addressed to me alone! Nobody asked my husband's opinion. They all talked to me about it, and always when he wasn't around. Because I was supposed to be the one to decide. Me and only me. I didn't have the strength to explain to everyone again and again that it would be his decision, and his alone. I was just nodding my head, overwhelmed by all this advice: how, what, when and with whom to give birth.

And my husband... well, he's a very practical man. Before he made his decision, he attended all the prenatal classes, he discussed the issues raised there, he asked questions and listened carefully. He read the part about childbirth and the postpartum period in the book "Mums to Mums," he asked colleagues who had participated in the birth of their children about their impressions. Then one evening he told me that he wanted to accompany me. He felt that I would feel safer and more secure if he was there. He just wasn't sure if he would last to the end. You can't even imagine (or maybe you can :)) how moved I was by these words.

The end of the story is simple. Matthew was at the birth until the very end. He supported me incredibly – I don't know if I could have done it without him, because it was difficult. And at the end, he cut the umbilical cord with great pride and care.

I wanted this story to see the light of day, because I'm pretty sure that I wasn't the only one who experienced such a situation. And as you know, the awareness that you are not alone helps in certain situations. Finally, some small advice: almost everyone we meet during pregnancy will have a ready-made solution or opinion for you, because it worked well for them, or good advice, because – after all – this has been happening since the beginning of time and there is nothing else to think about. And you... nod your head and listen. The most important thing is to talk with your partner! Then nobody and nothing will be able to break you and you will be happy. And that's all that matters! ◆

Daria – happy wife and even happier mum.

59. Occupation: Midwife

During your pregnancy you are likely to meet different midwives. They will be the women (and sometimes even men) who will weigh you and make an entry in your pregnancy card during your visit to the obstetrician. One of them will help you give birth to your baby and will visit you at home after the birth to answer your questions.

What is a midwife? Currently, in order to practise the profession of midwifery in most countries, you need to complete at least three years of bachelor's studies and receive the right to practise as a midwife. Midwives can work, among other places: in hospitals, birthing centres, at home births, in out-patient clinics (as a family midwife), in obstetric or gynaecological offices, lactation clinics, antenatal schools, as well as at universities (e.g. research projects) or local government bodies.

Choosing a midwife. Every woman, regardless of her age, should have a midwife. If you are able to have a choice you should choose your midwife consciously by submitting a written declaration of choice – in many countries you can do this at the office of the chosen midwife or at your GP practice.

When choosing a midwife, pay attention to the range of services she provides (e.g. whether she does prenatal education and home visits), whether she will come to your home if necessary, whether you get on with her well and whether she has time to tell you about herself and her care. How do you check this? It is best to meet her in person or, if that's not possible, talk to her on the phone. You can also consult other mums, but here you have to remember that everyone has different requirements and needs – something that will be great for one woman may not be right for another.

Midwife care during pregnancy. A midwife is fully competent to lead a pregnancy and visits to the midwife are not significantly different from visits to a obstetrician – during the visit the midwife will also carry out an interview, confirm the pregnancy, examine you, take a cytology test, measure your blood pressure, heart rate and weight, make a KTG/CTG record, issue referrals for blood and urine tests and assess those already done, and can often issue a certificate that you are pregnant, and if you have a suitable course, issue a prescription for certain drugs. In the case of abnormalities, she will refer you to an obstetrician. Generally she will also refer you to an obstetrician for an ultrasound examination because only a few midwives carry this out.

In most countries, you can choose between taking on a midwife privately or going through the national health system. Most midwives leading the pregnancy have their own office, which is very similar to that of an obstetrician's, and it is there that visits take place. You make an appointment with a midwife just as you do with a doctor.

According to the Guidelines of Perinatal Care, an obstetrician is obliged to refer every pregnant woman after week 21 to her family midwife for additional care (apart from the doctor leading the pregnancy). It is worth making an appointment with your midwife for prenatal education. In some countries you can have weekly appointments between week 21 and 31 and two appointments per week between week 32 and the date of birth.

Such appointments can take the form of both individual and group meetings (prenatal classes). If you want the same midwife to visit you after the birth, make sure that she also does home visits.

The role of the midwife during childbirth. If the birth is healthy, the midwife is responsible for guiding you through it from start to finish. The doctor often only appears if something irregular or concerning happens, and after the birth to assess the placenta and possibly stitch larger perineal wounds. The midwife guides you through every stage of the birth, performs the necessary medical activities, but also supports you emotionally, massages your back, helps you get into the best positions, coaches you in how to breathe properly, offers various forms of pain relief, and can help you feel that you are doing well.

It will probably be her, not the doctor, who will deliver your baby. She's the one who will show you your baby for the first time, put it up to your chest, and show the dad how to cut the umbilical cord.

In some hospitals and countries you can "buy" individual midwife care. Then the midwife will only have you in her care during the birth and can devote her full attention to you and your baby. A midwife who is on normal duty usually has two or three babies under her care (depending on the hospital). You may also be accompanied by a doula in the delivery room (▶ I – 60) – this is a woman who does not have a medical education, but has undergone the appropriate training.

In some countries, home deliveries by midwives are becoming increasingly popular. Unfortunately, this is not a free service. You should decide on a home birth early enough to have time to prepare for it (▶ I – 57), but also to find a midwife in your area who can take on the birth. The decision as to whether a woman can give birth at home is made at the end of the pregnancy by the midwife who is in charge of the birth.

The midwife's care after the birth of a child – home visits. Your midwife should visit you within the first 48 hours after you leave the hospital or on the next working day after receiving your application. The hospital should send a written notice to the midwife that a baby has been born and that her parents have indicated her as the chosen midwife. It is therefore a good idea to make the choice ahead of time and to notify the midwife by phone while you are still in hospital – this speeds up your first visit considerably. It varies from country to country, but in some countries the midwife can visit you 4 to 6 times during the first 6 weeks after the birth. The number of visits depends on your needs, but also on the health of the mother and child and the opinion of the midwife. Remember that home visits are a right for the mother and child, which they can (but do not have to) use, while for the midwife they are an obligation. This means that parents can (in writing) opt out of such visits at any stage, while the midwife must allow parents to have such visits if they wish, and must record any refusal in the documentation together with the signature of the child's mother or legal guardian.

During the visits, the midwife, among other things, collects the history of the mother and the newborn baby, reads the hospital records, assesses the baby, helps with any breastfeeding difficulties, checks the general condition of the mother, makes sure that the uterus is as it should be, that there is no problem with the breasts, that any perineal wounds or caesarean section wound heal properly. If she has completed the appropriate course, she can remove the stitches at home. She also assesses the mother's mental state, family relations, and the conditions in which the mother and child are staying. Of course, she is also an emotional support for you – she will answer the questions and confirm your conviction that you are good parents. The midwife notes everything in the documentation.

You can write and write about the midwifery profession. The most important thing is that you know that a midwife is for you. With her factual knowledge, emotional and spiritual support and warm words, she will help you at different stages of your life. So take a moment and just as you deliberately and carefully choose your obstetrician, choose your midwife to be your actual support and help. Meet her before the birth or pregnancy, so that you know what care you can count on, and don't be afraid to ask her for help. ◆

Isabel – qualified midwife.

60. Occupation: Doula

The word doula comes from the Greek word for 'woman's servant'. A doula is an educated and experienced woman who provides continuous, non-medical, emotional, informative and physical support for you and your family during pregnancy, childbirth and after the birth.

What does a doula add to the pregnancy and birth? Many women believe that the presence of a loved one is sufficient support during childbirth. Not everyone knows the difference between the support offered by a midwife (▶ I – 59) and a doula. It is up to you to decide who you choose to give birth with and depends mainly on how you imagine the birth and what you want from your surroundings. Both the midwife and the doula provide comprehensive care for you and their roles complement each other, while their responsibilities are completely different.

How many people can be in the birthing room with the mother depends on internal hospital regulations – sometimes when all the attendees can be in the room at the same time, sometimes they have to do it in such a way that only one person can be with the mother at any given time. A doula works in her own capacity, and is not bound by any contract with any maternity hospital or clinic. You sign the contract with the doula individually, and the choice of the contract is determined by your personal preferences and the availability of the doula during the period when the birth is due to occur. During home births, the number of accompanying persons is limited only by the mother – it is she who decides who she wants to have with her and how many people she needs during the birth.

This is what you can expect from a doula. She:
- is exclusive to you,
- provides continuous non-medical support during childbirth, regardless of its duration, course and end (medical intervention, instrumental birth or Caesarean section),
- follows your needs,
- takes care of your individual birth plan,
- provides support (non-medical),
  - provides you with information about maternity hospitals, acquainting you and the person accompanying you with the course of the birth, medical procedures, etc.,
  - mental – helps to recognize and determine your mental needs and focus on the most important ones; helps to create a birth plan,
  - emotional – helps to understand your emotions (sometimes surprising in their strength, sometimes contradictory) during pregnancy, childbirth and the postpartum period,
  - physical – helps with touch, massage (during pregnancy, childbirth and postpartum), uses non-pharmaceutical ways to relieve birth pain, can help with taking a shower or changing position,
  - unconditionally accepts all your needs, emotions, choices. A doula deals with your world of emotions, thoughts and beliefs.

A doula and a midwife do not work interchangeably, but they can complement each other perfectly in meeting your needs.

What do doula services include?
- One or two preliminary meetings, during which you get to know the doula, discuss the birth plan and agree on the conditions of your partnership.
- Accompaniment during childbirth. Usually you will keep her informed by phone about your symptoms, which may be a harbinger of the birth. You

discuss the moment when the birth begins and whether you need direct help. The doula arrives at your home, where you stay in case of a home birth or to the hospital/birthing centre together. Regardless of the duration of the birth, the doula accompanies you until the end of stage 4 of the birth.
- During the contract period, the mother is in constant contact with the doula.
- Often after childbirth, one more meeting is organised in order to discuss the birth and end the partnership.

To sum up: if you want multifaceted support on the road that is childbirth, a road which can be simple, but can also be winding and bumpy, and if you can afford it financially, it is worthwhile to opt for additional midwifery and/or doula services. Women who employ their services often enjoy a greater sense of security and comfort, knowing that in difficult moments they could count on their mental and physical help, and that the task of the accompanying persons was to ensure that their needs were respected and that the birth plan they had prepared would be taken into account. ◆

Alexandra – psychologist, doula, Shantal Massage Instructor, Babywearing Consultant; mum to Remy, Casimir, Flora and Frederic.

61. Birth plan — oxymoron or useful practice?

At first, the term "birth plan" sounds absurd. After all, birth is a force of nature. However, a good birth plan is neither a wish list nor an exact scenario of events. Instead, it can be an effective way to help communicate with medical personnel, and preparing it will help you define your expectations for the birth and broaden your knowledge of standard procedures and treatments. As Harriet said, a birth plan "helps to systematise our knowledge about the birth and lets us decide how we really want to give birth."

What does a birthing plan contain? It is a document in which you set out your preferences for care during the birth and describe your attitude towards medical procedures. For example, you may want to avoid induction or acceleration of the birth and administration of oxytocin, or you may want perineal protection and would like to take a vertical position during the second stage of labour. There is also room for non-medical aspects of care: requests to dim the lights, the possibility to play your music, limiting the number of people in the room and the presence of a companion. You can also write down your expectations for the care of your baby. Which treatments may be performed and which do you not want? Do you want your baby to be bathed (according to current guidelines, babies should not be bathed in the hospital unless the mother has HCV (hepatitis C) or HIV, in which case they should be bathed immediately after birth in a special liquid). Would you like to dress your baby in your clothes or hospital clothes?

When do you make the plan? The birth plan should be ready with the nursery. Starting in the middle of the pregnancy, you will have time to read through or watch some guidelines. The birth plan can also help you choose the place where you'll give birth, so it is a good idea to have it with you and discuss it with your midwife during your visit to the hospital.

Where do I start? Find out about your rights during the period around the birth and what the facility offers. You can find this information on government websites and it should be on your hospital's website as well.

Analyse the available options, risks and benefits of each solution. Imagine yourself in different situations and think about what will help you have a good birth experience.

Who can help you with the plan? It could be your doctor, or it could be the person who teaches at antenatal school, or the midwife or doula you choose to assist you at the birth, or your midwife (▶ I – 59, 60), as part of free prenatal education. This can also be the person who will accompany you during the birth. They should know your birth plan so that they can support you effectively in communicating with staff or provide appropriate care for your baby if, for some reason, you are unable to do so.

Ask for help, especially if you feel scared by the thought of medical interventions or if you are overwhelmed by the amount of information and feel like you want to quit all this planning.

What should be the plan? Best is for it to be short and clear, but also designed in an appropriate way. Two A4 pages should be fine. Divide the plan according to the stages of childbirth or aspects of care, and devote a separate section to each 'care'. Use positive words and phrases: "please", "I would like" instead of "I don't want". Consider the technical conditions in the hospital, like the availability of a bathtub for childbirth or a family room, as well as the availability of anaesthesia or epidurals. On issues of key importance to you, be firm. For example, you may not want them to feed your baby with formula milk without consulting you.

Plan A, Plan B and Plan CC? Be prepared for the possibility of a cesarean section. If this is already the plan, you may also have expectations of the care for you and the baby. A plan gives you more insight into the procedures at the hospital: when does the first skin-to-skin contact take place, when can the mother feed her baby for the first time, can an accompanying person kangaroo the baby, etc. Don't treat the birth plan as a dream scenario, but "use it to analyse all possible situations and options," as Beth says.

Presentation of the birth plan. When you arrive at the place you're giving birth, give them the plan. It will be attached to your medical records and then it will be placed in the delivery room with the midwife who will accompany you. Or you can give it directly to the midwife in the delivery room. The birth plan is in itself a message that you want to make informed decisions about you and the baby.

Difficulties in implementing the plan. Even if you expect your plan to be difficult to implement due to the way the staff work, try not to be negative. Make your expectations clear and make sure that your companion also knows what you want. During childbirth, you are a team and your goal is a successful birth. Ensuring you are comfortable with your birth plan is one way to do this.

Flexibility. When discussing the plan, a lot of mums emphasise that childbirth is a dynamic process. The implementation of the plan is not a goal, but it can help make the experience of childbirth as positive as it can be. Even if everything goes differently than you planned, you will have had an influence on the decisions made.

What if the birth plan is not respected? Preparation of the birth plan and the pursuit of its implementation by hospital staff is good practice, regardless of its legal status. My experience shows, however, that you are not always properly respected during childbirth, but it doesn't mean that once the birth is over you can't do anything about it. You can complain to the hospital management, to the Ministry of Health or the Patient Ombudsman. If they don't help, you can go to court. There are foundations and organisations you can turn to for help and support when writing your complaint.

Due to the dynamic nature of childbirth, the process of planning, preparing and rethinking certain issues may prove more valuable to you than the plan itself. ♦

Anna – mother of two children, enthusiastic about natural and home births.

62. Pack up! What to take to the birth?

Ideally you should have the delivery bag packed about 4-5 weeks before the due date. You will be calmer if the birth starts earlier and you don't have to run around the house in a panic to look for things at the last moment. You still have time to check what the hospital requires.

What documents do you need to take? The documentation is very important, and the lack of any documentation may cause you or your partner to be sent home from the hospital. Keep them with you at all times:
- ID card,
- proof of insurance,
- a pregnancy history card.

Attach the following test results to the documents:
- blood type and Rh factor, plus testing for anti-Rh antibodies (both for Rh- and Rh+),
- recent CBC (complete blood count) and urine test,
- results of virological tests from the third trimester of pregnancy: HBS, HCV, HIV, syphilis, CMV antigen. Toxoplasmosis and rubella tests are also useful – these may be from the first trimester,
- the results of all ultrasound examinations done during pregnancy, most importantly the last ultrasound,
- the result of GBS (Group B Strep), a routine vaginal and rectal swab test performed after 35 weeks of pregnancy,
- results of other important examinations or consultations, e.g. ophthalmology, cardiology, orthopaedics.

What kind of things need to be packed? Check the website of the hospital where you are going to give birth and read the hospital's guidelines for what you need to pack. If you live near the hospital, try to pack everything in one bag, dividing it into things for you, things for the baby and things for your companion.

MUST HAVES
Things for mum. You can divide them into things you need for the birth and things you need after the birth, with after-birth things at the bottom of the bag.
For the birth:
- clothes: shirt or longer t-shirt – what you feel best in, a bathrobe or a cardigan, warm socks, slippers,
- big thick pads,
- tissues,
- a hair tie or hairband,
- a cotton handkerchief or flannel to wipe your face,
- a moisturising lip balm (lips often dry out),
- non-carbonated drinking water,
- favourite snacks – just in case,
- cosmetics, shower slippers, towel, disposable panties – after birth you will have to wash up and prepare for the move to the postnatal room.

After the birth:
- buttoned or zip down shirt, comfortable to feed,
- a few pairs of underwear – preferably mesh ones that dry quickly, or disposable,
- toiletries (toothbrush, toothpaste, hair brush), cosmetics (mild body lotion, shampoo, hand cream),
- 2 towels and shower flip-flops,
- 20 large postnatal sanitary pads,
- a breastfeeding pillow – useful for feeding,
- 2 feeding bras and breast pads,
- nipple ointment,
- something to eat – if you give birth at night, you'll be waiting for a meal until morning,
- phone and the charger,
- camera,
- a book or magazine,
- coins for drinks or coffee from the vending machine.

Things for the dad or companion:
- comfortable clothes and slippers (sometimes a disposable set is required – apron, mask, shoe protectors – which are available in the hospital),
- coins for drinks or coffee from the machine,
- camera or a charged phone,
- sandwiches, drinks, snacks.

Things for the newborn for a three-day hospital stay:
- the smallest-sized nappies,
- 3 cotton T-shirts or bodysuits,
- 3 cotton hats or beanies and one warmer, without ties,
- 3 bodysuits or babygrows, long or short sleeved, depending on the season,
- 2-3 pairs of socks,
- newborn care cosmetics (▶ I – 15, 16), wet wipes,
- bath towel (may not be necessary. According to current standards of perinatal care, babies are not bathed in the hospital.),
- a blanket or a blanket wrap.

Remember, everything for the baby should be washed beforehand in delicate baby powder (read the ingredients!). How to pack them? Alexandra has some advice here, from her experience: "I recommend packing 3-4 baby sets (socks, babygrows, lightweight hats) into closable bags so that it's easy to take them out and have everything ready."

Extra things that might come in handy for you:
- cosmetic spray water to refresh your face,
- thermos for ice cubes,
- massage instruments, massage oil and your favorite essential oils,
- music,
- breast pump – decide whether you want a manual or an electric one, besides, as Ursula writes: "It's worth learning how to assemble it at home before you pack it",
- a spare blanket for the baby,
- coffee, tea, your own mug and spoon,
- a hairdryer.

You may want other, personal things. Martina writes: "For me a pregnancy sleeping pillow turned out to be a hit, suitable for feeding and for sleeping with my baby." Things that you don't take to the hospital, but may come in handy, arrange at home so they can be found by others more easily. It's worth involving your partner in packing your bag, so that he knows where everything is.

Things better not taken to the hospital:
- a postpartum belly wrap for the abdomen and silicon gel pads for your nipples- these may get you in trouble with your midwife,
- postpartum 'donut' cushion or pillow – currently it's not recommended by either gynaecologists or physiotherapists,
- ordinary cotton underwear – it can happen that the midwife tells you to change them for mesh underwear that are better ventilated (important after the birth),
- toys for newborns, mobiles over the cot, teddies – they are absolutely useless in this situation, and they will carry a bunch of hospital bacteria home with you.

Leaving the hospital. If you're coming home by car, don't forget the newborn baby seat. Dress your baby according to the season and the weather. Remember to pack looser clothes for you, you won't fit into your favourite jeans right away! ♦

Eve – mum of a patchwork family, raising two teenagers and a 3-year-old girl.

63. Is this it? How you know when the birth has begun?

As the due date approaches, fear starts to encroach on the joy you've been feeling. First time mothers usually have the greatest anxiety simply because they don't really know what to expect. Their most common question is: "How will I know it's time?"

The first symptoms of impending childbirth appear a few weeks before. Remember, however, that not every woman will show all the symptoms that herald an impending birth. Watch your body, and the changes taking place in it, carefully, as some are very subtle.

EARLY SYMPTOMS OF IMPENDING BIRTH
Small blotches. A few or several days before the birth, you may notice delicate pinkish or red streaks of mucus on your underwear. These are small, single blood vessels which colour the vaginal discharge.

Braxton-Hicks contractions. A few weeks before the birth, pregnant women may feel so-called 'false contractions'. The purpose of these contractions is to stretch the lower part of the uterus so that the baby's head can position itself on the pelvic floor. The Braxton-Hicks contractions are usually short and irregular and also cause pain in the lower abdomen. However, they are often eased by movement, body posture or bathing in warm water, which makes them different from birth cramps.

Diarrhoea. A harbinger of an approaching birth is also a loose stool, which often takes the form of diarrhea. This effect is due to the action of prostaglandins, which are secreted in the initial phase of labour. Emptying the large intestine is designed to help the baby get through the birth canal, which is adjacent to the large intestine.

A wolf's appetite. Some pregnant women have an unrestrained desire to eat a few days before the birth. It is likely that this is the body starting to store energy before a difficult task ahead.

The baby's weaker movements. A few dozen hours before birth, the baby can become much calmer and its kicks get lighter. This is a sign that the birth canal is starting to get tight and the baby is preparing for the effort of being born. However, if you are concerned about this, consult your doctor.

Pain in and around your lower back. Many future mums complain of a blunt pain in their back, thighs and groin a few days before the birth. It is caused by the head of a child putting pressure on your nerves and pushing themselves down into the birth canal.

It feels weird. A couple of days before the birth the feeling of being pregnant may change. Some women feel fear and anxiety, others euphoria. Some have growing fatigue, while others have a sudden surge of energy that makes them feel like doing something thorough like cleaning, washing windows, redecorating the house or shopping. This is a common "nesting" syndrome – preparing the family home for its newest member.

The mucus plug. Throughout the pregnancy the cervical outlet is closed by a layer of thick, compact mucus. It forms a barrier protecting the inside of the uterus against contamination, bacteria and viruses. When the cervix begins to dilate, the mucus is expelled. It is usually colourless, although sometimes it can be coloured with some blood.

The departure of the mucus plug does not necessarily mean that the birth is close, so you don't have to go to the hospital right away. It can happen anytime from two weeks to a few hours before the birth.

Lowering of the pelvic floor. A few weeks before birth, the baby's head moves towards the pelvic floor, taking a convenient position to lower the uterus. The lowering of the uterine floor makes it easier for the mother to breathe, as the enlarged uterus no longer presses on her lungs to such an extent. Before the birth, heartburn and stomach ailments often disappear as the pressure on the stomach also decreases. However, the lowering of the uterus may increase the feeling of pressure on the bladder.

Waters leaking or breaking. The moment fetal water (amniotic fluid) is discharged gives you the feeling of a watery, transparent liquid flowing out of your vagina – you may be surprised to see that it can drip for a long time. At the end of the pregnancy, wear pads so that you can check if it is urine or amniotic fluid (from the smell). You can also take a wet pad to the hospital with you so that the midwife can do the test, or you can buy special strips at the pharmacy to check for the presence of amniotic fluid. If the water hasn't broken, the birth may not happen quickly – the doctor will make a judgment. The fetal waters often break during the final stage of labour. Sometimes the doctor must help with this by piercing it with a special tool. This is not a painful procedure for mother or child. It can also happen that the waters burst a few or several dozen hours before birth. If the fetal waters are green, yellowish or brownish in colour, you should go to the hospital immediately, because a quick medical consultation is needed.

Cervical dilation. A few weeks or days before the birth the cervix begins to shorten and slowly dilate. The rate of shortening and dilation of the neck of the cervix is different from woman to woman. A full opening during childbirth is considered to be 10 cm.

How do you recognise birth contractions? From the moment the first contraction occurs, measure the duration of the contraction and the interval between contractions. The first contractions are usually:
- short, lasting about 30-40 seconds,
- occur every 15-20 minutes,

- not very painful, resembling menstrual pains; these will get stronger with time, but the rate varies from person to person.

It is important to observe the dynamics of your contractions. If, for example, you have two contractions every 20 minutes at the beginning and then two every 10 minutes and the next one every 5 minutes, it promises to be a fast birth and you may not have time to get to hospital. However, when the contractions are less frequent – every 15-20 minutes – and the frequency of the contractions does not increase during the following two hours, there's still some time until the birth. ◆

Marika – mother of three, midwife, lactation educator.

My story

What does birth look like? Remember what you saw in the movies and on TV. The heavily pregnant protagonist is walking down the street / sitting in a meeting at work / going shopping when suddenly she screams, grabs her stomach and shouts "I'm having a baby". Then she rushes to the hospital, and the next moment we see her with a delightful pink baby in her arms. If the scriptwriters want to add a bit of realism, they show a few more scenes with screams in a comfortable bed.

During antenatal classes, I was told that such scenes have little to do with reality. I heard that, when birth begins, young mothers – especially first-timers – can often panic terribly. I was told not to go to the hospital during the first contractions, but to take a few deep breaths and get in the bathtub. But if it's your first time, you don't know what to expect, and on top of this you're supposed to time the contractions…

So, when I felt something strange in my belly around midnight, I just thought to myself that Thai soup probably hadn't been the best idea. I completely didn't expect that I would be cradling my baby in less than three hours. After half an hour I was saying that I was in labour, but everyone told me not to panic. So I followed the advice I had been given and I got into the tub. That's when a memorable dialogue with my husband took place.

Husband: Maybe we should go to the hospital?
Me: No, they told me not to panic. Give me a moment.
Husband: Maybe we should though – doesn't it hurt?
Me: It hurts, but it's supposed to hurt. Don't panic.
Husband (quietly, but also nervously): The hospital?
Me: No, no, one more contraction.
Husband: Should I call the ambulance?
Me: CALL!!!

When I finally managed to convince the person on duty that I really did need an ambulance, the relief was so great that I hardly had any room for other emotions.

I realise that the thought of a sudden birth can seem terrifying. However, I'd like to frame it in terms of benefits. My whole birth took less than three hours. While waiting for the ambulance, I was terrified and convinced that in a moment, contrary to plan, I would give birth at home. But after the arrival of the paramedics, any fear evaporated. I arrived at the delivery room half-naked (it was November). The doctor was not very nice. I gave birth in a gynaecological chair. It was definitely too late for anaesthesia, so I didn't have to think about it. I did not use the services of a private midwife, because there was no time for that. But none of that mattered. The fact was that when other women were just starting to feel pain, I already had a newborn at my breast. ◆

Olga

---

64. Ouch! Methods for relieving labour pain

Pain is an inseparable part of every birth. Whether you give birth naturally or by caesarean section, birth always hurts. However, it is a kind of 'good' pain, after all it is thanks to this pain that your baby comes into the world.

The sensation of labour pain is highly influenced by your level of anxiety and stress. Stress triggers anxiety, anxiety causes increased muscle tension, and this makes the pain more marked – the so-called catch-22 situation. This is a kind of vicious cycle that most of us fall into, but... you can try to prevent it.

Which labour pain relief methods you choose depends mainly on you. If you have dreamed of giving birth naturally, you can use non-pharmacological methods to relieve pain, but if you are not so close to nature, you can use medical methods.

NATURAL METHODS OF RELIEVING LABOUR PAIN

Support – mental support can work wonders. Whether it be your partner, mother, sister, friend, doula or midwife, it is important to feel safe and cared for. If you would prefer not to give birth alone, try to find someone to accompany you. Forcing your husband to be with you, if he doesn't necessarily want to be there (not because he doesn't feel like it, but because he is simply afraid) is not the best thing to do, because instead of supporting you, he may actually annoy or upset you. Choose someone who you trust and whose support you can count on.

Relaxing the body (conscious breathing) – if you went to antenatal classes, you will know what I'm talking about. If not, the midwife in the delivery room will instruct you how to do it. Otherwise, your body will often tell you how to breathe. Try to breathe in through your nose and out through your mouth, slowly, calmly, at your pace. Breathing too fast, or vice versa, will only cause extra muscle tension and thus more pain.

Massage during childbirth – performed by your companion or the midwife. A massage of the sacro-lumbar region performed correctly (you can learn it at the antenatal classes or ask for instructions from a midwife or someone in the delivery room) can significantly relieve the pain and help you relax. However, remember that the midwife who is conducting the birth, despite her good intentions, may unfortunately not have time to do it, so ideally your companion will be able to do it.

TENS machine (Transcutaneous Electrical Nerve Stimulation) – consists of electrodes that are stuck to the lumbar and sacral region of your back. The low-frequency impulse helps to alleviate some of the labour pain very effectively. Unfortunately, not many facilities have this device, but you can rent it for a small fee in medical shops or physios and buy your own electrode pads.

The effect of hot and cold – mainly by means of wraps or a warm (not hot) shower. Small heat packs with cherry stones or wheat, which can later be used for your baby, can be great here. Hot or cold packs can also be used in the sacro-lumbar region or on the perineum.

Changing positions – it is an important point. You know how hard it is to stand in one position at the end of pregnancy, let alone when it hurts terribly! Be active, walk, crouch, wring your hips, kneel, sit, stand – whatever you want. If there are no obstetric indications to lie down, you are only limited by your imagination. Also consider giving birth in a vertical or horizontal position – on your side. There are several vertical positions, the most popular of which are: crouching, standing or kneeling. However, if you would like to give birth standing, but your legs refuse to obey you, don't insist – try another position. Discomfort also causes stress, and, combined with this anxiety and pain... and so on.

Equipment in the room – each delivery room should have birthing balls, stools, bean bags, mattresses and various types of wedges, which can be used to relieve labour pain. Try jumping on the ball, and if that doesn't help, lie down comfortably on the bean bag.

Water immersion – in the bathtub or in the shower. This relaxes you, helps empty your bladder, and adds a feeling of lightness. Before giving birth, find out what the hospital has available, as not every hospital has a bath (although some even have a whirlpool!). If you have dreamed of giving birth in water, be sure to find out if the place has this option, and be aware that it's not always possible – if, for example, you have a genital infection – then look for an institution or midwife who has experienced delivering such births.

Sounds – screaming, panting, groaning and even... singing! If it helps you, there are no limits to making any sound you wish. It is important, however, that in the second stage of childbirth all the sounds are converted into a thrusting force, because – with the screaming – precious air 'escapes' that you and your muscles need for the contractions to push the baby into the world. Some women remain silent during the entire period of childbirth, and silence can also be a 'remedy' for the pain of childbirth.

Music therapy, aromatherapy – in most hospitals there are music players available in the delivery room, and you can always take your headphones and player or phone with you. Favourite music relaxes, distracts and even motivates you. If you are particularly relaxed by a certain smell, if the hospital agrees to it, then go for aromatherapy – but the supply of it is entirely up to you.

Acupuncture, acupressure – they should be performed by qualified people.

MEDICAL METHODS FOR RELIEVING LABOUR PAIN
Painkillers and antispasmodic medication – administered only on the order of a doctor. If it is difficult for you to endure the pain and the contractions are getting stronger, you can ask your midwife for medication. It is extremely important to list in advance any allergies to medication which you might have. Most medicines during birth are given intravenously or intramuscularly. So if you want to use them, don't lean against the cannula. This is not only a way of administering medicines, but above all it is a safety net for you and your baby in an emergency, such as a life threatening situation.

Laughing gas – under the brand name ENTONOX, a mixture of nitrous oxide and oxygen in 50/50 proportions, often used in dentistry. It is completely safe for you and your child, and can be worth trying . Ask your midwife for instructions, because ineffective entonox breathing will not bring any results, only irritation.

Regional analgesia
- **Epidural Anesthesia** – most commonly used during childbirth. With appropriate dilatation, progressing birthand correct test results, you may be eligible for an epidural. You can ask the midwife for this anaesthetic, who will give your details to the doctors. The final decision is made by the obstetrician together with the anaesthesiologist. The standard operating procedure consists of puncturing the skin and inserting a thin catheter into the extradural space of the spine, through which drugs are administered. After delivery, the catheter is removed. The entire procedure lasts about

20 minutes and while it's taking place, cooperation between the mother and the anaesthesiologist is essential. Unfortunately not all women can use it. Absolute bans on its use are clotting disorders, some neurological disorders, allergy to drugs administered during anaesthesia, inflammation or a tattoo on the puncture site. The epidural provides the possibility of movement, and even though there is no pain, there remains the sensation of pushing. The dosage of the drugs by the anaesthesiologist is carried out in close cooperation with the midwife conducting the labour to spread their effects over time so that in the second stage of labour the anaesthesia works slightly less – all this so that you can push effectively. It is not true that the anaesthesia always slows down labour. However, if it is administered too early (poor systolic function, small dilation), it may actually slow down the labour action and then synthetic oxytocin will be necessary; however, very often during anaesthesia, women relax completely, which favours the development of dilation and labour progresses much faster. The most frequent complication of epidurals is a drop in blood pressure. The situation can be controlled quickly. The anaesthesia can also lead to a surgical birth (with the use of forceps or a vacuum), cause numbness in the legs or post-anaesthesia headaches. However, these complications are rare.

- Spinal block or anesthesia – consists of administration of a puncture to the lumbar-sacral section of the spine to the subarachnoid space. It is applied with a single puncture, without a catheter. Very rarely used during natural childbirth, in turn, usually used during caesarean sections.
- Combined spinal and epidural anaesthesia – combines the advantages of spinal blocks and epidurals. The subarachnoid component provides a very quick onset of pain relief and the epidural catheter provides quick extension of the relief and good postoperative anaesthesia. This anaesthesia is used for natural births and caesareans.

There are many ways to relieve labour pain. Whether you use them or not depends on you and your wishes. Preparing a birth plan (▶ I – 61) will certainly make it easier for the staff to choose the right methods for you, but remember that you can always change your mind during the birth and try something else. If you are in any doubt, talk to your midwife, your GP or the hospital before the birth. You will certainly receive accurate information, and this will keep you calm in the happy countdown of birth. ◆

Agnes – Pola's mum, midwife.

65. Cord blood — what we know to date

As parents, we do everything we can to protect our children from danger and disease – we transport them in the safest car seats, fit them with helmets, put safety gates on stairs and so many other things. Should we add umbilical cord blood collection and storage to the list? Or maybe it's just a business opportunity for companies engaged in it? What about public cord blood banks?

An objective approach to the subject is not easy in the maze of contradictory information and offers from cord blood storage companies. But let us try to understand the topic based on available scientific sources.

What is umbilical cord blood? Cord blood is the blood that's in the placenta and the umbilical cord connected to it. It is rich in haematopoietic stem cells, which can be used to treat certain diseases.

Other stem cell sources. Apart from umbilical cord blood, other sources of haematopoietic stem cells may be bone marrow and peripheral blood – not only for a child, but also for an adult. Another source, although ethically disputable, may be *embryonic stem cells* (ESCs). However, thanks to recent achievements in genetic engineering and biotechnology, stem cells can also be obtained from already differentiated cells like skin fibroblasts. They are called induced *pluripotent stem cells* (iPSCs) [1].

Conclusion: Cord blood is not the only source of stem cells and new methods of their acquisition are being researched.

Stem cell treatment. For some blood cancers (e.g. leukaemia, lymphoma, myeloma), as well as diseases such as haemoglobinopathy or primary immune deficiencies, a hematopoietic stem cell transplant can save a child or patient's life. The chances of success increase when the cell donor and the recipient (patient) have human *leukocyte antigens* (HLA) as similar as possible. In addition, if the antigens are fully compatible, the chances of success are slightly higher when using cells from umbilical cord blood than from bone marrow or peripheral blood. However it is important that the donor is healthy. For this reason, a sick child's cord blood will usually not help him or her, since most illnesses in which cord blood is currently used are genetic [2]. It is also worth noting that the amount of blood taken from one child's umbilical cord may not be sufficient for the treatment of an adult. For this reason, in adult transplants using cord blood, units of cord blood from various donors are usually used in order to maximize the chances of success.

There is growing evidence that hematopoietic stem cells can also be reprogrammed into cells of other tissues, which opens up further potential treatment options for diseases other than blood diseases [3], however, effective therapies may still be far away from being developed.

Conclusion: At present, blood stem cell therapy is applicable to only some diseases, mainly related to disorders of the blood and immune system. However, a child's umbilical cord blood can be collected for the exclusive use of the family if his or her siblings suffer from a disease that can be cured by a hematopoietic stem cell transplant.

Umbilical cord blood collection. The World Health Organization (WHO) recommends not cutting the umbilical cord earlier than 1 minute after birth, and preferably to wait between 1 and 3 minutes [5], unless a child needs immediate intervention. This recommendation is based on studies which indicate that the concentration of iron in the blood of a child is higher than in those with the umbilical cord cut earlier [6]. On the other hand, to obtain the highest amount and best quality of cord blood, it is important that this is done relatively quickly. Even a delay of 30 to 60 seconds has slight negative effects on its quality. However, waiting more than 1 minute for the cutoff significantly decreases its quality and volume [7].

Conclusion: the best moment to take new blood from the umbilical cord seems to be 1 minute before the umbilical cord is cut.

Private and public umbilical cord blood banks. Cord blood can be deposited in a private bank, for which you pay, and the blood is available to the child and his or her family. However, at present there is no convincing evidence for the efficacy of the use of one's own cord blood in treatments [8]. Moreover, many of the disorders that can be treated with the use of stem cells have a genetic background, so in this case the administration of your own stem cells may not only not help, but may even cause the relapse of the disease [9]. Research and clinical trials are carried out on the use of cord blood stem cells to regenerate other tissues. Moreover, cord blood can be donated to the public cord blood bank or for scientific purposes. Such a donation is free, but the exclusive right to its use is lost. Theoretically, it is available to patients from all over the world, whose antigens are similar, including the person who deposited the blood [10].

Thanks to public blood banking, it can be used by people who need it (including your child), regardless of whether they have donated blood to such a public bank or not.

However, some banks may still solicit such blood from their own funds or sponsors, so it is best to find out about this possibility in a hospital where you plan to give birth or directly in public cord blood banks in the area. If you are giving birth abroad, you can probably get this information from the hospital where you are planning to give birth in or from your doctor.

Stem cell transplants from cord blood, even in the absence of complete compatibility, are successfully used in the treatment of many severe haematological diseases, immunodeficiency disorders and hereditary metabolic diseases. The collection of umbilical cord blood in the case of healthy births is considered safe for the mother and her child. Cord blood collection for private purposes and storage in private/family cord blood banks is recommended when a family member (sibling or biological parent) suffers from a disease that can be cured by stem cell transplantation. In other cases, cord blood is not a guarantee and its storage is expensive. Please note, advertising for private cord blood banks can be misleading.

Umbilical cord blood donated to a public bank can be used for transplantation in patients who need it and have similar tissue compatibility. Additionally, it is worth adding that research on the reprogramming of 'normal cells' to obtain stem cells is very advanced, which opens up further possibilities for treating stem cells obtained directly from the patient or members of the patient's family. ◆

Kinga – passionate about research and scientific discoveries, mum to Maya.

66. The kid scored! About the Apgar score

The Apgar score was created by American paediatrician Virginia Apgar and is used to assess the general condition of newborns. The baby is evaluated in the 1st and 5th minute if it receives anything between 7 and 10 points on the Apgar score. If the newborn baby receives a medium score (less than 7 points) or severe (less than 4 points), then it is evaluated as many as 4 times, in the first, third, fifth and tenth minute of their life.

The assessment is made by a doctor or midwife, after the birth of the baby, at the moment when it is in contact with the mother's skin, or, if necessary, apart from the mother. Often parents receive information about their baby's Apgar score when they are informed about its birth weight and length.

A newborn baby is evaluated for 5 symptoms. A maximum of 2 points and a minimum of 0 points can be awarded for each criteria.

Newborn baby evaluation criteria:
- Skin colouring: 2 points are given when the baby is pink and 0 when it is blue.
- Heart rate: more than 100 beats per minute – 2 points, heart beat undetectable – 0.
- Reaction to stimulus (e.g. irritation of the foot): 2 points for crying or sneezing, 0 for lack of reaction.
- Muscle tension: correct tension gets 2 points, no tension or limp – 0 points.
- Breathing: correct breathing – 2 points, no breathing – 0 points.

Anything in between gets 1 point. A newborn baby can receive a maximum of 10 points.

What does the score say about his or her condition at birth?
- 8-10 points: the child born is in good condition,

- 4-7 points: medium condition,
- 0-3 points: severe condition.

If a baby is born in medium or severe condition, it is necessary to transfer the newborn to the neonatal pathology department or intensive care. Further action will be taken there.

It is important to remember that the Apgar score does not reflect the full health of the child. That is why various tests and examinations are performed in the hospital, such as a hearing test and a blood test for metabolic diseases. ♦

Kate – mother of a daughter, midwife, Certified Lactation Advisor. Since 2007 she has been dealing with issues related to infertility, efforts to have a baby, pregnancy, birth and breastfeeding.

67. Kangaroo care — wonderfully close to baby, straight after birth

You play the most important role in caring for your child, conveying your devotion, love and care even before the baby is born. And right after the birth, the best thing you can do is to convey all the positive emotions to your baby through a gentle, sensitive touch, creating an incredibly strong bond.

Kangaroo mother care (KMC), otherwise known as "skin-to-skin" contact. This term is "the result of observing the world of animals, especially kangaroos, which are born in an embryonic state and grow up and mature in their mother's pouch" [1]. In simple terms, kangarooing is "the handling of a child that enables direct skin contact between the mother/parent's and the child's skin by placing the child on the parent's body during and after hospitalisation (even applies to premature babies)" [2]. The originators of the kangaroo method were Edgar Rey Sambara and Hector Martinez Gomez, two extraordinary pediatricians who, in 1978, due to the lack of staff for the care of premature babies, were the first in the world to introduce this method of neonatal care in the hospital in Bogota, putting the premature babies on the chest of their mothers. This caused a sharp drop in the mortality rate of babies born prematurely! The method was also used in Europe in the 1970s, for example in Sweden. Scientific studies have confirmed the positive effects of the 'human incubator' on both children and parents.

Why "skin-to-skin"? The best developed sense in a newborn baby is touch, and the stimulation of the sensory system supports brain development in the baby. In the beginning, touch is the most important means of communication between a baby, its mother and the environment.

The benefits of KMC:
- for the child: reduces the risk of respiratory problems, supports lactation, promotes the exchange of bacterial flora with the parent, balances the heart rate and blood pressure, has a positive effect on thermoregulation and weight gain, reduces the frequency and length of crying, supports sleep, reduces stress levels, increases the level of endorphins, supports psychomotor and psychosomatic development,
- for the parent: reduces stress levels, increases endorphin levels, reduces the risk of postnatal depression, gets to know the child better through hearing, sight and touch, gives confidence. Kangarooing fosters a close relationship between the child and the parent, which satisfies the emotional needs of both.

How to kangaroo? A parent should take a comfortable semi-reclining position on an armchair or bed, a position which is optimal for the baby. It is best to position the newborn in such a way that its belly and legs rest on the adult's belly, so that it can better feel the movements of the parent's diaphragm. The baby's head should lie freely on its side in such a way that the cheek touches the mother or father's chest. A newborn baby is only wearing a diaper, so its bare breast lies on the skin of the parent.

Who can kangaroo and from when? This long-awaited moment of first physical contact should last at least 2 hours from the moment of birth, continuously until the first feed is completed, regardless of whether the birth took place naturally or by caesarean section. The performance of further procedures, such as delivery of the placenta, should not be an obstacle to kangarooing, and weighing and measuring the baby may take place later, after the first hugging and feeding is completed. According to general standards of perinatal care, "skin-to-skin contact may be interrupted if there is a threat to the life or health of the mother or newborn." In cases where the health of the child after birth requires medical intervention, kangarooing can begin in the following hours or days of the newborn's life.

Usually the first person to hug a newborn baby is its mother. However, if her health does not allow it, kangarooing may be started by the child's father or another person accompanying the birth.

How long can you kangaroo for? Carrying a child with you as close as possible, in the closest possible contact, can take place as long as the child and parent's physiological capabilities or household duties allow. Usually a newborn baby sleeps a lot in the first days of its life. Practically every nap can take place during skin-to-skin contact. You can kangaroo your baby while sitting, lying or even walking around, for example in a sling or baby carrier (▸ II – 36).

The natural need and desire for every person is to be hugged. Touch provides warmth, comfort, happiness and, consequently, a sense of security. The first moments after birth are very important and, at the same time, unique for the child and the mother, who, after an intensive effort such as birth, can feel warmth, rebalance their breathing and hear each other's heartbeat. It can be said that kangarooing is a method that allows you to return to the lifestyle of our ancestors, undisturbed by the development of civilisation. ◆

Agnes – mum to John, midwife, Babywearing Consultant.

68. Breastfeeding — preparation during pregnancy

You're probably wondering if you need to read about this subject. Fun fact: milk starts to be produced in the breasts as early as week 16, so if the baby is born prematurely, the mother is able to feed and the lactation can begin. If the breast milk of the mother of a premature baby and the mother of a full term baby are both tested, the composition would be different. The female body is full of magic and the composition of milk adapts to the baby's needs. Factors such as the season of the year or the health of family members are important in its production. If someone in the vicinity of a breastfeeding mother is ill, her body will automatically produce more antibodies in the milk. This is why babies who are breastfed are less likely to become ill or will have milder infections. Mums who are breastfeeding in tandem (i.e. older babies and younger babies at the same time) often observe that by pumping from both breasts at the same time, there will be slightly different-looking milk in each bottle, adapted to the individual needs of each of her children. Doesn't that sound like magic? That is why I encourage you to prepare yourself for breastfeeding. In fact, you are equipped with everything you need – breasts and, at the right moment, a small person.

Why prepare for breastfeeding? Unfortunately, because of factors such as media hype, 'family advice', women's lack of faith in their abilities, pressure and other things, breastfeeding can be more difficult than it should be. And this is not helped by the media presenting images of happy mothers easily feeding their babies. Some mothers will find it simple, but many others will encounter difficulties with their child attaching to their breast, and lactation problems can cause millions of doubts in the head of a young mother. At this point lots of advice appears. To find out what help is really beneficial in a given situation, it's important to know the basic principles of breastfeeding. After this, it's much easier to choose a trustworthy person to support you in your lactation journey.

Can you prepare yourself for breastfeeding? From my work and experience, I think you can, and the best time to learn is during pregnancy.

How to prepare for the 'milky way'? First of all, attend prenatal classes. There will certainly be a session on breastfeeding. The information given can very often be basic, but it's important. If you want to really get to grips with the topic of lactation, or if you want to dispel any doubts you might have, I recommend meeting with a community midwife or a certified lactation counselor. There are also women's groups which meet and talk about lactation. Look around your area, ask other mums. It is also very useful to read lactation guides and check out breastfeeding blogs. You will find different ways and approaches to breastfeeding.

There are plenty of books that are worthy of attention. One book I recommend is *Simply Breastfeeding* by Gill Rapley and Tracey Murkett.

What can surprise you in breastfeeding? Every woman is different. Breastfeeding is a science for both you and the baby. Early breastfeeding can take quite a long time and is repeated often, so women usually complain about pain in their nipples. It's worth taking care of them right away and, after breastfeeding, rub either a few drops of your own milk or lanolin on them. If you are in doubt as to whether your baby is managing properly, seek help from your midwife or a certified breastfeeding advisor right away.

Theoretical preparation for breastfeeding will reduce potential stress associated with lactation physiology. Women often worry that they 'don't have any milk'. But this is natural. In the first few days colostrum is produced, in relatively small quantities, but it's enough for the baby. After 3-4 days post birth (in the case of caesarean section, 5-6 days), a lot of milk starts to appear. Then a common cry is: "I have milk, but what should I do with it all?" The best solution is to feed your baby frequently.

Where to find help? If you are having problems and you are still in the hospital, ask your midwife for help. Go to the emergency room and ask if the midwife – or a certified lactation counselor – has a moment because feeding time is coming up in 10 minutes.

If you have already gone home you can get help from a community midwife, possibly during a paid visit. A list of midwives in your area will be online.

The problem is in your head. Statistically, most women can breastfeed. Only a small percentage of women will not be able to breastfeed their children. So assume you can breastfeed. Visualise a baby attached to your breast, in which there are hectolitres of milk. Take a calm, deep breath when putting your baby to your breast. If your baby cries, cuddle it and offer your breast again in a minute. Breastfeeding can take a lot of work, but it's worth it, because wherever you go with your baby, you'll always have milk on hand.

Find support. During pregnancy you can look for breastfeeding 'mates' or women who are at a similar stage of pregnancy to yours and will give birth at about the same time. Talking to other breastfeeding mums will give you plenty of support. Simply verbalising your difficulties and having someone listen to you will bring a lot of relief and motivation.

I wish you a happy 'milk journey' :) ◆

Kate – mother of a daughter, midwife, Certified Lactation Advisor. Since 2007 she has been dealing with issues related to infertility, efforts to have a baby, pregnancy, birth and breastfeeding.

THE POSTPARTUM PERIOD

69. The postpartum period — an important time after the birth. The physiological aspect

After childbirth a period known as postpartum (or puerperium) begins, which lasts at least 6 weeks regardless of your age, number of births, or the way the baby was born [4]. One mum, Magdalene, beautifully described postpartum as a time for 'lying down and regeneration', but it is also a period of adjusting to the needs of the newborn and entering into the role of a mother [11]. Magda writes: "This is a difficult time, sometimes worse than the birth itself. It is six weeks of getting back on your feet after the demands of pregnancy and birth."

The first day after childbirth — the hardest part can be the beginning.
The postpartum period can be divided into direct (first day after delivery), early (first week) and late (from week 2 to 8) [9]. This is a time of physiological changes, some of which may cause health problems that can impair your quality of life. The vast majority of complaints occur during the first few days and some can become more permanent. A lack of appropriate care during this time may result in the deterioration of a mother's health and that of their children, and sadly can even lead to death [11].

The postpartum period begins after the fourth stage of labour, which includes 2 hours after spontaneous birth or 4 hours after a surgical delivery (from the moment of birth, i.e. the placenta, umbilical cord and membranes [3]). If you have a natural birth in hospital, it is most likely that you and your newborn baby will be moved from the delivery room to the maternity ward. If the birth was by caesarean section, you will be transferred to the recovery room immediately after the completion of medical procedures. Then the newborn baby will be under the care of a family member or will be in the neonatal unit. A midwife will come to assist you with such things as breastfeeding and skin-to-skin contact (▶ I – 67). If you gave birth at home, you will be able to spend this time with your family in your own room.

In the first hours after the birth, you may experience ailments that affect you physically or psychologically [11]. You will probably be very tired, even exhausted, hungry and thirsty. You might be cold and shivery or you could be sweaty. Your body and shirt may be smeared with blood or amniotic fluid from the birth. After the birth you will experience vaginal secretions for several weeks which change colour and quantity, so you will need to wear large pads initially. These may fit into special disposable underwear. If you have had an episiotomy or caesarean section, you will have freshly stitched, healing wounds. You may have pain in your crotch and incision area, in the area of the abdominal wound after a caesarean section, or in your spine after the epidural. Some women feel pain from the contractions of the uterus muscle. There may also be some nipple pain during breastfeeding. You may have problems sitting on your own, standing, lifting, getting dressed, washing, using the toilet (you may feel anxious about having a poo) and be having problems breastfeeding. You may also feel many conflicting emotions, such as joy, euphoria, excitement and happiness turning suddenly to sadness, anger and anxiety (▶ I – 70). Your baby can behave in many different ways: it may be asleep and calm, or terribly hungry and constantly demanding to be breastfed.

Caesarean section surgery carries a four-times higher risk of complications for the mother than natural birth; therefore, after a caesarean section, the obstetrician will observe the mother closely [12]. This includes assessment of consciousness and observation of general condition including pulse, breathing, blood pressure, temperature, skin discolouration, increase of urination and faeces, assessment of the appearance of the abdominal dressing (which is removed on day 2 or 3, thereafter the wound is simply observed), assessment of obstetric condition (i.e. uterine contractions and genital bleeding) and finally assessment of the lactation process. If you give birth by C-Section, you will be given fluids and medicines as prescribed by your doctor, mainly pain relief, antibiotics, anti-nausea pills and, sometimes blood-thinners and others. Urine will be passed from your bladder using a catheter into a bag. The urinary catheter is removed on medical order, usually after the patient begins to have freedom of movement. The duration of your stay in the recovery room varies and depends on your condition and general hospital practices. Often it ends with the patient being discharged, at the earliest about six hours after surgery, sometimes after 10-12 hours [9].

Getting up and walking soon after the operation (and putting compression stockings on or using pneumatic pressure) is related to antithrombotic prophylaxis (drugs to prevent blood clots). There is not enough scientific evidence as to what are the optimal schemes of thromboprophylaxis in women after birth by caesarean section [10, 16]. Usually a patient, accompanied by a midwife, first gets out of bed several hours after delivery, balancing the need to rest after the operation with the amount of anaesthesia administered. Firstly, the sensory/motor blocking action of the anaesthetic has to recede. Anaesthesiologists have different opinions on the position in which the mother should lie on the bed after anaesthesia. Until recently, women have been encouraged to lie flat on their back; however recently some anaesthesiologists have allowed them to adopt any position except for that of bending the head to the chest and bending forward. At this time, drinking lots of water is beneficial. When first beginning to move, it is important to make small, slow movements, e.g. lie down on your side, then lower your legs from the bed and (with your hand against the bed) rise to a sitting position [20]. It's best to sit there for a few minutes, and if you feel well, you can try to stand.

The most important physical changes after birth and breastfeeding [9]. A woman's body naturally needs to gradually return to its former way of functioning. Some people call this process "dynamic equilibrium", because different changes take place every day, leading eventually to a return to normal.
- Cardiovascular system. The volume of blood circulating in the bloodstream decreases(from 5-6 litres to 4 litres in the third week of postpartum). In the case of twins there is an even bigger change. This is due to the loss of blood during and after childbirth, as well as the loss of excess pregnant tissue fluids through urination. Within 2 weeks after the birth, iron levels decrease. Your heart rate also accelerates but this normalises about a week after delivery.
- The reproductive system. During the postpartum period, there is an evolution, that is, a myriad of changes taking place in the reproductive system. As a result of hormonal changes and the reduction of blood flow, the uterus reduces its weight and size to reach pre-pregnancy condition around the sixth week. During this time the woman feels cramps of varying intensity and pain. Dead cells are also excreted through the faeces and the placenta. Through examination, the uterine separation (done by the doctor and midwife) can be used to assess the stage of repairing and shrinking of the uterus. The wound left behind from the placenta takes up to 21 days to heal, so it is important to maintain proper hygiene and check

your body carefully. Postpartum secretions from the reproductive tract in the period after birth change in colour and quantity at different stages of the postpartum period. At first it is bloody, then brown, then yellow and white, until it disappears completely. If you have given birth by caesarean section, you may have much less due to the doctor cleaning your uterus during surgery. If you are breastfeeding, you will notice an increased amount of vaginal discharge immediately after you have finished feeding your baby – this is due to the release of hormones during breastfeeding that cause the uterus to contract.

The cervix changes shape and closes. Depending on the birth canal it is formed differently. This is important information for women who use natural family planning methods. Suitable exercises can improve the muscle tension of the vaginal walls (▶ II – 106).

The muscles of the fundus of the uterus and pelvic diaphragm slowly strengthen and tense. Gentle, gradual exercises of the abdominal muscles (▶ II – 112) and pelvic floor muscles are beneficial. Stretched skin can slowly tighten, but it is difficult to fight or repair stretch marks as these are already cracked elastic skin fibres.

- Hormone system. Changes are also taking place in your hormones. The high concentration of hormones that sustained the pregnancy is no longer necessary so progesterone and estrogen go back to their pre-pregnancy levels. On the other hand, the concentration of prolactin – the hormone that determines the start of lactation – increases.

Self-observation and self-nursing during the postpartum period. Changes after childbirth usually proceed in a completely natural way, and each one has its own way. It's good to understand not only the changes after childbirth and why, but also what symptoms or events you should pay attention to in the postpartum period to maintain your health and well-being.

- Keep an eye on your temperature, heart rate and blood pressure. If you are dehydrated, especially immediately after childbirth, you may feel an elevated body temperature. After a week your heart rate should be slower and your blood pressure may drop. If you have a fever above 38°C you should tell a doctor. Drink plenty of water. Good hydration of the body increases blood pressure and makes you feel better. Pay attention to the

colour of your skin – look out for blue or yellow skin – and watch out for conjunctivitis or swelling.
- **Pay attention to your breasts.** They will change every day during the postpartum period. If your nipples are damaged, it is best to ventilate them and take care of them properly. Report any pain in your nipples or breasts to your midwife.
- **Watch your belly.** Is your skin taut? Are there stretch marks on it? Is your stomach still the same shape? Do you feel any pain anywhere? Your midwife or gynaecologist will examine your uterus. Pay attention to the colour and amount of discharge from the reproductive tract. If something is bothering you, tell your midwife or doctor. If you see no discharge, report it to your midwife or doctor.
- **If you gave birth naturally,** pay attention to your vagina. You can touch it or look in the mirror. If you had an incision in your vagina, take care of the wound, making sure it's dry, clean and ventilated. Special postpartum panties can help with this. The perineum may have developed petechiae (red spots), swelling or bleeding from the wound at the incision site, which must be checked by a doctor. You can give yourself relief with cold flannels or ice packs. The stitches dissolveafter 2 or 3 weeks. If traditional stitches were used, you will be advised to report to the hospital to have them removed at a certain time, usually on the fifth day after the birth.
- **If you had a C-section, watch your postoperative wound carefully.** This will be difficult at first, because it will be covered with a bandage. After the bandage has been removed by the doctor, pay attention to the appearance of the wound, which should be the same colour as the rest of your body. Keep the area dry and clean but the wound should not be covered by underwear. Stitches put in during the caesarean section should be removed around the 7th day after the birth. Detailed recommendations should be made in the discharge papers you receive on the day you leave hospital.
- **Check if your urine flows freely when you urinate,** and if you feel pain in your urethra. Make sure that the amount of urine you urinate is adequate for the amount of fluid you are drinking. Touch your stomach and take a moment to think about how you feel in your bowel area. Does it feel as if it's filled with gas? After pregnancy, the abdominal muscles are flaccid, which slows down bowel movements, making it difficult to defecate and

expel gas, leading to a risk of constipation. Your first bowel movement can be stressful. You may feel great discomfort or even anxiety [11]. Also examine the anus region for haemorrhoids. Cold compresses, ointments, creams, anti-inflammatory and analgesic suppositories or preparations which improve blood circulation may all be helpful. If you have worn stockings or compression tights during pregnancy and childbirth, you should also wear them in the postpartum period. Some are recommended blood-thinning therapy.
- Take special care of the hygiene of your whole body, including washing your hands. Remember to wash your breasts, especially your nipple area. You are free to touch the perineum, although it will be very sensitive. For intimate areas, use a gentle liquid, washing from the vagina to the anus. After washing, dry the body and perineum. Use disposable paper towels. In the first days after childbirth, large postpartum pads will be the best choice. During the day, try lying down as often as possible without underwear, which speeds up healing. You can put a hygienic underlay on the bed so as not to soil the bedding.

You'll probably lose weight in the first 2 weeks. The proper weight loss rate calculated from the body weight before birth is 8 kg in the first week, 9 kg in the first month, and a maximum 2 kg per month from the second month [7]. The first days, or even the first weeks and months after birth, are not the time for rigorous weight loss. Eat healthily and sensibly [14]. There is no special diet for a breastfeeding mother; however, it is worth adding that your body's demand for energy and nutrients is increased and you should (according to the standards of perinatal care) consume about 300 kcal more every day. With a daily calorie count of 1500 or less, the amount of milk produced decreases [7].

Moving around after the birth may be difficult, but – unless it's not possible – is very important. Physical activity reduces the risk of deep vein thrombosis, incontinence, pelvic and abdominal organ failure. You can start gentle and low impact exercise while lying down. It is particularly important to exercise the transverse abdominal and pelvic floor muscles, which can be started from the first day after natural delivery or the second day after surgery. The work of these muscles is closely related to each other. After the birth, you can gently massage the lower abdomen in the direction from the pubic junction to the navel. Over time, depending on your health, you can move your upper and lower limbs, which activate the remaining abdominal muscles. You may consider returning to targeted sports activities after the 8th week after natural delivery and 12-14th after surgery, after consultation with your doctor [20]. Be attentive and take care of yourself, not neglecting your emotional side either. Most importantly, ask and look for support. If something is bothering you, ask your midwife or doctor about it.

Problems in the postpartum period – what to look out for. The most dangerous situations are infection or inflammation: in the reproductive tract (the uterus or vagina), the abdomen, in the urinary tract or in the wounds of the vagina or abdomen after caesarean section. It is also dangerous to bleed or to have symptoms of thromboembolism, including pulmonary artery embolism. Unfortunately, in the postpartum period, thrombosis can occur. There is more and more talk about the dissociation of abdominal straight muscles (▶ II – 105) [18].

The first problems with breastfeeding may occur in the hospital, which can be solved with the help of a midwife or lactation advisor. Any disturbing complaints should be consulted with a physician [11].

In summary, symptoms such as: fever, fast heart rate, very low or high blood pressure, blue skin, swelling, heavy bleeding from the reproductive tract, disturbing appearance and smell of postpartum discharge, fainting or unconsciousness, dizziness, shortness of breath, palpitations, feeling pain located in a particular place (e.g. breasts, chest, abdomen, calf), headache accompanied by another symptom(visual disturbance, nausea, vomiting, convulsions, pain in the abdomen) or general malaise – should be checked with your doctor.

Postpartum visits and check-ups. You and your new baby's care is usually provided by a midwife. The midwife will make no less than four appointments after your birth, a maximum of 6 within 2 calendar months, including the first appointment within 48 hours. In the case of high-risk pregnancies with diagnosed malformations (according to the World Health Organisation's classification), you should be entitled to more visits. The midwife prepares an individual care plan, modified by the obstetrician and according to the health of the newborn baby and the situation in the home environment. If a medical problem occurs that is beyond the competence of the family midwife, she will pass this information on to the primary care physician. Once the baby is about 6 weeks old, the midwife passes the care on to the primary care nurse [4]. You should visit the person who led the pregnancy in the 6th week after the birth and book an appointment for a gynaecological examination. Depending on your condition, you may be referred for additional examinations. If you have a scar on your stomach or vagina after the birth, you can have a physiotherapist or osteopath help you mobilise the scar (or a midwife who specialises in this). With the right work on the scar (not only massage of this area, but also other physiotherapeutic techniques), blood supply to the tissue is improved,which speeds up healing [15]. The connective tissue softens and becomes more flexible. This prevents adhesions and discomfort or pain in the scar area [21].

The return of fertility. The moment when menstruation returns is determined primarily by the individual's predisposition (because fertility can return even 21 days after birth) and how much you are breastfeeding. Women who are not breastfeeding usually start their period between the 6th week and the 3rd month after birth. For breastfeeding mothers, the return to menstruation is usually later, and can vary between a few weeks or even up to 2 years after birth and beyond. The return of menstruation is a sign of a return to fertility.

Most researchers stress that breastfeeding alone does not protect against pregnancy. The World Health Organization has recognized breastfeeding as one of the methods of family planning, but there are other factors that determine its effectiveness. It is most likely that the fertility of a breastfeeding woman is influenced by the frequency and duration of breastfeeding by the baby, as well as the overall length of breastfeeding, the age of the baby, and the individual characteristics of the woman.

It has been estimated that breastfeeding has a 98% efficacy rate in pregnancy prevention, which means that 2% of women may become pregnant by the sixth month after the birth if they are not using other methods of contraception. High effectiveness is ensured by frequent and effective sucking of the breasts by the baby (at least six times a day, also at night), and also the age of the baby up to six months and lack of menstruation or other bleeding from the reproductive tract in the woman. The administration of other foods or medicine can interfere with the rhythm and frequency of sucking, which can reduce the effectiveness of this method. It is not good to prolong breaks between feeds, meaning that breaks longer than four hours during the day and six hours at night should be avoided. The total number of minutes spent breastfeeding per day is important (at least 100 minutes is recommended). It seems that a woman's nutritional situation is also an important variable in fertility. When her energy balance is good, the chance of getting pregnant is lower. ◆

Martina – mother of three girls, midwife, psychologist. She teaches women how to take care of their health and support them at every stage of their fertility and family life.

70. The postpartum period — an important time after the birth. The psychological aspect

Like all significant events in life, the birth of a child can give a woman a chance to develop and mature in terms of her personality. Just like opening Pandora's box, childbirth provides an opportunity to work through internal conflicts and relationships, to modify the image of oneself and others in a more or less conscious way. This is what can make a woman become a different and stronger person.

The first days and weeks after the birth is a time when a lot of fear can appear, often focused on the health of the baby. The woman feels the physical and mental fragility of the baby. The mother can also experience feelings of loss, including loss of her pre-pregnancy identity and the experience of becoming a mother can contradict her perception of herself during pregnancy. After giving birth, a woman can also be more sensitive, and any comments can be perceived as a criticism of her. In addition to feelings of loss, a woman may experience helplessness and an increased sense of dependence after giving birth – especially if she is focused on her career and ambitious to progress in it.

A mother's mental state after childbirth, after such a physically and emotionally demanding event, often evokes feelings of relief, exhaustion, disorientation and increased sensitivity in the woman. It is precisely this intensity of experience that can sometimes lead to postpartum depression (▶ II – 120, 121). The expectations of a mother can also change rapidly after the birth. During pregnancy a woman is usually treated in a special and attentive manner. After the birth, there is an expectation that the mother will manage on her own. During her pregnancy, a woman experiences care and attention from doctors, nurses and relatives. Immediately after the birth, practically all attention is redirected to the baby, and the mother is expected to recover quickly and take care of the baby.

Emotions after birth are very changeable. On the one hand, new mothers can feel a tide of love and happiness, and on the other hand, deep sadness. This is completely natural, it is worth trying to prepare for this even during pregnancy. Mood swings are a frequent phenomenon during the postpartum period, and sleep deprivation or exhaustion after the birth can contribute to this. It may also result from other factors, such as a lack of experience with a newborn baby, a sense of loneliness, a lack of support from the woman's environment, or an inability to take care of oneself. This is why it is so important to arrange support before the birth, and then be able to accept help when it is offered. It is a good idea to agree on the responsibilities and support of the partner – who plays an important role here – in advance. And finally rest after childbirth is essential to maintain your mental health and overall wellbeing. ◆

Alexandra – mum of Sophie and George, psychologist and psychotherapist.

TIPS & TRICKS

71. Organisational tips & tricks to make starting motherhood easier

This part is not about the baby's room, or nappies and blankets, but about the other, more meaningful things that you can prepare and do before the birth, which will make your life with the little one so much easier. More so than a designer bath or a fancy set of clothes for your baby.

Get a team together. When you're pregnant, you can be confident that you'll be able to handle the birth with your partner or support person. Without diminishing your abilities and desires, each of us, especially during the first days or even weeks with a new baby, can use the help of friends or relatives. Even before the birth, take time and effort to create a group of friendly people around you who can help you with the baby.

If friends ask you if you need something, don't be polite and embarrassed, and say: "No thanks, we can do it," because it's possible that you won't be able to make dinner, do the shopping, vacuum the apartment or take the dog for a walk. Try to make sure that your loved ones know exactly what kind of help you need, and you certainly don't want to be looking after them as well, when they come to visit. Prepare them for a role reversal – let them make coffee for you, and it's best they give it to you in bed, where you'll lie with your little one all day.

Cook good and nutritious food. As long as you're feeling well in your pregnancy and you have the strength and willingness to cook – build up a stock of meals! Preparing lamb chops for dinner? Make some extra and freeze them. Most dishes can be frozen, and upon heating, are as good as fresh. And most importantly, you have a complete meal ready in a few minutes. As one mum advises: "What else can you prepare when you're pregnant? Food supplies: frozen foods, jars, etc. Make a list of local lunch restaurants or cafes that deliver. Personally, I didn't prepare very thoroughly so I ended up living on sandwiches."

You can also stock up on products such as rice, pasta & legumes – they are quick and easy to prepare, and tins of vegetables also work well. Rolled oats, nuts, dried fruit – they can all be bought earlier. Try preparing a shopping list in advance and order delivery for a date of your choice after the birth.

Prepare important phone numbers and addresses. Keep them close by while you're in hospital. During emergencies there will be no time to look for specialists. It is worth having contact with a certified lactation counsellor. Some hospitals have them, but they may not have time for you. Midwives can, of course, help you with lactation-related topics, but it's generally best to have a professional consultation. You should also have a contact number for the nearest hospital and clinic, for the local paediatrician (especially the one who does home visits), for a certified taxi driver (one who has no problem with fitting car seats), for the person who takes the dogs out and the number of a mobile beautician if you can't live without your nails painted... Any contacts that make life easier will now be of great importance.

Get a collection of TV series, books, films, audiobooks, e-books, playlists together - anything that will make your time breastfeeding more pleasant. Yes, the fourth trimester is mainly about feeding, cuddling and sleeping in mum's arms, and – apart from staring at your little miracle – it's worth having a subscription to Netflix and a good book on hand.

Get some sleep! Let's be honest, you can never get enough sleep. What you can do is take a nap and sleep whenever you feel like it, without remorse. Are you sleeping during the day? There you go! Many pregnant women have very peaceful and blissful sleep, which regenerates you.

Dear Mum, prepare for what awaits you after the birth with a peaceful mind. Don't reject help, but make the rules and boundaries clear. ◆

Joanna – Kazik's mother, Panda's partner, caretaker of two dogs and a cat. She likes close parenting, being in the here and now – and loves baby wraps.

72. 20 things to do while you're pregnant

If it's your first child, you may have a little more free time and can celebrate every day. If you have older children at home, you'll have less time for pleasure. But let's assume that it's your first child and you can make the most of the 9 months of waiting. Relax, you'll be able to complete the baby's room, choose the hospital, go to antenatal classes, but for now think about relaxing and taking care of yourself! After the birth a lot will change and your life will look a little different.

1. Sleep until noon on Saturday, have a romantic breakfast in bed and have hot coffee.
2. Take a nap whenever you want.
3. Spontaneously invite your friends – no planning, no nanny, no cooking. Order pizza and watch your favourite movies until the morning. You can sleep afterwards.
4. "Take pictures of your tummy week by week or month by month," advises Marta. Watch it grow, write a diary of your pregnancy – what you felt, what you were afraid of. It will be a great souvenir for you and your baby.
5. Go to the cinema, to the theatre, to a concert.
6. A weekend out of town? Great! Take advantage of the fact that you can pack up everything in one small bag, leave whenever you want, make a stop where you want and listen to something other than children's songs in the car. "Trips, trips, trips and more trips! ...it is possible with a child, but it's not the same," writes Beatrice.
7. Maybe learn a new skill? A course, training, getting your driver's license or language learning?
8. Go shopping, but don't buy nappies and dummies – buy a dress!
9. Relax. Read books, listen to music.
10. Go to a restaurant for a romantic dinner for two.
11. How about fitness for pregnant women? Talk to your doctor about it.
12. Massage your belly with stretch mark cream up to 87 times a day if you feel like it.
13. Knitting, embroidering, sewing? Maybe it's time to renew your old passion?
14. Go on holiday! "Because a holiday with children is not all relaxing by the pool anymore," Amelie writes.

15. Finish the repairs and do some DIY at home.
16. Go for a night walk with your loved one, hold hands, look at the stars, come home whenever you want.
17. Go to the hairdresser, to the beautician, to the Spa – take care of yourself.
18. Wear your hair down whenever you feel like it without the risk of getting crispy corn or pasta in it.
19. A professional maternity photo shoot? It's a nice souvenir. The best time for it is probably in your second trimester of pregnancy.
20. Don't forget your partner. Enjoy yourselves, enjoy the time together.

And remember not to panic – you'll be able to do most of these things after the birth of your child, because the world will not end then. On the contrary, it is the start of a beautiful new chapter. Meetings, trips, hobbies, will still be possible, but it will require better planning, organisation and probably help from others. For now, enjoy the moments of waiting and squeeze as much as possible into them! As Eve advises: "Though your stomach is a little heavy, or you have terrible nausea, or you can't reach your shoelaces anymore – enjoy this special period. These 9 months will pass in a flash, and you will remember this time with great sentiment." I vouch for these words and wish you a wonderful 40 weeks. Good luck! ♦

Magda – mum of Victoria and Cornelia, author and blogger.

My story

Thumbnails of a mother. Half lighthearted, half serious.

Scene I. Before it all started...
The desire to have offspring fell on me like a thunderbolt from a clear sky on December 27th 2007 at 4 p.m. Till that moment I thought I would be a self-sufficient, independent unit, and an absolutely million percent childless woman...
Then he appeared – my beloved, a fairy tale prince on a white horse, my love and destiny. Okay, he came with his father's old half-breed, there were no fireworks, we were both tense and tired. But it was then that the thought germinated in my

head that it was time to think about duplicating my genes. Our candy trees fitted together, two halves of an orange found each other, we were soul mates joined together. I just knew that this man would become the father of our children.

Biology turned out to be inexorable for me. The desire to conceive possessed me completely. The strong will and pride that I had trained for years disappeared. Each topic that came up ended with the same question – when will we have a child? I didn't recognise myself. Whether I wanted it or not, I had entered completely new territory, started on a new path from which there was no turning back. A signpost with MOTHERSHIP written on it appeared in my head. In my imagination I saw small letters which read: "You will have hope, and it's beautiful." In fact it turned out to be something completely different:

"Abandon hope, all ye who enter here." Wearing my rose-tinted spectacles, ensconsed on the rushing train called life, I passed the signpost carelessly and… my whole orderly world turned upside down.

From Cupid's arrow to the birth of our firstborn was exactly 5 years, 104 days, 21 hours and 12 minutes. It took the lion's share of that time to convince my loved one that we were made to be dads and mums and that our child would be the eighth wonder of the world. Thanks to this you would think we managed to prepare ourselves thoroughly for our new roles. Nothing could be further from the truth – you can't prepare for it, it's simply a matter of survival.

Scene II. The adventures of an inexperienced truck

The first pregnancy was successful. Feeling as light as a bird, though in reality as heavy as an elephant, I ran joyfully to the university. It was the last year of my studies at the Faculty of Physics.

At one of the first classes of the semester, and newly pregnant, we were asked if any of us were expecting. I confirmed that I was – the only one. As students of medical physics, we had classes in the nuclear medicine centre, which was not necessarily safe for future mothers and their unborn babies – after the radiation therapy is finished, free neutrons can happily drift in the air. I was given restricted access to some rooms. I was amused by the reaction of a younger colleague who said: "I knew you were pregnant. I just knew." I was intrigued by his confidence. I waited to hear how he knew. "You have, like, very large and prominent breasts." Well indeed. Before I started to look like I'd swallowed a watermelon, I was the possessor of an amazing bust.

I felt good, so I didn't slow down. Everything was just perfect. Until...

Around the 32nd week of my pregnancy, I decided to change my doctor to one who was closer to the hospital where I was going to give birth. And here the fairy tale stopped. It was decided that I should have a caesarean section. For me it felt like the end of the world, a trauma, a one-act drama – just a nightmare. The thought of cutting through the shells of my stomach knocked me off my feet. All the way from the doctor to the house, I broke down. I was scared. Everyone tried to comfort me, saying that it wasn't the end of the world, that it was necessary, that it was for the safety of my baby and me. But I built barriers around me and I didn't hear them. I felt sadness, grief, anger, anxiety. Why me? What could I have done differently? It was only then that I discovered a Facebook group on this topic, but it was too late for me to do some exercises which might have helped my baby turn around. The little fellow was now too big and supposedly there was something wrong with the flows. The doctor decided to have a caesarean "cold", which is planned to be done before the action of childbirth starts. I was very nervous and it was making the staff anxious. I was afraid that I would feel the cut. Those stories where the anesthesia doesn't work well? Fortunately, I didn't feel anything. I could breathe again.

Scene III. Plans and reality

Motherhood has taught me one very important thing – flexibility. The plans that I had before my first birth have evolved. This is what they were, and what happened to them...

Assumption number 1: I'll give birth naturally, just like my mother and both my sisters. *Reality:* a planned (elective) caesarean. *Rational considerations:* more openness to various options for resolving the pregnancy. *Emotional thoughts:* next time I won't be cut anyway, but for now I'm harnessing my inner Buddhist monk with steel nerves and a great humility of spirit.

Assumption number 2: I will breastfeed the prescribed 6 months and that's it, period. *Reality:* I feed, and I feed, and I feed, and I feed... And that's how I've made it to over 5 years... *Rational considerations:* mother's milk is wonderful, rich in many nutrients, the best for my baby. *Emotional thoughts:* I will probably feed until my son replaces my milk with coffee; after all, he is my beloved and I cannot refuse him.

Assumption number 3: he will sleep in his cot. Reality: he sleeps with us. Emotional sleepwalking: you have to follow the needs of the child; closeness is very important for the little one's psyche. Rational considerations: after all, I wouldn't be able to get up a hundred times a night to a young kid lying in his cot. Assumption number 4: I'll give him a soother so that he can quietly, calmly, and joyfully sleep in his buggy while we go for a walk. Reality: he spits it out and he screams so loudly that I can already feel the welfare breath on my back. Rational considerations: on balance, a soother is not so good; closeness is very important, and yet the stroller separates us from each other very much. Emotional thoughts: it's good that they have provided a few benches; a quick boob to calm him down and we rush on – after all, the walk does not have to last two hours – a quarter of an hour is enough, and the run will do me good. Assumption number 5: I won't sit at home with my child for too long, I'll take care of my personal development. Reality: I'll look after my child as if I were his shadow. Rational considerations: for the mental health of the child it is worth being with him; closeness is really important. Emotional thoughts: he is my firstborn, I have to guard him with eyes in the back of my head; after all, nobody will be as good as me at taking care of my little prince.

And so, plans are plans, and life is life. Although I had some assumptions, I watched my child and followed his needs. That doesn't mean I gave up on my needs. They just changed too. I was satisfied with my actions and I wouldn't change anything, even if I could go back in time.

Scene IV. With a second child, it's downhill

Two lines, for the second time... I suddenly felt very stressed out. I wanted a second child, but I didn't know how to divide love into two. My son was the whole world to me, so how do you make this world bigger? Luckily, wise heads said that after all, the universe is constantly expanding, and love – when you share it – it multiplies. That's how it happened. I love my bairns very, very, very much. But what was completely different was my approach to motherhood with a second child.

As usually happens with a second baby, I embraced reality three times faster than the first time. The boob docked almost right away – hurrah, half the success. Bathing the newborn was no longer like disarming a ticking bomb. I was no longer scared to handle her.

I could also see how the younger one learns a lot of skills from the older one. It was great. Unfortunately, time with the second child started to flow much faster, for unknown reasons. Suddenly it turned out that my younger child is an overgrown and talkative 3-year-old. With the firstborn I was able to describe each of his skills and the age at which he reached them. The younger one – I think she was walking, talking and playing right away.

Epilogue. Being a mum is great

Even though I don't always get enough sleep, even though I had to let go of some things in my professional life, I feel like I'm doing what I love. My life would be incomplete without children. I love taking the challenge – motherhood fits in perfectly. Gripping two rascals while keeping an eye on the home, preparing meals and materials for work, can quietly compete with climbing high mountains in winter. It's a 24-hour rollercoaster without a break. Legend has it that you can keep your home tidy, drink hot coffee during your childrens' naps and look like a million dollars. I'll put that on the shelf next to the fairy tales, drink a sip of cold coffee and run to separate the fighting kids. Once I manage to control them, we'll hug, laugh and spend blissful moments doing nothing, together. ◆

Magdalene – privately the mother of Lucia and Nikodem, professionally a physicist and musician in one.

MISCARRIAGE
WE RECOMMEND THAT YOU
ONLY READ THESE CHAPTERS
IF THEY SADLY APPLY TO YOU

73. Losing your baby — the medical side

A miscarriage is a particularly difficult experience for a woman. Pregnancy itself usually awakens great happiness, hope and often joyful expectation. Unfortunately, one of the most frequent complications that can happen is a miscarriage. In medical language, it is the spontaneous expulsion of the fetus from the uterus before the 20th week of pregnancy. After that, it's called a stillbirth. Miscarriages affect about 15% of known pregnancies [1]. Three or more miscarriages are called habitual miscarriages. The highest percentage, as high as 50%, occurs before the embryo implantation (i.e. before the end of the 4th week of pregnancy), when we often do not even know about the pregnancy yet. After week 13, only 1% of pregnancies end in miscarriage. This can be caused by many factors, but you should never blame yourself, because as a mother you do what is best for your unborn baby.

What are the symptoms of a miscarriage? First of all, lower abdominal pain and/or bleeding. The more advanced the pregnancy, the stronger the symptoms will be. A miscarriage also indicates a decrease in hCG levels in the blood. Depending on the severity of the symptoms, there are several types of miscarriage:
- Threatening miscarriage – usually manifests itself in painless bleeding from the uterus. Such bleeding can also occur if you have a healthy, live pregnancy and does not necessarily mean the loss of the child, so any bleeding should be immediately reported to a doctor.
- Miscarriage underway – manifests itself with bleeding and significant pain in the case of an unsafe miscarriage. Such a miscarriage cannot be stopped.
- Incomplete miscarriage – means that the fetus was not spontaneously expelled within the expected period, i.e. about 8 weeks after confirmation of its death. Therefore, there are no characteristic symptoms, like pain or bleeding, because the body behaves as if the pregnancy continues. It manifests itself as a lack of uterine enlargement and the hCG values show a downward trend. The doctor detects them during the ultrasound examination, stating that there are no signs of the baby's life.

Regardless of the intensity of the miscarriage symptoms, the situation requires a gynaecological consultation. If bleeding occurs, report to the hospital immediately, as this is primarily a threat to life and health.

In the case of a diagnosed miscarriage, depending on the week of pregnancy, you'll go to a birthing ward or gynaecology ward. In early pregnancies, up to about week 6-8, the doctor will probably recommend waiting for the uterus to clean itself. In some cases, after a miscarriage, medical measures may be taken to speed up the process and prepare the cervix for the removal of the fetal sac. If the uterus does not empty itself, you will need to thoroughly clean the uterus cavity.

Complications after a miscarriage. After a miscarriage, in addition to feeling down, you may be weakened. There may be blotting and pain, as well as nausea, diarrhoea, and even fainting can occur if you have lost a lot of blood. If the symptoms intensify, seek medical advice. Also, pay attention to your body temperature, because an elevated temperature may indicate an infection that is developing and requires immediate treatment.

Causes of miscarriages. They can be divided into three groups:
- genetic: abnormal number or structure of chromosomes in the fetus or parents (chromosome aberrations, e.g. trisomy, triploidia), or low progesterone production,
- anatomical: congenital uterine defect, cervical insufficiency, uterine fibroids, intrauterine adhesions, minor pelvic endometriosis,
- immunological: disturbances in the balance of cellular responses, or the occurrence of the rare case of histocompatibility antigens (i.e. father and mother have a similar HLA system (human leukocyte antigen) and pregnancy is rejected as foreign tissue), antiphospholipid syndrome or other autoimmune disorders,
- other: serious infections (e.g. rubella virus, salivary gland infection, measles, toxoplasmosis and other infections with high fevers), all chronic diseases, untreated diseases, endocrine (thyroid disorders, diabetes), toxic factors (alcohol, smoking, drugs, etc.) or long-term mental stress.

Unfortunately, a woman's age can also influence the risk of miscarriage. The risk increases after a woman is 35 years old. Miscarriages in women over 40 constitute up to 50% of cases. The exact reason for this has not been established yet. It is assumed that the increased number of miscarriages at this age depends primarily on genetic defects and abnormal oocytes (ovary cells).

Any remains after a miscarriage (if any) can be examined free of charge in the hospital for histopathological reasons to determine the cause of pregnancy loss. Unfortunately, this is not always possible – the karyotype (set of chromosomes) of a miscarried embryo is usually unknown, so the genetic cause of the miscarriage cannot be determined. To determine the embryo karyotype, parents can perform a paid cytogenetic test on their own. To do this, contact a specialist laboratory and follow the guidelines received from the facility. You can also obtain detailed information from the hospital.

What tests should be performed after a miscarriage? After a miscarriage, you should perform basic tests such as morphology, a general urine test or vaginal swab. Some women lose a lot of blood, and these tests will determine or rule out anaemia and infections. Your doctor will also do an ultrasound to determine if your uterus is empty. It is necessary to have a general examination, and sometimes even a specialist examination, in order to know your health in detail and try to find the cause of the miscarriage. The first step is to have a non-invasive ultrasound, MRI or CT scan. Only later are invasive examinations such as hysterosalpingography, hysteroscopy or laparoscopy (e.g. to exclude anatomical defects) used. It is worth checking for infections (e.g. rubella, toxoplasmosis, cytomegalovirus (CMV), chlamydia), because – as mentioned above – they can also cause miscarriages.

In the case of recurrent miscarriages it is advisable to perform a karyotype test of both partners and a cytogenetic examination of the aborted remains. You can also perform an LH level test, progesterone test or an endometrial biopsy. You should also check the level of androgens (male hormones), as their excess in the female body can also lead to miscarriages.

Your doctor will help guide you with these tests. And if necessary, you will be referred to other specialists.

When can you try to have a baby again? A miscarriage is a great trauma for parents-to-be, and especially for the woman, who sometimes blames herself.

Nothing could be further from the truth. In this difficult time, turn for support to your nearest and dearest, if this is possible, or take advantage of the help of specialists (▶ I – 74). If the gynaecologist gives the "green light" after a miscarriage, you can try for another child even after 3 to 6 months, depending on the duration of the pregnancy. Everything depends on your mental and physical condition. ◆

Agnes – Pola's mum and midwife.

74. Losing your baby — the psychological impact

Have you experienced miscarriage? Maybe your colleague, cousin, someone you know, or your best friend has? No matter who has been affected, it's worth knowing what this kind of loss means, what kind of reactions can come up, and, perhaps most importantly – how to help yourself or someone else.

Miscarriage as a loss of hope. Losing a child is one of the most difficult situations you can experience in life, and it doesn't help that many people don't understand it, and of course don't know about it. A miscarriage is a specific and difficult loss for several reasons. One is the fact that from the moment you find out you are pregnant, a number of processes related to your identity as a future parent start to happen [3]. You immediately start imagining what your baby will look like, what name you will choose, whether it is a boy or a girl. You create images of the future, images of moments to come. All this evaporates when a miscarriage happens.

Losing a child in the prenatal period is complex and difficult, and describing certain issues in detail definitely goes beyond the scope of such a text. We have tried to select a few important threads from the point of view of mothers who have experienced a miscarriage, but also from the point of view of women who accompany other women close to them in experiencing this trauma.

It's a very difficult blow for both parents. The fact that miscarriages occur relatively frequently does not diminish the pain that can occur in the parents. The prevalence of a given phenomenon in society does not diminish its impact on individuals.

Every story of loss is different. It is different when a couple who have been trying to get pregnant for 6 years have a miscarriage, and different when the pregnancy was unexpected. It is different when it occurs in week 5, and different when it occurs in week 20. It is different when there are already children on the scene, and different when it's the first pregnancy. There could be many more statements like this. None of these situations are automatically connected with greater pain. Pain after loss is very difficult to measure or compare and there is no reason to do so. Pain is pain.

Men and women suffer loss differently. Although a miscarriage concerns both the mother and the father, studies show that there are some differences in the response to loss between women and men [3]. Often, especially at the very beginning of the event, a woman can be confused and doesn't understand what is happening to her. She is afraid. She is the one in hospital and it's her body it's happening to. The loss affects her tangibly, more directly. Her partner usually feels helpless. Men are very focused on helping and supporting their partner, and less focused on themselves and their emotions. It is also harder for them to talk about loss later on, and sometimes talking about this experience is what a woman needs most from her partner. The male pain also occurs, but it is often more hidden and inaccessible [1].

Mourning and all its phases. Mourning is usually associated with the loss of someone we had with us. It is inscribed in our social functioning, is culturally accepted, and has its rules and rituals. It is important from a psychological point of view and gives time to experience the loss, to get used to the pain. While this process is taken for granted in the case of a relative or close friend, when it involves a child who was not yet born, the process of mourning is often surprising. From a psychological point of view, individual – and sometimes even all – elements of mourning can occur. Elisabeth Kubler-Ross has identified five successive phases of mourning [4], which could be explained by the following sentences:
- DENIAL: It can't be true!
- ANGER – Why me?
- BARGAINING – If I had taken better care of myself, it wouldn't have happened.

- ♦ DEPRESSION – It makes no sense at all.
- ♦ ACCEPTANCE – I can't change it, I have to accept it.

Of course, not all phases have to occur, and the order may differ. In the case of a miscarriage, women can bargain for a very long time, looking for the causes of what happened, and very often look for faults in themselves (especially when the cause of the loss is unclear). It is very important to allow oneself to experience the different emotions that appear at successive stages, giving oneself the right to sadness, regret and anger. Experiencing all these emotions accelerates the return to balance.

Difficult comments. There are words and comments that women and couples, after having had a miscarriage or other types of loss in the prenatal period, hear exceptionally often, and they are phrases which they find difficult, sometimes even traumatic [3, 7]. They are spoken by friends, family, sometimes even doctors and midwives – almost always with good intentions. Even if there is a grain of truth in each of these sentences, they are often said too early, when parents are not yet ready to hear them. These include:
- ♦ You're young. You still have time to have children.
- ♦ Fortunately, it was only the second month.
- ♦ Better now than later.
- ♦ It's better that it ended like this, than for the baby to be born sick.
- ♦ What doesn't kill you makes you stronger.
- ♦ God gives and God takes away.
- ♦ You'll have another child and then you'll forget about this.

In the case of the last comment, the danger is that if parents believe in such a scenario, their next child can be perceived as a kind of "substitute" and not a new person [5].

What can help?
- ♦ Knowledge of your rights – especially those relating to staying in hospitals, the possibility of obtaining the baby's body regardless of the stage of pregnancy, employment rights after the event of a miscarriage (► I – 73).
- ♦ Gestures and presence – research shows that sometimes gestures are more comforting than words, like touching an arm. Even silence and just being there can be important.

- Reaching out for help and support – it is important to be able to turn to people for help, support, and sometimes to seek specialist help if needed.
- Giving yourself time – many couples want to get pregnant again quickly. It's worth stopping and thinking whether more time is needed.
- Small but important signs, symbols and rituals – some people are helped by hanging an ultrasound picture in a frame at home, others by a small box with several mementoes such as a pregnancy test or the first pair of socks bought, often supported by certain rituals, such as lighting a candle for the unborn child or putting out an extra tiny plate at Christmas Eve.
- Listening to yourself and taking care of yourself – it's worth seeking out what will help a couple move through the experience of loss, and identify what would be too difficult or not supportive at that moment (e.g. a nephew or niece's first birthday party).

A miscarriage is always a very difficult life experience, regardless of the circumstances. If it happens to you, remember that it is worth asking for help; support can make it easier to go through the process of grief. If you want to help a person who has lost a child, simply ask how you can help. ♦

Mary – wife to Tom, mother to Sophie, Margaret and Matthew, psychologist.
Monica – philosopher, artist, author of the novel "The End of the World". Mary's mum.

My story

19.01.2017
Life brings me a lot of surprises, which usually shake my world to the core, but often bring about positive changes. Recently, however, it has brought me something that is still difficult to talk about. I was supposed to be a mum. This time I'm not going to be...

When I became pregnant before Christmas, I was very happy. It was hard to believe that it had happened so quickly! I immediately shared the good news with my family and friends. I was slowly getting used to the idea that our child would soon appear in the world. The fear I felt were the usual worries of a first pregnancy. There were stains, some abdominal pain, but I didn't want to panic. Unfortunately, it turned out that these were not symptoms of a healthy pregnancy...

On Sunday night from January 15 to 16, the nightmare began.

My bleeding woke me up. I quickly ran out of the house to the ambulance, which took me to the hospital. My husband couldn't come with me, and I didn't even know where they were taking me. I was lying in the ambulance, the lamp lights were flashing out of my window and I was crying and praying. The doctor who took me in quickly did an ultrasound and it turned out that it was all over. She said it happens in the early stages of pregnancy, if the embryo doesn't develop properly. The crying I experienced was different to anything I'd experienced – so internal, like howling. I didn't know I had such a voice inside me...

They kept me in the hospital. Nurses, midwives, doctors – everyone was so kind. Someone stroked me, said a few warm words. I got a drip, I was lying alone in my room that first night. I could not sleep. I was waiting for the hospital to get going in the morning so I could find out when the doctor would come, when my husband would come. I called my parents. I will remember their voices for the rest of my life. I couldn't even call my mother-in-law... When I woke up the next day in the hospital, it was my birthday, and I didn't know how to put myself together. Fortunately, help came from every possible angle. I talked to the hospital psychologist, but the most important thing was the support of other people – my family, my close friends, but also others. When I told them what had happened, they wrote, called and prayed for me. It lifted my spirits, gave me hope that it would be better. Suddenly I found myself on the other side: here I am, someone who likes to support others, to inspire them to fulfil their dreams, not to be afraid to live the life they want. I had to ask for help. Thanks to this, I found out how many people support me and how many I could count on, just like they do on me. I don't know what I would have done if it wasn't for them.

I lost my pregnancy. It's a terrible experience, no matter how early. Because a new life appeared for a moment and then disappeared, taking with it our plans and dreams, a piece of ourselves. Our world as we knew it ended. A new one began and we have yet to learn why. And for this to happen, you have to go through a stage of deep sadness, to get used to what happened. It takes time. I know it'll get better someday, it has to. I don't know why it happened to me. Maybe someday I'll find out. Or maybe it'll remain unknown forever...

19.01.2018, one year later

I'm in exactly the same pregnancy pathology ward as last year. The difference is that next to me, there's a small, healthy, beautiful girl on the bed. We're not lying here because of any complications, but because there's no room in the newborn ward…

I became pregnant three months after my loss when the process of mourning was over. Surprisingly, I was much calmer with this pregnancy than in the previous one. I had great results, I felt great. I had a good birth. I have a lovely little girl!

The experience of loss has taught me not only that it is worth asking for help, but also how to support others who are suffering. I organised a meeting at our parish for women who suffered miscarriages. I understood that life and death are inseparably intertwined, that if you experience great joy, you are also open to great pain. And that's what you can call the fullness of life. ◆

Monica – philosopher, artist, author of the novel "The End of the World". Mary's mum.

My story

We are parents of 3 angels and 3 children.

We got married 10 years ago. We had known each other for 2 years, and planned our wedding for a year and a half. We were young, in love and happy. What more do you want? At first we wanted to have children a few years after the wedding. After a year and a half, however, we decided that there was no need to wait. It took us about 3-4 months. When I saw two lines on the test, I was very happy. My husband too. My parents and siblings found out right away. We didn't hide it – we were so happy.

Unfortunately, our happiness did not last long. One day in the afternoon I started to bleed, got scared and went to the hospital. My husband was not at home but my mother was with me. I guess I've never been so scared in my life. The doctor did not give me any illusions – he immediately said what the situation looked like. He also offered a pill to support the pregnancy, to see what it looked like the next day. There wasn't even a heartbeat. That night in the hospital wasn't easy. The next day I had another examination, which confirmed that I had started to miscarry. I remember that the nurse came, she gave me some documents to sign. It was about matters related to the funeral, but we did not go into it. I didn't have the headspace for it. There is not much left in my memory from those days – the main memory from the hospital is tears. I have the impression that I cried the whole time.

My husband and I didn't talk about what happened. There were days when I wanted to talk to him, but he hid all his feelings inside. I was very worried about the next pregnancy and that the situation might happen again.

We decided to try again after a year. We felt joy. Just like before, my husband wanted to brag about it. I hid my fear under a mask of happiness. I was constantly afraid that we would lose our child again. This time, from the very beginning, I took supplements to support my pregnancy. When I went to the gynaecologist in week 9, I was very upset. During the ultrasound, the doctor stared at the screen for a very long time, and I felt more fearful with every second. Eventually, the doctor said that his equipment was old and I had to go to the hospital, but he suspected that there had been a miscarriage. After leaving his office I couldn't stop the tears. I immediately called my husband to inform him. At the hospital they confirmed the bad news and prescribed me some pills to help speed up the miscarriage. This time it was different, I felt completely different emotions. I didn't cry so much anymore. I was just waiting for the pain. Because it was a second miscarriage, the gynaecologist referred us to genetic testing. Fortunately, the results turned out to be good, although it didn't change the fact that we still didn't know why we had a miscarriage. Despite this, the positive results gave us comfort.

After a while, we felt we were ready to try again and I became pregnant within a couple of months. I was nauseous from the beginning, and it was so annoying. With hindsight, I can see that I felt calm in this pregnancy, as if I knew in advance that everything would be fine this time. There were problems and I was in hospital several times but in December, we welcomed our daughter. Soon afterwards, we decided to try for another child – we didn't want a big age difference. When my daughter was nine months old, I became pregnant again. Everything was fine at first. It wasn't until week 8 that the doctor said he didn't see anything in the bubble. I was to come back for another ultrasound in a few days. Nothing had changed. Once again hospital and surgery. This time there was no sea of tears. Maybe I had already accepted that our way was not easy. Maybe it was meant to be. That's what I thought then. I tried to be positive.

Once again, we waited for some time, and once again we became pregnant immediately after we started trying. The pregnancy was difficult and took all my strength, but after 9 months we welcomed our son into the world. We felt very happy.

When he was one and a half years old, we started thinking about another child, but we waited for a bit longer. Then once again, we succeeded immediately. The beginning was different, with no nausea. On the one hand, it bothered me a little, on the other hand, I was satisfied – nausea is never pleasant. This time I also felt calm, or maybe I accepted our losses and that the past could repeat itself. Until week 10 everything went smoothly – and then there were complications. This time we did not miss a visit to the hospital and our daughter was born in week 40.

So after six pregnancies, we are parents of 3 angels and 3 children. How does it feel? It depends. We try not to think about our angels too much. There are days when involuntary thoughts lead to them. I still wonder why it happened to us, but we'll never know the answer. I once read that God gives us as much difficulty as we can bear. Is there something in that? If it helps someone, then why not? ◆

Eve – mum of Emily, Sebastian, Rosa and three Angels.

Us Mums, we are strong! You are too, though you might not know it yet. Good luck, you'll be fine!

Dear Mum,
My wish for you
is that you feel your own power,
have a calm childbirth,
keep your head free of anxiety and fear,
experience and appreciate the varied emotions of motherhood,
and hold onto your enthusiasm, even after a sleepless night.
Let your intuition guide you and give you the confidence not to accept 'wise' advice from others.
And then, when your child first attempts to say that magic word, 'Mummy',
let your heart embrace that beautiful word, that beautiful moment.
Magda – grateful mum of two amazing children.

Dear Mum, your life will change completely from now on. Your new "boss" won't give you a vacation or a lunch break, he or she won't pay you for your work. He or she will use you unscrupulously, and you will still feel happy.
Eve – a mother of two sons and a daughter

I wish all mothers a lot of patience, strength, nerves of steel, distance and a moment to sleep.
Monica – mum to Stanislas

Remember, you're the best mum for your baby. Despite many moments of doubt, don't forget it! Just be. Be there for your baby when it needs you. Support and love it as much as you can!
Kate – Wojciech's mum

Dear Mum, take care of yourself! – Kate

When raising your child, don't follow what "kind people" say to you. 'Good advice' often drowns out our most precious gift – motherly instinct and intuition. Surround

yourself with kind people, and only listen to those you trust. Who are they? You will judge for yourself over time.
Monica – Pola's mum

A beautiful childbirth that will give you strength throughout motherhood, a peaceful delivery and a whole village of support, that you will never feel alone.
Anna

Remember, you can be a good enough mum. – Monica

Don't be afraid. The most beautiful and precious thing you can live your life with is right in front of you.
Kate – Polly's mum

In difficult times, remember, it will pass! One day you will miss those sleepless nights ;). – Milo's mum

Dear woman! You don't have to be perfect. Always remember, you're good enough. And keep your head up! – Alexandra

I wish for you that you can count on the support of your loved ones, trust your intuition and believe in yourself when moments of doubt come.
Joan – Lena and Jonny's mother

Mum, you know best what's good for your baby.
Edith – Dorothy's mum

Mum! Remember to take care of yourself, and everything will be fine :).
Monica – Cuba and Simon's mum

Enjoy motherhood! :) – Maria

It's (almost) over...

There are many topics related to motherhood, and hopefully – after reading this book – you will feel more confident that you will manage.

The important thing is to believe in yourself and to remember that you are the best mum for your child. It is worth listening to the advice of others, but accept only the advice which you feel is right for you. Children are different, mums are different and there is no universal recipe for good motherhood. **Make your own choices and respect the choices of others.**

You will face difficult moments and doubts as to whether you are doing the right thing – sometimes even guilt or remorse. This is normal. Us mums, we are what we are :). Trust yourself.

At the very end, a few kind requests from our group of 1,200 authors. If you think that our work has helped you and the book is worth recommending, then:
- Take a picture of the book, mark us **@mumstomums** and publish it on social media – we want to meet our readers and hear what you have to say
- Share your opinion with us:
    - on our Facebook: facebook.com/MumsToMumsBook
    - at goodreads.com (each volume of the book is evaluated separately)
    - write to us at contact@MumsToMums.com
- Give information about the book to people you think would enjoy or benefit from it. Or maybe you want to give it as a valuable gift to a friend or loved one?
- Give information about the book to people you think would enjoy or benefit from it. Or maybe you want to give it as a valuable gift to a friend or loved one?
- You can also buy a charity copy www.MumsToMums.com
- Find us at:
    - www.MumsToMums.com
    - facebook.com/MumsToMumsBook
    - instagram.com/MumsToMums
- We're planning more projects for mums. Why don't you take part with us? :)

- Write to contact@MumsToMums.com, with what you liked about the book, what you didn't like, what to correct or add, and what's out of date – let this guide live and be up-to-date. You will soon join this group of mums, so help us create this compendium of knowledge, which will make it easier for new mothers starting the motherhood journey.

With love :)
1200 authors and mums

What's next?

In this first book you have read about preparing for the birth of your baby. Now there are other equally important chapters ahead of you. They deal with motherhood and raising a child. The same group of mothers and authors have contributed to the second volume of the book **"Mums to Mums. Motherhood – how to succeed in the most important role of your life?"** and we have prepared over 160 topics about motherhood.

Attention! It's really worth reading while you still have the time. After having a baby, life suddenly accelerates and sometimes it's hard to catch your breath ;).

Examples of chapters from Volume II: **"Mums to Mums. Motherhood – how to succeed in the most important role of your life?"**
- Learn it by heart! First aid for babies and young children.
- Cot death – how to reduce the risk of this tragedy.
- Pacifier – to give or not to give? That is the question…
- Sleeping the whole night through – every parent's dream.
- Caring for your baby – a physiotherapist's perspective.
- Infant colic – how to survive it.
- Wearing your baby – the advantages of a sling.
- A healthy lollipop? Children and dietary supplements.
- Added sugar? The traps in children's food.
- An extremely needy child. High need babies.
- Hug me Mum, hug me Dad! The importance of physical contact for a child's development.
- Let her cry… The negative consequences of leaving a baby to cry.
- Are you sure you want a 'good' baby? The consequences of reward and punishment.
- (no) Love at first sight. Why you don't always fall in love with your child straight away.
- Overweight and obesity in children. Causes and prevention.
- Your female power centre – the Pelvic floor muscles.
- Can I eat this too? The science behind the lactation diet.
- Support and rejection. How relationships change after the birth of a child.

- Woman to woman. Relationships between mums.
- Maternal burnout – when a mother has had enough.
- Stay home with your baby or go back to work? Dilemma of a working mum.
- Like cats and dogs, or inseparable birds? Helping siblings build positive relationships.

These are just some of the 160 topics that we cover in the second volume of **"Mums to Mums. Motherhood – how to succeed in the most important role of your life?"** The full list of chapters can be found at www.MumsToMums.com.

You can buy the book at: www.MumsToMums.com.
Or do you have a loved one for whom it would be a valuable gift?

BIBLIOGRAPHY

Classic or modern? Choosing a name can be tricky

1. Statistics on names, 07.03.2018, www.gov.pl
2. The Great Book of Names – The Meaning of Names, 07.03.2018, www.ksiegaimion.com
3. Recommendations for civil registry offices concerning the giving of names to children of Polish citizens and of Polish nationality, published in the "Communications of the Committee on Language Culture of the Committee on Linguistics of the Polish Academy of Sciences", No 1(4)/1996, 13.02.2018

I'm growing and growing! The main stages of your baby's development during pregnancy

1. Obstetrics and Gynaecology, G. Breborowicz, Warsaw 2015
2. Clinical Embryology, H. Bartel, Warsaw 2009
3. Can The Fetus Feel Pain, Gynaecol. Pol., no. 82/2011, pp. 133-136
4. K. Kosinska-Kaczynska, M. Wielgos, O. Walusinski, Fetal Yawning, Front. Neurol. Neurosci., No 28/2010, pp. 32-41.
5. The Conception of a Child, B.Barczynski, www.ciaza.mp.pl, accessed 13.09.2011
6. Pregnancy Week by Week, W.R. Harmset, www.mayoclinic.org/ healthy-lifestyle/pregnancy-week-by-week/basics/healthy-pregnancy/hlv- 20049471 (12.07.2017)
7. Prematurity, E. Helwich, www.pediatria.mp.pl, accessed 02.01.2013

Playing with the little one in my belly. Supporting your growing baby

1. Stress in Pregnancy and Intelligence of the Child, Anonymous, www.republikakobiet.pl/psychology (17.03.2018)
2. Prenatal Pedagogy. New Area of Education Sciences, Dorothy Kornas-Biela, Lublin 2009
3. Around the Beginning of Human Life, Dorothy Kornas-Biela, Warsaw 2004.
4. "There is a way to increase a child's intelligence!", Magdalene Mrozowska, www.kobieta.pl
5. What to eat to support a child's development, Martha Novik, www.mjakmama24.pl (17.03.2018)
6. What does your baby like in the belly – we know how to make them laugh! Catherine Pinocchio, www.mamotoja.pl (13.03.2018)
7. Child Psychology, H.R. Schaffer, Warsaw 2014
8. Psychology of Human Development, Janusz Trempała, Warsaw 2011

Hello, it's Mom! How do you build a relationship with your baby during pregnancy

1. Traumatic Experiences in the Womb. Doris Brombach, Recognition and release, ed. Franz Ruppert, Warsaw 2016
2. Haptonomy. Wonderful Touch of the Tummy, www.znana-polozna.pl 18.03.2018
3. Prenatal Pedagogy. New Area of Education Sciences, Dorothy Kornas-Biela, Lublin 2009
4. Around the Beginning of Human Life, Dorothy Kornas-Biela, Warsaw 2004
5. Love them when you're pregnant and they'll grow faster, Kate Pinkosz, 05.10.2015, www.mamotoja.pl 19.03.2018

Negative effects of stress on the child during pregnancy

1. Why Love Matters: How affection shapes a baby's brain, Sue Gerhardt
2. Psychological Adversity in Pregnancy: what works to improve outcomes? Vivette Glover, Jane Barlow, Journal of Children's Services nr 9.2/2014, p. 96–108
3. Pregnancy. Backstage of the Inner World, Joan Raphael-Leff

4. Programming intrauterine as a cause of chronic diseases in adulthood, Agnes Seremak-Mrozikiewicz, Magdalene Barlik, Chris Drews, Explanatory Works, Gynaecol Pol. no. 85/2014

Cancer prevention – how to reduce the risk of cancer in the child while pregnant?

1. Cancer Prevention, Recommendations and public health and policy implications 2018, World Cancer Research Fund/American Institute for Cancer Research
2. Diet, Nutrition, Physical Activity and Cancer: a Global Perspective, Continuous Update Project Expert Report 2018, World Cancer Research Fund/American
3. Institute for Cancer Research
4. Nutrition Recommendations in Pregnancy and Lactation, group work 2016, www.ncbi.nlm.nih.gov/pubmed/29842836, accessed 16.02.2020
5. Chips off the Old Block: How a Father's Preconception Exposures Might Affect the Health of His Children, C.W. Schmidt, Environ Health Perspect. 2018, www.ncbi.nlm.nih.gov/pmc/articles/PMC6066336/ accessed 16.02.2020

The nesting instinct – fact or excuse?

1. Nesting Instinct, Margaret Uścińska, 26.01.2015, www.mamotoja.pl

An oasis of peace and development – arranging your new baby's room

1. Ergonomics of the Home, Etienne Grandjean
2. Minimalism is fun, Francine Jay
3. The Magic of Feng Shui Order, Karen Kingston
4. The Life Changing Magic of Tidying. The Japanese Art of Decluttering and Organizing, Kondo Marie
5. The Last Child in the Woods. Saving Our Children From Nature-Deficit Disorder, Richard Louv
6. Understanding Montessori, Margaret Miksza. Maria Montessori on bringing up children, Krakow 2014
7. The Color Revolution, Dagny Thurmann-Moe

Making your home safe for your baby

1. The European Child Safety Alliance, Amsterdam 2007, www.childsafety-europe.org/publications/info/factsheets/childhood-home-safety.pdf

Baby essentials – do we have it easier than our mums?

1. Agnes Skoczylas www.bliskodziecka.com.pl

Putting it all together

1. The economic baby essentials – not without pleasant madness, Anna Chomiak, 18.09.2017, www.nieidealnaanna.pl
2. A taste of motherhood, Anna Stachura, www.smakimacierzynstwa.pl
3. Margaret Grzegorzewska, October 2017, www.facebook.com/lisekopl/videos/997730923699416/

Baby essentials – clothes

1. Aqademia.pl, Materials used in materials for children, 26.09.2016,www.aqademia.eu, Maria Gorecka, How to complete a layette for a child, 11.10.2013, www.mamygadzety.

pl, Manchak Martha, Baby Gloves – useful or unnecessary? 22.10.2015, www.dziecko.siostraania.pl

Baby essentials – cosmetics. The basics of baby grooming

1. SCCS – Scientific Committee on Consumer Safety, 1999b. Opinion of the Scien- tific Committee on Cosmetic Products and Non-Food Products intended for Consumers concerning ACRYLAMIDE RESIDUES IN COSMETICS adopted by the plenary session of the SCCNFP of 30 September 1999. www.ec.europa.eu/health
2. Office of Cosmetics and Colors, March 20, 2006, www.fda.gov

Baby essentials – the pharmacy

1. Lactobacillus reuteri strain DSM 17 938 reduces the severity of infant colic, Bozena Dubel, 4.02.2013, https://www.mp.pl/pediatria
2. Newborn and infant care creams, Ana Krysiewicz, 17.05.2018, www.matkaaptekarka.pl
3. List of products – layette for a newborn baby by Mother Pharmacist, Ana Krysiewicz, 4.08.2017, www.matkaaptekarka.pl
4. Mugga vs. Essential oils. What to choose?, Ana Krysiewicz, 7.06.2018, www.matkaaptekarka.pl
5. Probiotics in drops necessary for toddlers from the first days of life, 7.09.2017, Ana Krysiewicz, www.matkaaptekarka.pl
6. Vitamin D: essential element of a diet, or clear marketing? Ana Krysiewicz, 18.06.2018, www.matkaaptekarka.pl
7. Preventing hives, Piotr Sawiec, www.mp.pl/pediatria

Baby essentials – equipment. Objects you didn't even know existed

1. www.hafija.pl
2. www.mamafizjoterapeuta.pl/2018
3. www.wymagajace.pl
4. www.wymagajace.pl

Baby essentials – car seat

1. www.fotelik.info (as of 27.02.2018).
2. www.sikkerautostol.dk (as of 02.03.2018)

Sugar and spice... A few words about gestational diabetes

1. Gestational Diabetes Mellitus. American Diabetes Association. Diabetes Care. 27 Suppl 1/ 2004, p. 88–90, www.care.diabetesjournals.org, accessed 11.04.2018
2. Pregnancy diabetes. What are the causes, how to diagnose it and how to deal with the disease? K. Korczak 26.12.2016, www.znana-polozna.pl, accessed 23.03.2018
3. Standards of the Polish Gynaecological Society for the treatment of women with diabetes – update. Gynaecol. Pol., no. 85/2014, pp. 476-478
4. Clinical recommendations for the management of diabetes mellitus patients 2017. The Polish Diabetological Society. Practical Diabetology, Volume 3, supl. A, 2017, pp. 53-55

A pregnant woman walks into a pharmacy... Basic principles of medicine use during pregnancy

1. Safety of Pharmacotherapy during Pregnancy, "Pharmacy Co-op", No. 2/2008, p. 109-115

2. The use of paracetamol by pregnant women can harm the baby, PAP, 03.07.2016 www.mp.pl

You mean folic acid isn't enough?! What supplements to take in pregnancy

1. Recommendations of the Polish Gynaecological Society for the use of vitamins and trace elements in women planning pregnancy, pregnant or nursing, Agatha Karowicz-Bilińska, Gynaecology and Practical Perinatology 2014, 5/2014, 85,p. 395-399
2. Folate supplementation during pre-conception, pregnancy and postpartum. Recommendations of the Polish Society of Gynaecologists, Obstetricians, Gynaecology and Practical Perinatology 2017, Volume 2, No. 5, pp. 210-214, Dorothy Bomba-Opon, www.perinatologia.umed.pl
3. Expert position of the Polish Society of Human Genetics and the Polish Society of Gynaecologists and Obstetricians on commissioning and interpreting the results of tests for genetic variants in the MTHFR gene, Gynaecology and Practical Perinatology 2017, volume 2, no. 5, p. 234-238, Hannah Moczulska. www.journals.viamedica.pl
4. New recommendations for the admission of foliates in women of childbearing age, 19.05.2018, Nicole Sochacki-Wójcicka, www.mamaginekolog.pl
5. Vitamin D – an essential element of diet or pure marketing? Ana Krysiewicz, 18.06.2018, www.matkaaptekarka.pl
6. Diagnostics and treatment of thyroid diseases in pregnant women according to guidelines of the American Thyroid Association 2017. M. Ruchała, E. Szczepanek-Parulska, Płaczkiewicz-Jankowska E. Med. 2017; 12: p. 48-59
7. Questions to experts. Principles of omega-3 fatty acids supplementation, Hannah Szajewska, 1.08.2011,www.mp.pl
8. Demand for iron in pregnant women, Andrzej Bacz, 15.09.2011, www.ciaza. mp.pl
9. Does vitamin B12 supplementation only have to be pharmaceutical? Vegetarians are reluctant to use it. What can they use? 01.03.2014, www.mp.pl

Pregnancy isn't an illness. Lifestyle choices during pregnancy

1. All the rest, Dagmara Hicks, 22.03.2018, www.calareszta.pl/ciaza-to-choroba/
2. Pregnant Brain, shocking discoveries by scientists!, Dominica Wojsz, 20.03.2018, www.mamalekarz.pl
3. www.cytaty.pl, 20.03.2018
4. Birth in Love, about the Birth Into Being method, 22.03.2018
5. www.birthintobeing.com.pl/birth-into-being
6. Father's blog, Kamil Novak, 22.03.2018
7. www.blogojciec.pl

Nourishing both of you, without eating for two. A healthy diet during pregnancy

1. Nutrition and nutritional treatment of children and adolescents, ed. Hannah Szajewska and Andrea Horvath, Krakow 2017
2. Nutrition for the healthy and the sick, ed. Jan Gawęcki, Marian Grzymisławski, Warsaw 2012
3. Dietetics. Nutrition of a Healthy and Sick Man, Helena Ciborowska, Anna Rudnicka, Warsaw 2007
4. The Importance of maternal diet on the infant's immune system during gestation and lactation, P. V. Jeurink, K. Knipping, F. Wiens, K. Barańska, B. Stahl, J. Garssen & B. Krolak-Olejnik. 2018. ISSN: 1040-8398 (Print) 1549-7852 (Online) Journal

5. Breastfeeding: A Review of Its Physiology and Galactogogue Plants in View of Traditional Persian Medicine, Breastfeed Med. Javan R., Javadi B., Feyzabadi Z. 2017 p. 401-409
6. Hafija – blog of a breastfeeding mother, www.hafija.pl

Pregnancy diet for vegetarians and vegans
1. The pregnant vegan, Yvonne Kibil, E-book 2016
2. Position of the Academy of Nutrition and Dietetics: Vegetarian Diets, J Acad Nutr Diet, Melina V., Craig W., Levin S., nr 116(12)2016, s. 1970–1980
3. Vegan-vegetarian diets in pregnancy: danger or panacea? A systematic narrative review, Piccoli GB et al, BJOG, nr 122(5)2015, s. 623–633

Munching cucumber with chocolate. The science behind pregnancy cravings
1. Polish language dictionary, Witold Doroszewki (ed.), www.sjp.pwn.pl, accessed 26.03.2018
2. In anticipation of the baby. Guide for future mothers and fathers, Murkoff Heidi E., Eisenberg Arlene, Hathaway Sandee
3. Pickles and ice cream! Food cravings in pregnancy: hypotheses, preliminary evidence and directions for future research, Orloff Natalie C., Hormes Julia M., 23.09.2014, www.ncbi.nlm.nih.gov, accessed 26.3.2018
4. A test of four evolutionary hypotheses of pregnancy food cravings: evidence for the social bargaining model, Caitlyn Placek, 18.10.2017, www.ncbi.nlm.nih.gov, accessed 26.3.2018

How much coffee can a mother-to-be drink? Stimulants and pregnancy
1. Too young to drink. Violation of the right to life and health of a child by pregnant women drinking alcohol, Barbara Barnfeld and Jacek Mazurkiewicz, Wrocław 2016, p. 4-7
2. Position of an Expert Group on the impact of alcohol on pregnancy: state of the art for 2014, R. Dębski and others, downloaded 08.07.2018: www.ciazabezalkoholu.pl
3. Food Standards Agency – New caffeine advice for pregnant women, 03.11.2008, 07.07.2018. www.webarchive.nationalarchives.gov.uk/20111206123508 www.food.gov.uk/news/pressreleases/2008/nov/caffeineadvice
4. How alcohol affects the brain of a child, Margaret Klecka, 02.09.2008, www.opoka.org.pl
5. Alcohol and Pregnancy, 13.07.2018, www.ciazabezalkoholu.pl
6. I am pregnant, 10.07.2018, www.jakrzucicpalenie.pl
7. The influence of drugs on pregnancy, mamoniebierz.pl, 05.07.2018, www.mamoniebierz.pl
8. sosrodzice.pl, Pregnancy caffeine, 07.07.2018, www.sosrodzice.pl
9. Influence of caffeine intake on the course of pregnancy and fetal development, Perinatology, Neonatology and Gynaecology, Regina Wierzejska, No. 5(2)/2012, pp. 110-113
10. Hazards related to caffeine consumption during pregnancy, Margaret Wisniewska-Lowigus, Polish Nursing, no. 1(47)/2013, p. 28-33

Pregnancy in motion. Physical activity during pregnancy
1. Why exercise during pregnancy?, www.czasdzieci.pl, accessed 16.04.2018

2. Exercises during pregnancy are safe and beneficial for the foetus, www.osesek.pl, accessed 12.04.2018
3. Pregnancy exercises affect the development of the child's brain, Margaret Przybylowicz-Nowak, 20.11.2013, accessed 13.03.2018
4. Recommendations of the Polish Gynaecological Society for prenatal care in pregnancy, 17.03.2018, www.femmed.com.pl
5. Physical activity during pregnancy, Dorothy Torbè, Andrewj Torbè, Dorothy Ćwiek, "New Medicine" 4/2013, p. 174-179

Pregnant yoga – exercise for health!

1. Pregnant Yoga: action and contraindications. Yoga exercises for pregnant women, Anna Sierant, www.wformie24.poradnikzdrowie.pl (16.03.2018)
2. 50 shades... of a future mother, that is, pregnant sex.
3. Pregnant sex – prohibition of entry, Caroline Piotrowska, 02.02.2017, www.karolinapiotrowska.com
4. All About Pregnant Sex, Agnes Kurczuk-Powolny, Eve Zeromska, 20.03.2007 www.edziecko.pl

A pampered mum-to-be. What cosmetic treatments can you have during pregnancy?

1. Cosmetic and beauty treatments suitable for pregnant women, Marzena Krzewicka, www.mjakmama24.pl
2. Massage in women in preparation for pregnancy, during pregnancy and in the postpartum period – methods of exercise, indications and contraindications, Gynaecology After Diploma, Gregory Lewandowski, No. 1/2012, pp. 43-48.
3. Hydrotherapy for pregnant women, Rehabilitation in Practice. Magda Piecha, Agnes Opala-Berdzik, Daria Chmielewska, 1895-4146. No. 3/2013, pp. 50-53
4. Kinesio taping as a new form of physiotherapy for pregnant women, Kate Zieba, 2006, www.docplayer.pl
5. The role of aromatherapy in medicine, Family Medicine & Primary Care Review, no. 4/2014, Zygmund Zdrojewicz, Kate Minczakowska, Christopher Klepacki, p. 387-391
6. Chinese bubble massage for a pregnant woman, Claudia Zwiorek-Czech, www. portal. abczdrowie.pl

It's not always rosy. Getting through a difficult pregnancy

1. Conditions and consequences of postpartum depression, Magdalene Chrzan-Detkos, "Psychotherapy" 2012, no. 2, p. 57
2. Maternal Representation of a Child – its significance for the relationship with a child, Gracka-Tomaszewska, "Psychiatry and Clinical Psychology" 2006, No. 6, p. 199
3. Depression in Pregnancy?, Downloaded from www.badania-prenatal.pl
4. Born together and naturally, Irene Choluj, Wrocław 2009
5. Ways to Motherhood, Milena Gracka-Tomaszewska, Warsaw 2014
6. The Motherly Representation of a Child and its significance for the relationship with a child, Milena Gracka-Tomaszewska, "Psychiatry and Clinical Psychology" 2006, no. 6
7. Deep in the Continuum, Liedloff, Warsaw 2010
8. Childbirth Depression in Women, Monica Wasilewska-Pordes, Kraków 2000
9. Euphoric runner – what is it? When does it appear? www.wformie24.poradnikzdrowie.pl

Meditation and the well-being of the future mother
1. Alterations in brain and immune function produced by mindfulness meditation, R.J. Davidson, J. Kabat-Zinn, J. Schumacher. "Psychosom Med" 2003 www.ncbi.nlm.nih.gov
2. Wherever you go, there you are, Jon Kabat-Zinn, Warsaw 2014
3. Mindfulness for Beginners, Jon Kabat-Zinn, Warsaw 2014

Lions and tigers and bears, oh my! The fear of giving birth and other pregnancy worries
1. Being and time, Martin Heidegger, Warsaw 2004.
2. Between fear and anxiety. How to be afraid as much as necessary, Wojciech Imielski, Kielce 2017
3. The Concept of Anxiety, Kierkegaard Søren, Kety 2000
4. Thus Spoke Zarathustra, Friedrich Nietzsche, Kęty 2004
5. Thoughts, Blaise Pascal, Poznań-Warsaw, 1921

Shopping with your bump... and not necessarily replacing your entire wardrobe
1. Binding of the abdomen with a sling during pregnancy, www.pl.lennylamb.com, accessed 15.07.2018
2. Essentials for mum, www.parenting.pl, accessed on 15.07.2018

Mum's essentials. 'Must haves' in the home medicine cabinet
1. Recommendations of the Polish Gynaecological Society for the use of vitamins and trace elements in women planning pregnancy, pregnant and nursing, Gynaecology and Practical Perinatology 2014, Agatha Karowicz-Bilińska et al, 5/2014, 85,p. 395-399, www.ptgin.pl
2. Lanolina = rescue for a breast-feeding mother, Ana Krysiewicz 11.05.2018, www.matkaaptekarka.pl
3. Hospital delivery bag for mum, Ana Krysiewicz, 27.08.2017,www.matkaaptekarka.pl

Safe in a two-pack. How to ensure safety during pregnancy
1. Time for change, Eve Koziol, www.zielonyzagonek.pl accessed 19.03.2018
2. 13 Myths about Pregnancy – True or False, Martha Miłosz, www.dziecisawazne.pl, accessed on 10.03.2018
3. What you can't eat when you're pregnant, Kate Moritz, www.dzidziusiowo.pl, accessed 12.03.2018
4. Your Home, Health and Safety during Pregnancy, Beatrice Pawelec, www.poradnikzdrowie.pl, accessed 18.03.2018
5. Sister Anna, Margaret Przybyłowicz-Nowak, 12.03.2015,www.ciaza.siostraania.pl, accessed 11.03.2018
6. Can pregnant women ride a bicycle, Luke Przechodzen, 14.02.2014, cycling advice, www.roweroweporady.pl, accessed 12.03.2018

On the plane with a baby bump! Travel during pregnancy
1. MEAVITA Medical Center, Pregnancy Air Travel, www.meavita.pl, accessed 07.06.2017
2. Concentration Problems in Pregnancy – why is it so difficult to concentrate while pregnant? Eliza Dolecka, 18.01.2018, www.poradnikzdrowie.pl
3. Is it safe to fly when pregnant? www.mozgi.pl
4. Traveling Pregnant, Justina Sobolak, 04.08.2017, www.medicover.pl

5. Holiday women's dilemmas, Nicole Sochacki-Wojcicka, 17.07.2017, www.mamaginekologist.pl

The baby shower – your child's first party
1. Baby shower, www.dzidziusiowo.pl, (30.03.2018)
2. Baby shower, or stork shower, Sylvie Kawalerowicz www.baby-shower.pl (30.03.2018)

Crazy for animals – preparing pets for a baby's appearance
1. Well born Association, Statistics 2010-2015, 06.04.2018, www.dobrzeurodzeni.pl/statistics.html
2. Ministry of Health, Maternity Care Standards, 09.05.218, www.gov.pl/zdrowie

Attitude matters – preparing mentally for childbirth
1. Active delivery, Janet Balaskas, Independent Publishing House, 1997, Warsaw, p. 12

The different forms of childbirth
1. Obstretics and gynaecology, vol. 1, Gregory Breborowicz (ed.), Warsaw 2008
2. Practical obstetrics and obstetric surgery, Joachim Dudenhausen, Willibald Pschyrembel
3. Natural Childbirth, Group Childbirth, Ina May Gaskin, Warsaw 2012
4. Natural Childbirth, Kate Oles, Lodz 2014
5. The Labor Progress Handbook, Penny Simkin, Ruth Ancheta, 2005
6. Rhythm and Time of Childbirth, Barbara Baranowska, Anna Otffinowska, www.rodzic-poldzku.pl, accessed 15.08.2018
7. On Childbirth Pain and Methods of Relief, Ursula Kubicka-Kraszynska et al., www.rodzicpoludzku.pl
8. Crotch Incision – Necessary or Routine?, Ursula Kubicka-Kraszynska, Anna Otffinowska, www.rodzicpoludzku.pl
9. The Most Important Moment in Life, Anna Oslislo, Anna Otffinowska, www.rodzicpoludzku.pl

Choosing the best place to give birth
1. Birth at home is safe! Results of a study covering 529 688 births of low-risk women: Around Childbirth, Barbara Baranowska, www.rodzicpoludzku.pl, accessed: 10.07.2018
2. House of Birth, www.szpital.szpitalzelazna.pl, accessed on 03.08.2018
3. Alternative Places of Birth, Ursula Kubicka-Kraszynska, "Nurse and Midwife Magazine", no. 1-3/2004
4. Natural Childbirth, Kate Oleś, Warsaw 2018
5. Human Birth: Choosing where to give birth, www.rodzicpoludzku.pl, accessed 13.07.2018
6. Human Childbirth: Birth at home, www.rodzicpoludzku.pl, accessed 13.07.2018
7. Human Childbirth, Birth outside hospital, www.rodzicpoludzku.pl, accessed 11.07.2018

Occupation: Midwife
1. Who's the midwife? Dorothy Fryc, www.porody-domowe.pl, accessed 18.08.2018
2. Ordinance of the Minister of Science and Higher Education on education standards for fields of study: medical, dental, pharmacy, nursing and midwifery, Journal of Laws of the Republic of Poland, Warsaw, 9 February 2018, Item 345
3. Act of 15 July 2011 on the professions of nurse and midwife, Journal of Laws of 2009 No. 151 item 121

4. Known Midwife, Who is an Independent Midwife?, 23.08.2015, http://www.znana-polozna.pl/articles, accessed 14.08.2018
5. See, Understand – More respect for nurses!, 30.01.2017, www.zobaczzrozum.wordpress.com, accessed 14.08.2018

Birth plan – oxymoron or useful practice?

1. Childbirth plan to download, Kate Lodygowska, 20.07.2017, www.matkaprawnik.pl, accessed 11.03.2018
2. Natural Birth, Birth plan, www.rodzicpoludzku.pl, accessed 11.03.2018
3. Ordinance of the Minister of Health of 20 September 2012 on the standards of medical conduct in the provision of health services in the scope of perinatal care provided to a woman during physiological pregnancy, physiological childbirth, puerperium and neonatal care, www.prawo.sejm.gov.pl, accessed 11.03.2018

Pack up! What to take to the birth

1. Natural Births Foundation, Bag to Hospital, www.rodzicpoludzku.pl, 2017, www.rodzicpoludzku.pl
2. Wyprawka – what is worth taking to the hospital for a newborn baby? Kate Plaza-Piekarzewska, www.blog.zapytajpolozna.pl, 16.12.2014
3. What you really need to take to the hospital to give birth, Agnes Roszkowska, www.mjakmama24.pl, 31.10.2017

Ouch! Methods for relieving labour pain

1. Obstetrics & Gynecology, G. Breborowicz, PZWL, Warsaw 2015
2. Painkillers – guidelines
3. Standards of labour pain relief
4. Recommendations for pain management in gynaecology. Treatment of pain in pregnant, parturient and postparturient women

Cord blood – what we know to date

1. Induction of Pluripotent Stem Cells from Adult Human Fibroblasts by Defined Factors. K. Takahashi et al. Cell, 2007. 131(5): p. 861-72
2. Cord Blood Banking for Potential Future Transplantation. W. T. Shearer et al., Pediatrics, 2017. 140(5)
3. Cord Blood Banking Standards: Autologous Versus Altruistic. S. Armitage, Front Med (Lausanne), 2015. 2: p. 94
4. Therapeutic Application of Pluripotent Stem Cells: Challenges and Risks. U. Martin, Front Med (Lausanne), 2017. 4: p. 229
5. in Guideline: Delayed Umbilical Cord Clamping for Improved Maternal and Infant Health and Nutrition Outcomes. 2014: Geneva
6. Effect of timing of umbilical cord clamping of full-term babies on maternal and neonatal outcomes. S.J. McDonald, Evid. Based Child Health, 2014. 9(2): p. 303-97
7. Impact of delayed umbilical cord clamping on public cord blood donations: can we help future patients and benefit infant donors? Transfusion, 2018, 58(6): p. 1427-1433
8. Cord Blood Banking for Potential Future Transplantation. W.T. Shearer et al, Pediatrics, 2017. 140(5)
9. www.mamalekarz.pl/krew-pepowinowa-6-prawd/
10. Cord Blood Banking Standards: Autologous Versus Altruistic. Front Med (Lausanne), S. Armitage, 2015. 2: p. 94

Kangaroo care – wonderfully close to baby, straight after birth

1. Kangarooing – recommended first direct contact of the newborn with the mother's body, Hygeia public health, 2014, Anna Bajek, George Marcinkowski, Jadviga Rzempowska, Camilla Gawlowicz, 49 (3), p. 417-420
2. Kangarooing (KMC – Kangaroo Mother Care) as an element supporting the process of lactation and natural feeding and part of a comprehensive
3. "Neonatal care system and early developmental stimulation" (System of developmental care, care and support of the child's functional competence maturation) – recommended for Neonatal Intensive Care Units (II and III reference level), Magda Bednarczyk, Magdalene Lewandowska, Pauline Stobnicka-Stolarska and others, Medical/Pediatrics Standards, 2014, 11, p. 21-25
4. Journal of Laws of 2016, item 1132, p.14
5. Kangarooing as a method of early developmental stimulation, Kate Janik, Jagiellonian University, Cracow, 2008
6. The influence of close contact (skin to skin) of a child with its mother shortly after birth on the later behaviour of the newborn, Kate Maria Kornacka, Practical Medicine – Pediatrics, 2004, 113, p. 858-865
7. Skin on skin contact and kangarooing of newborns – a momentary fashion or a scientifically proven method?, Anna Stodolak, Alexander Fuglewicz, Perinatology, Neonatology and Gynaecology, 2012, 5 (1), p. 19-25
8. The importance of touch in supporting children's development and its application in selected types of therapy, Beatrice Zagorska, Culture and Education, 2013, 5, 179-192

Midwifery – an important time after the birth. Psychological aspect

1. Spilled milk, Joan Raphael-Leff, Gdansk 2013, Imago Publishing House
2. Pregnancy. Backstage of the Inner World, Joan Raphael-Leff, Warsaw 2018, Ingenium Outbuilding
3. Natural Childbirth, Ina May Gaskin, Warsaw 2012
4. Psychodynamic Current in Prenatal Psychology: Selected Problems in the Area of Procreation, Dorothy Kornas-Biela, PSYCHOLOGICAL OVERVIEW, 2003, Volume 46, No. 2, p. 179-196

Losing your baby – the medical aspect

1. Obstetrics and Gynaecology, G Breborowicz, Cracow 2015
2. Does obesity increase the risk of miscarriage in spontaneous conception: a systematic review. C. Boots, Stephenson M.D., Semin. Reprod. Med., nr 29/2011, p. 507–513
3. Vitamin supplementation for preventing miscarriage. A. Rumbold, Ph. Middleton, C. A. Crowther: Cochrane Database Syst. Rev., nr 1/2011
4. Treatment of early pregnancy loss. Guidelines of the Royal College of Obstetricians and Gynaecologists
5. The investigation and treatment of couples with recurrent first-trimester and second-trimester miscarriage
6. Royal College of Obstetricians and Gynaecologists Green-top Guideline No. 17, April 2011

Losing your baby – the psychological aspect

1. Similarities and differences in couples' grief reactions following a miscarriage; Results from a longitudinal study. M. Beutel et al., Journal of Psychosomatic Research, nr 40/1996, s. 245–253

2. Obstetrics and gynaecology. Volume I, G. Breborowicz (ed.), Warsaw 2012
3. Interrupted Waiting. Guide for women after a miscarriage, G. Cozza
4. On Death and Dying, Elizabeth Kubler-Ross
5. Pregnancy after stillbirth or neonatal death: psychological risks and management, E. Lewis, S. Bourne; Spilt Milk. Perinatal Loss and Breakdown, J. Raphael-Leff (ed.)
6. Gender differences in reactions to perinatal loss: A qualitative study of couples. M. R. McCarthy, Dissertation Abstracts International. B.; The Science and Engineering, Vol. 62/2002, p. 3809

The Authors of the book "Mums to Mums"

The authors of chapters in volume I (Pregnancy) and II (Motherhood) are mums and experts in their fields – including doctors, pharmacists, midwives, doulas, psychologists, dieticians and lawyers. They often worked on the book at night, spending every spare moment outside of their day job and childcare.

Ada Krynicka (I, II)
Adrianna Jagodzinska (II)
Agatha Banaszak (II)
Agatha Major (I)
Agatha Potapska (II)
Agatha Smialek (II)
Agatha Zieleznik-Szarek (I, II)
Agnes Bienkowska (II)
Agnes Bukowczan-Rzeszut (II)
Agnes Czmyr-Kaczanowska (II)
Agnes Krzyzak-Pitura (II)
Agnes Liszewska (I, II)
Agnes Maliszewska (II)
Agnes Parobek (II)
Agnes Stazka-Gawrysiak (II)
Agnes Stepien (II)
Agnes Wal (I, II)
Agnes Wojdat (II)
Agnes Wrona (I)
Alexandra Czun (II)
Alexandra Hytros-Kiwala (II)
Alexandra Krzywinska (I)
Alexandra Odalska (I, II)
Alexandra Polanowska-Lenart (II)
Alexandra Wierzejska (I, II)
Alice Dzierzak (II)
Anna Krysiewicz (I, II)
Annette Kopytko (I, II)
Annette Olkowska (I, II)
Annette Wojciechowska (II)
Anita Bachowska-Peczak (I, II)
Anna Frackowiak (I)
Anna Kehl (II)
Anna Ksiazek (I, II)
Anna Kwiatek-Kucharska (I, II)
Anna Lose (II)
Anna Labedz (II)
Anna Labno–Kucharska (II)
Anna Stawiarska (I)
Anna Szymik (I)
Anna Sliwinska (II)
Anna Wrzochal (II)
Joanna Michnicka (I, II)
Barbara Falenta (I)
Beatrice Meinguer (I)
Beatrice Napierała (I)
Bozena Szymanska (II)
Camilla Wlodarski (I, II)
Dagmara Chmurzynska-Rutkowska (II)
Dagmara Lipkowska (II)
Daria (I)
Dominica Gajewska (I, II)
Dominica Naborowska (I)
Edith Zalewska (II)
Elizabeth Luczak (II)
Elizabeth Slusarczyk (I)
Eve Bolesta-Mroczek (I, II)
Eve Cetera (I, II)
Eve Gos (II)
Eve Majewska (I, II)
Eve Szczygieł (I)
Isabel Frankowska-Olech (II)
Isabel Sztandera (II)
Isabel Dembinska (I)
Isabel Ksyta (I, II)
Jagoda Sikora (II)
Joanna Banys (I)
Joanna Barczuk (II)
Joanna Bogdan (II)
Joanna Gotfryd (II)
Joanna Kalinowska (II)
Joanna Olejarczyk (II)
Joanna Ostrejko-Sochal (II)
Joanna Pstragowska (II)
Joanna Suchowska-Oruba (II)
Caroline Bury (II)
Caroline Janowska-Kroner (II)
Caroline Rowinska (I, II)
Caroline Stanczyk (I)
Catherine Golabek-Drapiewska
Catherine Burzynska (II)
Catherine Laddach (II)
Catherine Mirek (I)
Catherine Osadnik (II)
Catherine Płaza-Piekarzewska (I)
Catherine Ring-Andrzejczuk (II)
Catherine Turchan (II)
Kinga Polchlopek (II)
Kinga Kalinowska (I, II)
Lydia Kardasz (II)
Lilla Maslanka-Pawlik (II)
Linda Czechowicz (II)
Magdalene Gajewska (I, II)
Magdalene Stolarska (II)
Magdalene Hul (I)
Magdalene Lozinska (I, II)
Magdalene Skiba (II)
Margaret Bronska-Krzyzanowska (I)
Margaret Jonczy-Adamska (II)
Margaret Sarnecka (II)
Margaret Zawilska-Rospedek (II)
Mary Hornowska-Stoch (I)
Mary Karkosik-Fritzsche (I)
Mary Mirowska-Jon (II)
Marika Kaczmarek (I, II)
Mariola Ciach (II)
Marlene Grajek (II)
Marlene Stola-Wojt (II)
Martha Dembska (II)
Martina (I)

Martina Kukawska (I)	Nina Wojtyra (II)	Tatiana Szafraniec (II)
Marzena Pilarz-Herzyk (I, II)	Olga Walkuska (I)	Ursula Rozko (I, II)
Monica Kasperczyk (II)	Pamela Bozek (I, II)	Violet Stachacz (I)
Monica Kroenke (I, II)	Pauline Milonas (II)	Violet Michta (II)
Monica Margaret Lis (I)	Pauline Tarachowicz (II)	Susanna Angelosanto (I, II)
Monica Trocha (II)	Pauline Wilczynska (I, II)	Susanna Wędołowska (II)
Monica Zalewska (II)	Sylvia Anderson-Hanney (II)	Susanna Szuminska (I)
Natalie Fedan (II)	Sylvia Nowak (I)	
Natalie Lublinska (I, II)	Sylvia Wlodarska (I, II)	

Co-authors of the book – participants in the "Mums to Mums" project, who took part in exciting and emotional discussions, shared their knowledge and experiences, and worked on the vision of the book and its content with the greatest commitment.

Aga Mal	Alexandra Olka Olkowska	Anna Jasinska
Agatha Bator-Mysłek	Alexandra Pluciennik	Anna Catherine
Agatha Geppert	Alexandra Stefanska	Anna Catherine Goszczynska
Agatha Gieryn	Alexandra Szpiegowska	Anna Ksiazek
Agatha Organistka	Alexandra Walkuska	Anna Kulis
Agatha Potapska	Alexandra Wierzejska	Anna Kwiatek-Kucharska
Agatha Rokosz	Alexandra Wronska-Zych	Anna Lewczuk
Agatha Sosnowska	Alexandra Zydron	Anna Lose
Agatha Szarek	Alice Dzierzak	Anna Samsel
Agatha Szczygiel	Alice Liddell	Anna Sarnecka
Agatha Smialek	Alice Malkowska	Anna Stawiarska
Agnes Bojar	Alice Zet	Anna Szymik
Agnes Bukowczan-Rzeszut	Alina Alberska	Anna Sliwinska
Agnes Gryszowka	Ame Osi	Anna Wloszczynska-Lewinka
Agnes Kacban	Amelie Bucko	Asja Michnicka
Agnes Krynska	An Ru	Barbara Dudzik
Agnes Lesz	Ana Krysiewicz	Beatrice Meinguer-Jedlinska
Agnes Liszewska	Annette Beza	Beatrice Napierala
Agnes Pieczynska	Annette Kardasz	Beatrice Nowotnik
Agnes Polska-Bachurzewska	Annette Kierlanczyk	Bogna Krzyzanowska-Glab
Agnes Prawdzic	Angelica Molas	Bogumila Bogna
Agnes Redzik	Anna Balabuch	Bozena Szymańska
Agnes Stazka-Gawrysiak	Anna Barska	Bozena Warpas
Agnes Stepien	Anna Bobowska	Camilla Wlodarski
Agnes Wal	Anna Es	Dagmara Lipkowska
Agnes Wojdat	Anna Macios	Danute Kowalska
Agnes Wojcik	Anna Oka	Daria Kapica
Alexandra Banasiak	Anna Sokolnicka	Daria Kiersnowska
Alexandra Cybulska	Anna Szopa	Daria Kowalska
Alexandra Handk	Anna Witczak	Daria Ziewiec
Alexandra Kaczmarek	Anne Mioduszevska	Diana Putko
Alexandra Krzywinska	Anne Sza Ja	Dominica Gajewska
Alexandra Kuczynska	Anna Baginska	Dominica Naborowska

Dorothy Wołkowska	Camilla Jaros	Magdalene Szczepanska
Edith Bator	Camilla Niewiadomska	Magdalene Szczukiewicz
Edith Bielatowicz	Camilla Osiadacz	Magdalene Zawadzka
Edith Kaminska-Pacha	Karina Olga	Maya Wrzos
Edith Zalewska	Karina Szwarc	Malwina Slowik
Elizabeth Luczak	Caroline Bury	Malwina Sopyla
Evelyn Parole	Caroline Grzesiuk	Margaret Bronska-Krzyzanowska
Eve Bolesta-Mroczek	Caroline Kozubek	Margaret Jarosik-Jankowska
Eve Brazewicz	Caroline Małecka	Margaret Jonczy-Adamska
Eve Ciesielska-Baran	Caroline Rowińska	Margaret Sarnecka
Eve Gos	Caroline Stanczyk	Margaret Wachala
Eve Kajstura	Caroline Styczen	Margaret Zielonka-Wielanek
Eve Kazimierczuk	Caroline Sucharska	Margaret Zawilska-Rospedek
Eve Szczygieł	Joanna Niemyjska	Maria Mirowska-Jon
Eve Thori Urbanska	Kate Andrzejczuk	Marika Kaczmarek
Evelyn Cichowska	Kate Burzynska	Marika Kieruzel
Evelyn Uljanicka	Kate Fratczak	Mariola Ciach
Gienia Canis	Kate Gorzenska	Mariola Rutkowska
Hannah Maria Pochwala	Kate Olbrycht	Marlene Kawczynska
Hortensja Kuczynska	Katherine Blaszczyk	Marlene Murawska
Yvonne Zabierzewska	Katherine Bolęba-Bocheńska	Marlene Pe
Isabel Idzikowska	Katherine Karczmarczyk	Marlene Stola-Wojt
Isabel Ksyta	Katherine Kuczer-Koszuk	Martha Dembska
Jagoda Bogaczewicz	Katherine Laddach	Martha Gargas
Joanna Banys	Katherine Mirek	Martha Konars
Joanna Guga	Katherine Pruszkowska	Martha
Joanna Jakubiak	Katherine Ptaszynska	Ksiazkiewicz-Piotrowska
Joanna Jamiol	Katherine Stepien	Martha Madeja
Joanna Kilańska	Katherine Turchan	Martha Maria Mega
Joanna Krempa-Szameto	Keight Wojdyna-Szliserman	Martha Podemska
Joanna Musialowicz	Kinga Kalinowska	Martha Rusek-Cabaj
Joanna Nowak	Claudia Lapa	Martha Wozniewicz
Joanna Olczyk	Claudia Urban	Martina Brzozowska
Joanna Ostrejko-Sochal	Claudia Zacharczuk	Martina Kukawska
Joanna Wiater	Lydia Kardasz	Martina Pawelec-Szczepaniak
Joanna Jakubiak	Lilla Maslanka-Pawlik	Martina Stasiniewska
Julia Burska	Linda Czechowicz	Mary Karkosik-Fritzsche
Julia Hladiy	Magda Gajewska	Mary Nicpon
Justina Formela	Magdalene Koltun	Marzena Flis
Justina Gromada	Magdalene Piasecka-Kaczmarek	Marzena Pilarz-Herzyk
Justina Kazmierczak	Magdalene Dratwa	Marzena Piotrowska
Justina Kudas	Magdalene Glodek-Marciniak	Monica Dorenda-Czuchaj
Justina Ogrodnik	Magdalene Kizewska	Monica Fabiańska
Kayah Grochowalska	Magdalenel Lozinska	Monica Fołta
Kalina Iwanek	Magdalene Peszko-Doktor	Monica Garnek
Camilla Andrychowicz	Magdalene Skiba	Monica Huntjens
Camilla Anna	Magdalene Stolarczyk	Monica Kasperczyk

Monica Kroenke	Patricia Fabijanska	Sylvia Nowak
Monica Malgorzata Lis	Paula Nikolov	Sylvia Pokorska
Monica Rozner	Paula Staniszewska	Sylvia Stalewska
Monica Skuza	Pauline Debosz	Sylvia Stepien-Osiecka
Monica Stankiewicz	Pauline Kurcz-Hersztek	Sylvia Telka
Monica Trocha	Pauline Milonas	Sylvia Wlodarska
Monica Wilczewska	Pauline Miszka	Tatiana Szafraniec
Monica Zalewska	Pauline Smoczkiewicz	Theresa Ha
Monica Zycka	Pauline Stepien	Ursula Ger
Natalie Alina Marcinka	Pauline Wilczynska	Ursula Rożko
Natalie Czekalska	Renata Czarnecka	Ursula Urszula
Natalie Fedan	Sandra Mackowska	Ursula Ulka Dobrogowska
Natalie Kosiacka	Sandra Myrun-Kraszewska	Ursula Ida Twarowska
Natalie Lesniewska	Sara Misan	Violet Stachacz
Natalie Lublinska	Sophie Bielska	Violet Michta
Natalie Lukasiak	Sylvia Anderson-Hanney	Xiaotai Bai
Nina Wojtyra	Sylvia Ly	Susanna Gloeh
Pamela Bozek	Sylvia Malesa	Susanna Szumińska

Notes

Notes